"In *Moving from I to ...* prophet, he calls us ou... ministry. As an exhorter, he lifts us up to believe that we can live out a biblical vision. As a leader, he shows us the way to get there. If we pay attention and let the Holy Spirit lead, we will discover better ways to be the body of Christ and join Him on His redemptive mission in our world with power, joy, and fruit."

—DR. TIM ROEHL, director of church health and multiplication,
The Wesleyan Church

"Paul Ford sees God's vision of moving displaced leaders into a synergy that will generate transforming impact and bring organic living into the body life of Christ's bride. This is God's relentless goal to empower every part of Christ's church to reveal His grace in various forms with 'grace-filled love through life-giving relationships,' as emphasized throughout the book. This is God's design for the church to be dominated by spirit."

—REV. SIMON PETER EMIAU, general superintendent,
Pentecostal Assemblies of God, Uganda and all of Africa

"In this book, Paul Ford calls leaders in the body of Christ to a new posture: together. One facet at a time, he causes the reader to look at the implications of relationally interdependent leadership. Whether you agree with every argument he makes or not, you cannot step away from this book without considering how you might walk and work more deeply interdependent with the leaders God has placed around you."

—GARY MAYES, vice president and director, ChurchNEXT,
Church Resource Ministries

"This book is of utmost importance for ministry and church members, existing leaders, leader teams, and anyone serious about following Jesus faithfully. *Moving from I to We* is not just nice-to-know theory; it really works and it is vital for us who seek to hear our Lord say, 'Well done, good and faithful servant.'"

—DR. STACY RINEHART, founder, MentorLink International

"Dr. Paul Ford has hit a home run with *Moving from I to We*. It is filled with insight and wisdom that leaders need to pay more attention to, especially as the 'I' culture continues to prevail in organizations and the workplace. Paul's direct experiences with countless leaders around the world provide the rich context for the points he shares. I highly recommend this book for any leader who has a heart desire to partner with those they lead in more impactful ways."

—BRIAN G. BURNETT, president, Bohannan Huston, Inc.

"Paul Ford, after years of work across multiple cultures, is no mere trifler of words. He has lived and continues to live the concepts in *Moving from I to We*. If heeded, this book can assist the church in actually accomplishing its mandate to fulfill the Great Commission in a way that exemplifies Christ's desire for us to love one another."

—S. G., strategy leader, International Mission Board, Central Asia

"At moments, reading this book will be as much fun as finding prizes in your cereal box as a child. You will find delights buried in each chapter, insights into our deepest yearnings that are like small gifts on the page. Yet turn another page, and it will be as much fun as opening your worst report card. It will only remind you of the numerous ways in which your attempts to play church have led into religious activity that bears little resemblance to the plan and guidance of our servant-shepherd Jesus. I found myself alternatingly irritated, humbled, saddened, and ultimately grateful that God is still moving me from 'I' to 'We.' Paul helped me acknowledge that my self-protective, air-conditioned 'life pod' is not as fun as the enlivening challenge of being organically bonded into a 'We' community of others who have accepted Jesus' invitation to follow Him in authentic relationship."

—STEVE HOKE, leader development specialist, Church Resource Ministries, coauthor of *Your Guide to Cross-Cultural Service*

"Paul Ford humbly but forthrightly speaks to the issues of leadership within the body of Christ in such a way that the reader is challenged to reexamine the traditional models and teachings most of us have grown up with. My challenge and desire to be a more godly, body life–centered leader is heightened by the content of this book."

—DR. JOE HALE, president, Network of International Christian Schools

"This book challenges the dominant model of centralized church leadership woven into the fabric of North American church life. In contrast, it offers a tenaciously biblical, practical, and organic alternative for being a community shaped by the Holy Spirit. *Moving from I to We* is for any leader who knows that something must change. Take the risk!"

—GRADY D. KING, senior minister, Mansfield Church of Christ; vice president, Hope Network Ministries

"Paul Ford explains what happens when we over-focus on individual roles and ignore God's organic genius and synergy. It's not so pretty. I strongly encourage you to fasten your seat belt and hang on for this crucial relational journey toward fruitful interdependence as God intended."

—DENNIS STOKES, director, Leadership Services into the Body

DR. PAUL R. FORD

Moving from
I to We

Recovering the Biblical Vision
for Stewarding the Church

Discipleship Inside Out®

NavPress is the publishing ministry of The Navigators, an international Christian organization and leader in personal spiritual development. NavPress is committed to helping people grow spiritually and enjoy lives of meaning and hope through personal and group resources that are biblically rooted, culturally relevant, and highly practical.

For a free catalog go to www.NavPress.com
or call 1.800.366.7788 in the United States or 1.800.839.4769 in Canada.

ISBN-13: 978-1-61291-390-2

Cover design by Arvid Wallen
Cover image by Shutterstock

Some of the anecdotal illustrations in this book are true to life and are included with the permission of the persons involved. All other illustrations are composites of real situations, and any resemblance to people living or dead is coincidental.

Unless otherwise identified, all Scripture quotations in this publication are taken from The Holy Bible, English Standard Version (ESV), copyright © 2001 by Crossway Bibles, a division of Good News Publishers. Used by permission. All rights reserved. Other versions used include: *THE MESSAGE* (MSG). Copyright © 1993, 1994, 1995, 1996, 2000, 2001, 2002. Used by permission of NavPress Publishing Group; and the *Holy Bible, New International Version*® (NIV®). Copyright © 1973, 1978, 1984 by Biblica, used by permission of Zondervan. All rights reserved.

Ford, Paul R.
  Moving from I to we : recovering the biblical vision for stewarding the church / Dr. Paul R. Ford.
    pages cm
  ISBN 978-1-61291-390-2
  1. Christian leadership. 2. Church. I. Title.
  BV652.1.F625 2013
  253--dc23
                                    2012039071

Printed in the United States of America

1 2 3 4 5 6 7 8 / 18 17 16 15 14 13

To Kemit and Sarah Baumgardner, whose investments in the lives of Paul, Julie, and Stephen Ford are too numerous to mention. How I love you and thank you, dear friends.

Contents

Foreword

I have known Dr. Paul R. Ford for about twenty years. Because he is a world traveler, strikes up conversations with strangers, and knows half of the world personally, I assume most readers already know him. But for the other half who may be reading this, I'll describe him for you. He looks like a "Paul," not a "Dr. Paul R. Ford." Nobody really uses the whole "Dr. Paul R." thing except people who call him on the phone and haven't seen him or heard his highly relational way of speaking. Most of the time his hair is uncombed in sort of an absent-minded-professor way, but his eyes usually have the wild-eyed look of an inventor rather than the sophisticated look of a college don. It is not a look that is easy to categorize. Paul is a cross between an eccentric genius and a teddy bear, or between a motivational speaker and a backwoods lumberjack. But do not be fooled.

Paul is an exhorter. Like Paul the apostle of the Bible (see 2 Corinthians 10:10), people say Dr. Paul R.'s letters and books are strong and in your face. Unlike the Paul of the Bible, Dr. Paul R. is also strong and in your face when he is actually in your face. Yet it's always more about encouraging you intensely, not just confronting you. He says things you wish you believed about yourself. Then he keeps saying them over and over again, month after month, year after year, until you start to believe they are true. Almost by accident, you find yourself doing the things he challenged you to do, not out of shame but out of the belief that God really loves you and you really want to do what God desires. As readers, you will not get the full-orbed impact of this gift that has challenge wrapped in encouragement. I wish you could. For those of us who see Paul often, it is a blessing beyond blessings.

Paul first started sharing these things with me in the 1990s, when I was serving as the president of Leadership Network. Leadership Network was founded in part by Peter Drucker, a management consultant who wrote widely read books on management, structure, planning, goals, and leadership. We created forums for large-church leaders to talk about many things, including organizational structure, strategic planning, and personal leadership skills. You will soon discover that Paul is fairly unimpressed with such things. At times, I found myself getting defensive. Paul was talking so radically that his ideas seemed unrealistic for those of us with "real" leadership responsibilities.

Yet over time I realized that while my job required a lot of strategic planning and organizational structure and leadership skill conversations, Paul helped me see a deeper reality. The more we spent time doing strategic planning, the more it was obvious that it was the conversations during the planning process that directed our work, not the resulting plan on paper. It was the growth in people's understanding and trust during the planning process that created new goals and changed behavior, not the report that recorded our new goals and actions. Paul was on to something.

While it may appear at times in this book that Paul is dead set against structure, planning, and organization, he's not. He is actually pointing out that God, working through relationships, is the one who creates those realities. As much as leadership, planning, and structured activities build relationships and trust, it is then that they are valuable.

If you feel yourself getting defensive as I did, remember the Polish-American scientist and philosopher Alfred Korzybski. He once said, "The map is not the territory." Think of Dr. Paul R. Ford as the Korzybski of the church world. For Paul, written plans, organizational charts, and leadership titles are merely the map of the community that forms the true reality. As organizational leaders, we spend so much time working on the plans that we can be fooled into thinking that they are the actual territory rather than merely a map of it. Paul will give you new insights into the difference between the plan and the planning relationships.

You will discover that Paul intensely believes what he is writing about, and that he has developed these ideas in the midst of many relationships in many cultures. This book is written from a cross-cultural perspective to a cross-cultural audience. If you are from a more community-based culture and hear Paul talking about individualistic cultures, don't relax and think he is pointing the finger only at others. No matter where we live in the world, there is a thing called selfishness and it brings up the issues of "I" quite well. Paul does an excellent job of illustrating the problem of "I" by contrasting cultures, but it doesn't mean that any of us gets a free pass to avoid being convicted about our need to change.

We all know change is hard, especially for leaders. But if we want to move from *I* to *We,* we'll have to change the way we work, relate to others, see ourselves, and approach God. But relax; while this book includes practical steps for applying change, the real power is in changing perspective. Specifically, understanding we are people in community and giving up the notion of self-discovery as a separate task from community discovery.

So lesson one is to read this book with others. The answer will be found in the dialogue, not in the reading. You're not even to the first chapter and you already have a homework assignment. Buy more copies; give them to some friends; set a time and location for when you will have your discussion about the first three chapters.

BRAD SMITH
President, Bakke Graduate University

Acknowledgments

As I wrote a book about the joy, challenge, and opportunity in body life and organic, shared leadership, it seemed wise to practice what I am preaching in the process.

I rejoice in how God has brought Steve Hoke and John Blake alongside to help me understand a "Three Musketeers" approach to building and extending the body of Christ. Steve has edited and rebuilt every outline I have developed in the last four years, and John has brought equal wisdom and creativity to the principles developed in this book. Thank you, dear brothers, for your profound investment in my life, and for helping me so clearly grasp God's prophetic call during this season. Thank you also, John, for providing a major edit for this book, making certain that my words speak to the next generation. You two are my full brothers in body-life crime.

I offer heartfelt thanks as well to Brian Burnett and Michael Mangum, two long-time friends and businessmen who helped me to more broadly grasp the implications of *Moving from I to We*. Your friendship, "iron sharpening iron" counsel, and faithfully, patiently standing alongside over the past twenty years mean more than words can describe.

I am also overjoyed by the investment made by those who provided what I call my "body-life edit" in the preparation of this manuscript. A special thanks goes to body-life editors Nancy Boecker, Peter Drypolcher, Wayne Einfeld, Steve Hoke, Betsy

Howard, Chris Madigan, Michael Mangum, Vince Rutherford, and Judy Winje. To body-life readers checking my biblical content, I thankfully acknowledge Elaine Abrams, Hal Burke, Robin Dugall, Rod Gibson, Steven Gilbert, Toby Joeckel, Bruce Lininger, Del Owyoung, Boyd Pelley, Langdon Reinke, Stacy Rinehart, Neil Tibbott, and Dick Winje. Special kudos to Boyd for his creative offering of questions at the end of nearly every chapter. I thank you for helping me to be a good steward—and equally effective wordsmith—of the principles God has given herein.

Other ministry associates are duly noted, though it seems wiser to call them companions. Their influence in *Moving from I to We* with me has been significant: Tom and Janet Williams, Simon Peter and Rose Emaiu, Sam and Agnes Abuku, Hal Burke, Anarbek and Gulbanu Akhylbekov, Steven and Liz Gilbert, Dave and Rachel Wetzler, Dennis and Ellen Stokes, Joey Chamberlin, Stacy Rinehart, Brad Smith, Bob Rummel, Carl and Linna Peterson, Lanny Wirth, Ron Ward, and Steve Potter.

All else pales to the influence, honesty, and grace revealed through my wife, Julie, and the joy we are experiencing as our son, Stephen, matures into manhood. Thank you, my love, and Stephen—your friendship continues to be a cherished treasure.

Introduction

Speaking the truth in love, we are to grow up in every way into him who is the head, into Christ, from whom the whole body, joined and held together by every joint with which it is equipped, when each part is working properly, makes the body grow so that it builds itself up in love.

— EPHESIANS 4:15-16

Long before the seismic generational and cultural shift to the new millennium took place, a great conflict was already underway—a clash between the individual, I-focused Western worldview and the community, We-centered approach of the tribal and relational cultures that dominate the rest of world.

I is winning.

The powerful forces of individualism, social networking, and pervasive personal technology at work today create a dynamic, I-energy that has nearly wiped out vital community in the Church. Facebook, Twitter, and an avalanche of personal electronic devices have created alternate communities and fantasy realms where our personal "status" ranks at the top of the latest "news feed," our thoughts from moment to moment are broadcast to thousands, and many more thousands are left stranded, isolated in the predigital yesteryear. Insatiable self-interest, with its entitlements and indulgences, commonly overshadows the We-forces of relationship and the needs of the community.

In response to this cultural, generational, and ideological scuffle, we will attempt to grapple with the key issues and get at the very heart of how God designed us to function together as Christians and how His economy of purpose calls us instead to boldly move the other way—from "I to We." We will discuss the vision of the prophet Ezekiel announcing God's dismissal of I-focused shepherd leaders and the promise that His people would become a We-focused, Spirit-filled, powerful army. We will see the promised Good Shepherd Jesus, representing His Father, come to live, die, and rise for the sake of His sheep, present and future. In sending His Holy Spirit, He reshapes us into a life-giving body commissioned and empowered to change the world. Together we become His hands and His feet, the very place from which God will live and move and have His way.

I-Church History

No vehicle of change on earth is more affected by the force of individualism than the Church. (And by "Church" I do not mean the institution or organization that the Church has often become, but rather the kinship-designed body of Jesus Christ.) This life-giving organism has seldom had full opportunity to become the Spirit-breathed, life-giving force in culture that it was designed to be. The people of God all too often became the church of kings and priests and ministers, while the bulk of the people never really discovered what being a part of the body of Christ could be.

Both historically and today, the Church has generally taken an organizational form featuring a dominant hierarchy, systems, policies, and programs. This structural approach has always led to another common cultural occurrence: the raising up of individuals who become leaders. While God designed a people for His own purposes, each with essential Kingdom roles, so often the individuals become leaders who neglect and diminish the importance of the body of Christ.

While the desire to free the Church to be the dynamic, life-giving body of Christ the New Testament describes was one of the core precepts of the Reformation—referred to theologically as "the priesthood of all believers"—it was never fully activated in the Church. Spiritual authority, direction, and leadership were seldom allowed to be a part of body life functioning as the Bible describes. Both then and now, even with so many people desiring real community, so often the individual's desire to rise into self-importance obstructs true body-life ministry.

In watching many denominations, mission organizations, and cultures worldwide over the past twenty years, I have been stunned to observe one other major shift in the attitudes of church and missional leaders. Today more than ever, young and midcareer leaders want to become "great Kingdom leaders" rather than focus on equipping and releasing the body for the ministry of multiplication. It fits with the trend toward making everything of importance in the Kingdom about leadership.

One new pattern, correlating closely to this change, has emerged that will help us see this "I versus we" battle more clearly. The role that leaders play has grown in importance as strategic planning has now become a crucial value alongside leader-driven training models in nearly every Christian organization. Many appear to believe that their strategies for church-planting movements and raising up the right kind of leaders will help God fulfill His purposes. Often, the drive to fulfill biblical tasks in this way unintentionally devalues and subverts relationships and creates disharmony on the very team tasked to fulfill Kingdom objectives. And the cost is beyond imagination in broken relationships, split teams, and lessened impact of the gospel.

Here in the United States, a country that glorifies the personal spotlight, many people seeking to find their place in the body of Christ fall to the temptation of seeking the glamour that comes with becoming a noteworthy leader of some kind. We encourage this by placing an excessively high value on such leaders and forgetting that the leader is actually representative of so many others. The leader sometimes forgets this as well, and loses perspective on the critical role of empowering them.

Having closely worked with over ninety organizations in more than twenty cultures, I can vouch that the more a leader, minister, or missional church planter is the focus, the less likely that body ministry will take place among most of the teams or ministries in that organization. The approach an organization takes toward leadership and leadership development tends to define if and how much the whole body of Christ is released in that context.

> The approach an organization takes toward leadership and leadership development tends to define if and how much the whole body of Christ is released in that context.

In recent history, many Christian organizations trained toward a distinctive style of leader, with "pastor/shepherds" sought after in the sixties and seventies, "teachers" in the eighties and nineties, and now "visionary" leaders beginning in the late eighties and gaining strength throughout the nineties. Over the past five to ten years we have seen a move toward "missional" and now even "apostolic" leadership. Yet there is more to God's plan for reaching the world than determining the one right methodology driven by a single type of leader. There is more to discerning God's organic purposes than trying to train everyone toward one or two dominant ministry roles, or to support those "special" roles. One size does not fit all in the body of Christ.

For the record, it sounds like a great idea, this one-model, one-distinctive-leader-type approach. After twenty years of watching ministries in so many cultures representing all theological types and flavors, though, I am confident in saying that no such person or model exists. But I do not say that here for pragmatic reasons. I say it here for biblical, body-life reasons. The body of Christ, in the whole or in the parts, was not designed to function with just eyes and mouths—and, perhaps, big heads.

> The body of Christ, in the whole or in the parts, was not designed to function with just eyes and mouths – and, perhaps, big heads.

I-Realities

Whenever I work with Christian ministries and teams in the West, I expect certain things to be true. Every setting will be dominated by people who are I-thinking and I-acting in their behavior versus people who are more We-thinking and We-acting. The body of believers more often is a group of individuals wanting to be seen and valued as strong entities who have potential to "move up" within their ministry organizational structure. Or, they want to be valued for their unique, independent approaches to life and work. My working definition of an American Christian team, in fact, is "a group of people who happen to be in the same place at the same time, each doing their own thing." All of these trends tend to disable organic, life-giving body ministry among people designed by God to fulfill specific functions as they find their fit.

Compounding the I-problem is the growing trend in many ministries to become more "corporate," modeling themselves after secular companies. The temptation to adapt to best practices in management and administration without grappling with the body-life implications can detract from what God is doing. The pressure to conform to these models may come from the need to merge certain systems, roles, or departments because of dropping income. It may be further aggravated by the board's call for more efficiency or increased effectiveness. It may come in the form of greater accountability demanded, with more specific measurements for evaluating both programs and personnel.

God never intended for us to put faith in our well-developed systems or in our strategic plans. He never planned for us to set up training models that focus on one or two key skills and then to train the whole body as if they were each the same. He did not design individual uniqueness for self-glory or the spotlight, but rather for finding authentic fit in the We-body of Christ.

The Missional Man and His Organic Plan

In the Upper Room, just before Gethsemane, Jesus could have plotted a detailed plan of action that would have placed each of the twelve in intentional, strategic roles, laying out the next steps toward the building of a powerful, growing, and multiplying Kingdom. He could have spotlighted certain individuals as the model leaders. That did not happen. There was no discussion of church-planting movements or how to multiply strategic-thinking missional leaders. He knew their mixed motives and their internal battles to rise to importance in the eyes of men.

Rather, Jesus washed His disciples' feet, revealing to His followers a humble, downwardly mobile servant position. Then, in John 17, He prayed to the Father for unity among all of His followers so that the world would believe the Father had sent Jesus. Disciples of Jesus were to live out their days together, forming the actual dwelling place of God and the living, active body of Jesus. Finally, He told the disciples to wait for power from the Holy Spirit. They were not to dynamically "move out" in their own strength, attitudes, tactical plans, or actions. Spiritual power would come to drive God's strategic Kingdom purpose through a multiplicity of giftings, preaching, and fellowship, all portrayed in Acts 1 and 2. Even today, those whom our Lord brings into every situation and how He moves among them often show just how organic and unplanned—in human terms—His missional tactics are. There is more to His plan for reaching the world than a right methodology. One-size-fits-all corporate schemes are not part of a biblical strategy.

Where *We* Are Headed

My concern about the leadership ladder and its effect on body life worldwide resulted in my writing *Knocking Over the Leadership Ladder* four years ago. Some of the assumptions and concerns addressed in this book have their basis in the experiences and convictions that grew from the research and writing of this earlier book.

The purpose of this book is to give you a distinct glimpse of God's design for us in the world of the We-body of Christ rather than the entitled, self-focused, spotlight of the I-world. The Church, in all its forms, has become the place God has chosen to work out His will in a lost world.

We begin with a look at God's prophetic plan of action in Ezekiel 34–37, as He removes the shepherd leaders and creates a new economy of shared life and ministry among His people through the Holy Spirit. We will discover afresh how God raised up a new Davidic shepherd to lead His people in the person of Jesus. We will see again how Jesus left His people to create a Spirit-driven community called the body of Christ. After we catch God's vision of leadership and body life, we will take a time-out to examine how we got off track through a series of key misunderstandings and worldly beliefs. Finally, we will seize the opportunity to discover what body life could be if it were less leader driven and more body-life driven. Together, we'll consider such questions as . . .

What if stewarding the organic, relational body of Christ became a core strategy for ministry organizations?

What if the I-focus of Western cultures were redirected to a We-focused stewardship?

What if the emphasis of development was placed on helping individuals to soberly discern their fit in the whole body of Christ that God is raising up?

What if shared leadership really is the best means of multiplying body life into new cells and churches?

How can we prepare our structures to allow movements of God the Holy Spirit among us, as He grows us together into maturity into Himself?

What are the implications if maturity in body life is really an issue of individual holiness?

Enough to get your head spinning and turn your leadership worldview upside down?

The good news is that none of us needs to be the next, great Nehemiah. The body of Christ now carries the shared responsibility of fulfilling a multiplicity of leadership and ministry tasks. We will look at one helpful model of body-life leadership that may affect the way you think about spiritual leadership — and, more importantly, the way you determine to train leaders and teams or groups from this point forward. The concept of body-building roles defines the biblical model of leadership that grows out of our shared life together as Christians.

Leadership in the body of Christ is a series of functions to be fulfilled by a group of people. Yes, there are still individual leaders or elders to whom we must submit, but the *functions* of leadership are to be shared, like every other body-life role in this gifted household of God. By His design, in order to create organic, relational multiplication, everyone has a part to play and God gets the glory for how His strategies change the course of human history.

Something of substance has been misplaced along the way for many who are a part of the twenty-first-century Church, and it is the heart and soul of who we are together in Christ. *Moving from I to We* will, I hope, be a start in your journey to new, renewed, or deeper movement into the purposes of God for you and those whom God has placed around you.

Part 1

Ezekiel's Vision of We

God set up life and work to be best accomplished in the context of community and relationships. Long ago, God spoke through the prophet Ezekiel on this very subject. In an unforgettable vision, God defined the movement that must take place in preparation for the new covenant. As God reveals His intention to be Lord of His household there must be a move from the I-centric, weak leaders of Israel to the great We-body of a people coming alive in the power of the Holy Spirit.

His plan? He wanted to provide personalized care for His people and infiltrate them, individually and collectively, with the Holy Spirit, making them His new place of residence. This process of change would profoundly affect how the people of God would live and work together in the future – and become the essential framework for today. The course of action God started in Ezekiel will likely surprise you. It may also change the way you understand and enact body life with believers around you. Finally, it may change how you understand Christian leadership and its functions in the community of faith.

Through Ezekiel 34–37, God unmistakably prepared His people for Spirit-driven, relational community. He moved directly from the I-acting of leaders in chapter 34 to the releasing of the new We-acting of His body in chapter 37. No message is more needed today as cultural values and technology change the landscape of how we live in – or out of – community as Christians. The result of our response will affect the unsaved world, one way or the other.

Chapter 1 looks at this mighty move of the Holy Spirit that shook up a valley of dry bones into unity and fullness of the Spirit in Ezekiel 37. Herein God also promised to be the primary caregiver for His people from that point forward in history. Chapter 2 will review Ezekiel 34 and 36 and the dynamics that led to this tumultuous, unifying event in the valley of dry bones. In chapter 3 we identify the promised new shepherd king, Jesus, and the body of work He left behind. In fact, that discovery will drive us to potentially new conclusions about this Spirit-breathed army. Simply stated, this very day we are in process of being built together as the place where God lives and moves to reveal His purposes.

Receive His wise instruction, given thousands of years ago. Watch, listen, and learn. He wants to live and move among us as we move from Jerusalem to Judea, then to Samaria and the ends of the world (see Acts 1:8). Lord, we are watching and waiting for You. Together.

Chapter 1

Kingdom Weather

Rattling Bones and a Breath of Fresh Wind

It has to be centralized; there has to be a king, or there has to be an emperor, or there has to be a something.

— ORI BRAFMAN AND ROD A. BECKSTROM[1]

Dry bones have little hope of ever living again. Hopelessness in life is real. Truly, events happen in our lives that can create an overwhelming sense of despair, where direction and clarity cannot be found. Captain Ernest Shackleton and his team of seamen and scientists on the ship *Endurance* understood this. They became trapped in the snow and ice of an unforgiving Antarctic winter in 1914. They spent a lost year huddled together, caught in an ice jam. Their failed goal had been to make the first-ever crossing of the unexplored Antarctic continent.[2] Their exploration of Antarctica was filled with excitement, but it came at the highest cost.

Imagine the potential sense of aloneness on the *Endurance*, as Dennis Perkins suggested in his book describing the journey, *Leading at the Edge*: "You will be out of touch with the rest of the world; your family will have no idea whether you are dead or alive; and you will be hungry to the point of starvation."[3] A newspaper advertisement soliciting crewmen for the venture captures the same sense: "Men wanted for Hazardous Journey. Small wages, bitter cold, long months of complete darkness, constant danger, safe return doubtful. Honour and recognition in case of success."[4]

That promo makes you want to jump on board the *Endurance* immediately, does it not?

As weeks trapped in arctic temperatures dragged on, we might expect despair and bitterness to descend on this crew of twenty-eight people. As the ad had forewarned, there seemed little hope of even staying alive. The rest of the story, though, reveals something very different. Perkins described the surprising scenario aboard: "Teamwork, self-sacrifice, and astonishing good cheer replaced lying, cheating, and rapacious self-interest. It was as if the *Endurance* existed not just in a different polar region, but in a different, contrary parallel universe."[5] Not only did all of the men live through the harrowing experience, but the bonds of unity and friendship that remained were set for a lifetime.

Far from the southern pole and long before Shackleton's ill-fated journey, the prophet Ezekiel depicted an unforeseen transformation no less amazing than the spirit on the *Endurance*. The "parallel universe" is introduced in the pages of Ezekiel's prophecy in gripping, bold detail. It is a stirring vision that changes the course of God's long-standing relationship with His people. In fact, this scene of new life breathed into dry bones in Ezekiel is so moving that it is among the earliest and most frequently depicted in early Christian art.[6] And why not? Picture the earth-shaking imagery from Ezekiel 37:1-4:

> The hand of the LORD was upon me, and he brought me out
> in the Spirit of the LORD and set me down in the middle of the
> valley; it was full of bones. And he led me around among

them, and behold, there were very many on the surface of the valley, and behold, they were very dry. And he said to me, "Son of man, can these bones live?" And I answered, "O Lord GOD, you know." Then he said to me, "Prophesy over these bones, and say to them, O dry bones, hear the word of the LORD."

God wants to make certain that the dry bones listen to His Word. Imagine that! God's people were a maze of spiritually dry bones, lying randomly around. What the Lord had to say rattled them in ways that would change redemptive history.

Before the wind of the Spirit began to blow among those dry bones, consider briefly the broader context. Ezekiel, in the sixth century BC, was speaking to a group of displaced royal and priestly leaders, and thousands of the dislodged people of God who had been removed from their homeland in Jerusalem and Judea. Thus we see people in a tremendous season of turmoil and uncertainty, caused by unforgivable idolatry found in both leaders and people. The drama of this setting is so traumatic that in chapter 10, Ezekiel elaborately explained how the glory of the Lord had left the temple.[7] As commentator John Taylor said, "These were a shattered remains of a people in exile . . . people who had lost hope and truly felt cut off from God."[8] The hopelessness, however, was about to dramatically change.

The Wind of Change

The universe-shaking transformation that God prophetically commanded over His people and enacted through Ezekiel began in chapter 37:

Thus says the Lord GOD to these bones: Behold, I will cause breath to enter you, and you shall live. And I will lay sinews upon you, and will cause flesh to come upon you, and cover you with skin, and put breath in you, and you shall live, and you shall know that I am the LORD. (verses 5-6)

The vision of the future came to the broken, despairing people of God in the form of breath, which is likely to have two meanings. First, the word for breath in the Old Testament, the Hebrew word *ruah*, means wind. But it is not just the movement of wind blowing, but rather the dynamic energy released in the movement of that wind. Think of the wind power created in valleys as huge propellers spin mightily. The second meaning is spirit—in this case God's Spirit, the third person of the Trinity. His almighty, all-pervasive Holy Spirit is linked here in the movement toward a new covenant people to be revealed as the New Testament body of Christ.[9]

These two meanings flow very closely together, as we see in John 3:8: "The wind blows where it wishes, and you hear its sound, but you do not know where it comes from or where it goes. So it is with everyone who is born of the Spirit." The Greek word for wind or spirit, used there, *pneuma*, carries this same dual meaning.[10] This dynamic wind of God carries His Spirit, bringing it from the four ends of the earth to move His people from death to life. Note a key point: He was not merely reviving individuals here but rather the people as a whole.

Then it happens as we continue in Ezekiel 37:7-10:

There was a sound, and behold, a rattling, and the bones came together, bone to its bone. And I looked, and behold, there were sinews on them, and flesh had come upon them, and skin had covered them. But there was no breath in them. Then he said to me, "Prophesy to the breath; prophesy, son of man, and say to the breath, Thus says the Lord GOD: Come from the four winds, O breath, and breathe on these slain, that they may live." So I prophesied as he commanded me, and the breath came into them, and they lived and stood on their feet, an exceedingly great army.

Who says that our God doesn't have a flair for the dramatic? The powerful Holy Spirit wind from the four corners of the earth creates a rattling. The rattling begins the construction for God's new body of work to be revealed in His people. This new work is a changed existence for the people of God, a complete restoration that lays the foundation for the Kingdom of God on earth. The wind of the Holy Spirit in Ezekiel leads ultimately to Jesus in the flesh among us.[11]

They say you truly know an artist best by his or her whole body of work. There is no place on earth where this is more accurate than in the Creator God's intimate touch through the Holy Spirit. The Holy Spirit creates a dynamic, new community—an army if you will—revitalized in a completely new and unexpected way. God's working body, newly revealed in Ezekiel 37, is a very fluid one, where His power brings new life into a whole army of dry bones. Let's take a look at a creature in nature to further understand this dynamic communal concept.

The Starfish

God designed an unusual creature with a similar touch of lively, organic wholeness—the starfish. Its physical design is an open system without a centralized brain center. The intelligence is somehow spread throughout the system.[12]

As authors Brafman and Beckstrom described in *The Starfish and the Spider*, the starfish is a most wonderful organism, a life-giving group of cells that actually can adapt and change to context and need. Its decentralized design allows it to share functions across its whole organic structure. *Organic* means simply that all parts share a unique relationship together that almost supernaturally allows it to ebb and flow in new circumstances in or on the edge of the water.[13] Since its intelligence is spread throughout its whole structure, it has the uncanny capacity to adapt from any point on its bodily frame, just as God designed it.

> *Organic* means simply that all parts share a unique relationship together that almost supernaturally allows it to ebb and flow in new circumstances.

Amazingly, should a starfish be cut in half, soon you will have two fully intact starfish. Its major organs are replicated in different parts of its body. In fact, if the Linckia starfish loses one of its legs, the separated leg does not die because it has been severed from the larger body. It actually grows into a whole new starfish. Did you get that? The one-legged wanderer gets cut off from the mother ship, and it starts building its own fleet. Such decentralized, "open systems" sneak up on you, because they just don't function like so many other living creatures. They can change, adapt, and create newness according to whatever context they move into because their Creator designed them that way.[14] The relationships among the creatures' organic parts are truly life giving, able to multiply themselves because God has designed them so. Now that is my idea of flexibility.

A starfish can achieve this magical regeneration because, in reality, it is a neural network. That is, it is a network of cells that work in different ways simultaneously, according to the various environments and stimuli that affect it.[15] Such is the true nature of organic cell life: life-giving cells designed to fit the need, creating or adapting accordingly, as prepared by the Creator. They can do this because their knowledge and power are decentralized.

I enjoy membership in a small gym that embraces this starfish concept. My gym has an unusual approach to membership. When you join, you get a key that lets you into the locked gym 365 days of the year. This trusting approach by Mike the owner creates a sense of ownership in me and the others. We feel as though the gym is ours. Oh, we are still only renters paying a monthly fee, but we watch out for the place much as caretakers would. We still have clear rules and guidelines, yet Mike is not the only one who cares for the place. We welcome potential members when they come knocking at the locked gym door. Our sense of shared ownership creates a feeling of both power and freedom for us members. We are stewards of the gym, entrusted by Mike through that little key each of us received. Because of this, we share a relationship that makes this much more than a place to exercise. We are a starfish of sorts, where we all have a share in the day-to-day life of our little gym.

So it is with this Spirit-charged "open system" that God initiates among His people. Consider this New Testament hint from 1 Corinthians 12:27: "Now you are the body of Christ and individually members of it." Watch and listen carefully, as this open system will blow among us from the four corners of the earth, creating life-giving structures that are often more organic than organizational. God has prepared His people, and the wind is powerfully moving. In this neural network, the Creator is still very much involved with its life-giving, multiplying activities: "And I will put my Spirit within you, and you shall live, and I will place you in your own land. Then you shall know that I am the LORD; I have spoken, and I will do it, declares the LORD" (Ezekiel 37:14).

> Watch and listen carefully, as this open system will blow among
> us from the four corners of the earth, creating life-giving
> structures that are often more organic than organizational.

Unity Reengineered for the People
To grasp the whole of what God is doing in Ezekiel, we must continue into the second half of chapter 37. The issue of unity is never far from the center of God's heart, and immediately we see why. If you have experienced the despair of separation as the crew of *Endurance* did, God's words here will be of particular encouragement for you. The prophetic hope continues in verse 19. After hundreds of years of war, separation, isolation, and estrangement, the healing of His people begins.

> Say to them, Thus says the Lord GOD: Behold, I am about to
> take the stick of Joseph . . . and the tribes of Israel associated
> with him. And I will join with it the stick of Judah, and make
> them one stick, that they may be one in my hand. . . . Behold,
> I will take the people of Israel from the nations among which

they have gone, and will gather them from all around, and bring them to their own land. And I will make them one nation. . . . And one king shall be king over them all, and they shall no longer be two nations, and no longer divided into two kingdoms. (verses 19,21-22)

This prophetic move of God's Spirit is not about land or new real estate for a kingdom. It is not a new, unified military strength rising up with a new king. Instead, it is about relationship and dependence upon God. It is about finding a place to live together in unity as Lord and people. It is about God the Father being the initiator—again as so often in the past—and the pursuer of His sinful, lost people. This is so clearly expressed in Ezekiel 37:27-28: "My dwelling place shall be with them, and I will be their God, and they shall be my people. Then the nations will know that I am the LORD who sanctifies Israel, when my sanctuary is in their midst forevermore."

How often I have forgotten that God not only wants to be the Lord of His people, but also their leader and even their dwelling place. All the other nations had a king, but Israel would not need one because of this special covenant relationship. Consider the history of God and His people for a moment. He would lead them and they would follow and remain close relationally, both in worship and sacrifice. They could totally depend on Him. He even provided one of the twelve tribes, the Levites, as the priests separated unto God. They would be the ones who would approach Him on behalf of the people. Later He provided Moses and then the judges to supply guidance for His people, and prophets like Samuel, Elijah, and Elisha to speak on His behalf. He eventually—though reluctantly—allowed them to have kings, and had Solomon build a great temple. There they could come and offer praise and worship just outside the Holy of Holies, where God's very presence could be found. All along, He wanted to live with His people and lead them as no other nation. But the Israelites wandered away, again and again, eventually breaking the twelve tribes into the separate kingdoms of Israel and Judah. That brings us to the realities of Ezekiel 37 and two sticks needing to become one—the gathering of a people without hope now spread among many nations.

The Desire for a King

Despite God's desire to lead them as His very own, the people wanted an earthly, I-king to lead them just like all the other nations. Take note of what happened.

Samuel was a prophet and judge who followed in the footsteps of Eli, just before the season of Israel's kings. In his later years, in 1 Samuel 8:5-8, the elders of Israel confronted Samuel:

> [They] said to him, "Behold, you are old and your sons do not walk in your ways. Now appoint for us a king to judge us like all the nations." But the thing displeased Samuel when they said, "Give us a king to judge us." And Samuel prayed to the LORD. And the LORD said to Samuel, "Obey the voice of the people in all that they say to you, for they have not rejected you, but they have rejected me from being king over them. According to all the deeds that they have done, from the day I brought them up out of Egypt even to this day, forsaking me and serving other gods, so they are also doing to you.

After this unfortunate decision, Samuel explained the serious consequences that would come for the people by choosing an earthly king. Soon, though, he still proclaimed Saul as the Lord's choice to be king over His people. But it was not long before the people realized the seriousness of their sin. In the midst of Samuel's farewell address to the people, they confessed openly what they had done: "Pray for your servants to the LORD your God, that we may not die, for we have added to all our sins this evil, to ask for ourselves a king" (1 Samuel 12:19).

But it was too late, the deed was done, the path had been laid, and the years of wandering under both godly and godless kings had begun. It would continue until all kings of Israel and Judah were defeated and many thousands of people displaced from both kingdoms. The truth is that no earthly leader could provide what God had. This defining event in 1 Samuel 8 reflects an attitude in the people—from their elder leaders no doubt—that belittles God's place relationally with His people. They clearly did not want His leadership over their daily lives. Their desire for intimacy was nonexistent, and they said "no thanks" to God.

God made the issue ever so explicit in the words to Samuel just quoted, immediately after the people's demand in 1 Samuel 8:5, saying in essence, "Samuel, this is not your fault. They are rebuffing Me, not you. They are denying My leadership, not yours. They are snubbing all that has gone before in our relationship and My constant efforts to love, discipline, and restore them over so many seasons. They are discarding their unique place among nations as the one people under God in a very personal way. They are trading it in for the earthly model—a human king."

Clearly this was both a deeply personal offense to their God and an unbelievably stupid human decision. Sometimes the short-term decisions we make seem so wise, but time reveals that the long-term realities are much more painful than anticipated. The people of Israel wanted a man-made, man-driven system that let them see, touch, and interact face-to-face with their leader. Interestingly, this takes us back to the very first concerns that Samuel shared with God's people just as they had chosen to go this human route of leadership in 1 Samuel 8:10-18. He forewarned them of this pain in one last attempt to reason with the elder leaders. He explained to them exactly what would happen under the I-leadership of countless kings. Using *The Message,* I will summarize Samuel's warnings in 1 Samuel 8:10-18:

- He'll take your sons and make soldiers of them.
- He'll put some into forced labor on his farms and others to making weapons of war.
- He'll put your daughters to work as beauticians and waitresses and cooks.
- He'll conscript your best fields, vineyards, and orchards and hand them over to his special friends.
- He'll tax your harvests and vintage to support his extensive bureaucracy.
- He'll take your prize workers and best animals for his own use.
- He'll provide a structure where *all* will be put to work.
- He'll lay a tax on your flocks and you'll end up no better than slaves.

The final insult to injury came in verse 18: "The day will come when you will cry in desperation because of this king you so much want for yourselves. But don't expect GOD to answer" (MSG). What was the people's response? We see it in verses 19 and 20: "But the people refused to obey . . . Samuel. And they said, 'No! But there shall be a king over us, that we also may be like all the nations, and that our king may judge us and go out before us and fight our battles.'"

It is fair to say that Samuel warned them, but the people only stubbornly restated their demand. The era of the kings began with the deeply flawed monarchy of Saul and proceeded through the up-and-down kingdoms of Israel and Judah, ending in the utter failure of both. God was spot-on in His whole-picture evaluation of the situation. The I-institution of kings won this round over the We-life empowered by the Holy Spirit to follow God together. The starfish, organic model of leadership and community was blatantly disregarded, but thankfully the game was not yet over.

The Spider

Israel's leaders embraced the spider model more than the starfish concept. The principle of the spider is that "there has to be a king, or there has to be an emperor, or there has to be a some-thing."[16] In contrast to the starfish and its open system described earlier, the spider reflects a leader-driven system. It helps us understand what happened to the Israelites.

Most of us know that a spider is a creature with eight legs extending from a central body. The control center for those eight legs and a good-sized abdomen is a very small head. There is no question about who is running the spider show: that little brain in that diminutive head with its eight tiny eyes.[17] The spider's knowledge and control is concentrated in the head. It is able to adapt in many situations, but all direction comes from its head. If that little head is clipped off, the rest of the body dies.

In the same vein, Samuel cautioned the Israelites that standard, system-wide realities orchestrated by the king were about to become their new norm. The king would give them a face-to-face judge and guide, but at a high organizational cost to the people. Some people would be put in positions that fit them, while others would find themselves unfit for their roles. Many would wish for others' jobs.

I have spent many hours talking about leadership issues with my friends in Uganda. There the issue of being the king or tribal chief is very real. To be seen as the primary leader—and to be adored, respected, and greatly honored by others as such—is the highest goal. Given that cultural backdrop, when Ugandan pastors are trained for spiritual leadership, they often want to be the top leader. Culturally, they want to be the "boss." They want to be seen by their peers as the one who is in control as well as in the spotlight. They want others to respect them and seat them in places of honor.

Because of this, they often have difficulty sharing ministry responsibilities of substance because they don't want to lose their place of importance. They are afraid that if they share leadership, someone may take their seat of cultural and relational importance. So they limit others' involvement, preferring to give orders rather than sharing work and encouraging others in their work. They prefer being like the head of the spider, directing without fear of anyone taking their place or trying to lead without them.

The starfish, on the other hand, allows flexibility to grow in decentralized ways. With its cell framework, knowledge and power are shared, making it easier to adapt to circumstances. In the spider, you find greater rigidity and less freedom because all of that knowledge and power flow from but one point: that little head. The starfish has a network of interreliant parts that influence the direction and growth of the whole. The spider's growth, continuity, and ability to change comes from its one source of control—the head.

The Israelites had made their decision: Let some pinhead rule them! Their choice of a king meant their lives would change. A new system took over, and direction was handed down to them by an earthly leader. It brought some things for which they hoped, but other realities they had not expected.

Change Is Coming

Yet the Lord remained a relentless pursuer of His people at the end of the Ezekiel 37 prophecy. He desired to return to a quality of relationship with them that would cause wonder in the other nations. His desire for unity with and among His people continues to drive His actions toward us today, as we hear in the powerful words of the soon-to-be-crucified Jesus in John 17:21: "That they may all be one, just as you, Father, are in me, and I in you . . . so that the world may believe that you have sent me." The God who has been rebuffed by His people time and time again never gave up on them. He offered these words in Ezekiel 37:23-24: "I will save them from all the backslidings in which they have sinned, and will cleanse them; and they shall be my people, and I will be their God. My servant David shall be king over them, and they shall all have one shepherd."

The Word of the Lord continued, conveying the renewed depth of His covenant commitment to His people. He also created an intriguing vision of how that relationship would emerge in coming generations: "My dwelling place shall be with them, and I will be their God, and they shall be my people.

Then the nations will know that I am the LORD who sanctifies Israel, when my sanctuary is in their midst forevermore" (verses 27-28).

He not only saved the people from backsliding again, He also promised the reign of a future king driven by the outpouring of the Holy Spirit wind of transformation among dry bones. The messianic implications of this passage are also profound, since Ezekiel also called David "their prince" in verse 25. We know, though, what the Israelites hearing these words did not, that the Kingdom never would be set up quite as Ezekiel envisioned, that "the visible head of a united people never set up his throne in David's place."[18] Israel would never again have that earthly king who would lead them back to greatness among the nations.

But there is a coming king and prince who will live among His people as His sanctuary. Is this a reference to the coming Kingdom of God, where the Holy Spirit will build His people into the very temple of God? Is this the living body of Christ that reveals the very presence and power of God?[19] We will look at this more deeply in the chapters ahead. The starfish and the spider have much to teach us about the Kingdom of God and the prophetically promised body of Christ that will come.

Before this, however, we will review what happened in Ezekiel 34 and 36, the events leading up to the dynamic wind of the Holy Spirit that changed everything. What caused this dynamic wind of change and created God's intent to live anew among His people?

Summary

Ezekiel 37 shows us polar ends of the spectrum concerning the new covenant community. First we see the people's life energized as the "dry bones" are filled with the Spirit of God. They were to be cared for and led by Him to show the world whose people they are. Then, toward the end of the chapter we see a reference to God-appointed kingly leadership to again rule over His people. Against His wisdom in 1 Samuel 8, God had allowed His people to have their own king, so they could be like other cultures. They did not want God as their leader, but after centuries of broken kings and kingdoms, God again pursued His people and offered new hope, new land, and a "new David" to again confirm them as His own. All of this was so that God could lead His people and, by the Holy Spirit, live among them as His new sanctuary. Given these new covenant promises, how did God intend to live among and lead amid His people?

One thing is crystal clear: The Lord of all the nations wants to live and move and have His way again among us as an organic whole, not a petty fiefdom ruled by a feeble and flawed king.

Application Steps

1. Find a peer, mentor, or next-generation friend with whom you can read this book. Discuss it as you go, chapter by chapter. Model moving from "I to We" even as you read the book.
2. Form a small group of peers, local or long-distance, to discuss the book in the same fashion. A group of elders or deacons, a small group, or a leadership team could walk through these chapters together, praying, talking, and seeking application.
3. Create a simple chart with the word "Spider" on one side and "Starfish" on the other. Under the corresponding title, list your current groups, organizations, or connections that fit one or the other. What do you observe? Discuss your findings.
4. Do an Internet search for the old spiritual "Dem Bones."

If you are unfamiliar with the song, a YouTube search will give some context. Try singing along and let the powerful, joyful words sink in now that you appreciate their context.

Questions for Discussion

1. Consider the starfish and the spider. What ideas or images came to mind concerning these different types of organic life? What applications?

2. Why do you think the Israelites wanted an earthly king as their boss instead of God? What application does this have for today, if any?

3. What "dry bones" in your church, ministry, or organization are currently frustrating you?

4. What would body life look like in your fellowship, ministry, or church if all the bones were connected and working together? How would it be different?

1. Ori Brafman and Rod A. Beckstrom, *The Starfish and the Spider* (New York: Penguin, 2006), 33.
2. Dennis N. T. Perkins, *Leading at the Edge* (New York: American Management Association, 2000), xiii.
3. Perkins, 2.
4. Perkins, 2.
5. Perkins, xiii.
6. Walther Zimmerli, *Ezekiel 2* (Philadelphia: Fortress, 1983), 263.
7. Samuel L. Adams, "Between Text and Sermon," *Interpretation* 62 (January 2008): 304.
8. John Taylor, *Ezekiel: An Introduction and Commentary* (Leicester, England: InterVarsity, 1969), 234.
9. Colin Brown, *The New International Dictionary of New Testament Theology*, vol. 3 (Grand Rapids, MI: Zondervan, 1978), 690.
10. Brown, 692.
11. Carl Freidrich Keil, *Prophecies of Ezekiel* (Grand Rapids, MI: Eerdmans, 1970), 127.
12. Brafman and Beckstrom, 39.
13. Brafman and Beckstrom, 39.
14. Brafman and Beckstrom, 40–41, 50.

15. Brafman and Beckstrom, 35, 49.
16. Brafman and Beckstrom, 33.
17. Brafman and Beckstrom, 34–35.
18. G. A. Cooke, *The Book of Ezekiel*, International Critical Commentary (New York: Scribner, 1937), 402.
19. Richard Averbeck, "A Biblical Theology for Spiritual Formation," *Journal of Spiritual Formation and Soul Care* 1 (Spring 2008): 52–53.

Chapter 2

Kingdom Calamity

God's Anger Management

You are my sheep, human sheep of my pasture, and I am your God, declares the
Lord.

– EZEKIEL 34:31

[Jesus] is the head of the body, the church.

– COLOSSIANS 1:18

Do you ever find yourself angry? Of course. Do you ever find
yourself angry enough to give up on someone because of his or
her treatment of others? Ezekiel 34 gives us a bird's-eye opportunity to watch this very thing happen to the Lord of the universe.
God's anger management issues here relate directly to His people,
the same people who would soon find God's Spirit poured out
among their dry and weary bones.

The Leader Problem Creates a People Problem

While preaching recently in Soroti, Uganda, I experienced a
vision from the Lord unlike anything before in my life. As I was
speaking from the pulpit on a high platform, I looked to the back
of the long sanctuary. I could see the legs of the body of Jesus,

stretched out at the back of this jammed worship center. *The people were His legs.* Then, in the wider part of the worship area closer to me, I could see the arms of His body reaching out. *The people were His arms.* Then I realized that I was standing in front of the people. I looked as if I was the head of Jesus' body. Keep in mind, all this was going on while I was preaching about body life to seven hundred people at this 7 a.m. service.

It was difficult at first to grasp God's intent. Then it became clear: Because of where I was standing, the people were confused about who was—and is—the head of the Church. In this vision, I wanted to yell out, "People, I am not the head of Jesus' body. I am not the leader of His Church. *He* is!" Then, very quietly as I continued speaking to the body gathered, the Lord said ever so clearly to me, "Now you understand the problem."

Today we are often confused about who leads the Church, how that leadership functions, and how this affects the whole body of Christ as the priesthood of all believers. It appears that

God was angry about this issue in Ezekiel 34, except there was no confusion regarding the problem. God was upset with the shepherds for abusing their place of leadership. From this point forward in Israel's history, the people of God would have a new leader, One who would change everything.

Leadership Questions

Before we dig into Ezekiel 34, let's consider some related issues in the Christian world today. Everywhere you look, leadership seems to be *the* issue for organizations, including Christian mission agencies and churches. A recent survey of more than one thousand Christian leaders from the Lausanne Movement, a noted Christian organization, summarized this reality: "Leadership development is one of the most popular subjects in the world today. You notice by glancing at airport bookstores where entire shelves are dedicated to the newest one hundred titles on the subject. . . . Similarly in the Christian world the subject of leadership development seems to be on everyone's lips."[1]

In the Christian arena, though, we seem uncertain about what Christ-centered leadership really is. Many organizations are greatly confused about this issue. According to the Lausanne survey, most still think leadership is strategically important[2] and "unless we find, make available, promote and multiply the very best in leadership development opportunities throughout the Church, the results will be tragic."[3]

Christians in the larger body of Christ are also bewildered. In the West, many are perplexed by the developments of the past thirty years, in which there has been a fusing of business and organizational management principles with visionary-type spiritual leadership. At the same time, the importance of moving up in leadership is understood as commonplace in both the church and the business world. But whether it be in positional significance or through loyalty, tenure, education, results, or even relationships, we struggle to identify the appropriate ladders.

Given this, so many Christians don't know how to act. Why? Many organizations have joined this quest to make great, multiplying, strategic visionary leaders out of their followers. The greatest concern appears to be that not enough of the "right kind of leaders" are being raised up. Many next-generation ministries focus on raising up church planters who have some rare combination of vision and strategy, and then orchestrating leadership capacity within them.

> But what if the issue is more about the people of God than the leaders of God? What if the leadership question is really a body-life stewardship question?

Present-day attempts to discover and train the right kind of leader now reach all the way down to summer "leadership camps" for elementary-school children. This all comes on the heels of nearly five hundred post-Reformation years during which churches and other ministries have regularly disqualified the "priesthood of all believers" in their ministry models as they search for new Moseses, Josephs, and Nehemiahs. The perceived need for strong leaders dominates the church, as the Lausanne survey clearly showed.

Tribal cultures around the world experience a similar issue. It usually comes in the form of strong, authoritative spiritual leaders who will not share ministry functions or roles with others. I have seen this style dominate time after time in a number of African and central Asian tribal cultures. Pastors or leaders who "hear from God" and direct the people are the most important, like the tribal chief who speaks for all in his tribe. I find it so intriguing that most of the discussions today are about Christian leadership. Apparently we are not raising up enough of the right kind of leaders. The select few are supposedly the "make or break" people to lead local church missional impact, team ministry, and church planting.

But what if the issue is more about the people of God than the leaders of God? What if the leadership question is really a body-life stewardship question?

In Ezekiel 34, God spoke to an early leadership problem and set out steps to address this question. From here forward, we will call this God's "economy"; that is, His plan to work His Kingdom purposes through relationship. As you will see, this new economy began with God's outrage at His shepherd leaders. But God's concern was not primarily about the shepherd leaders, but rather about the whole body of His people. He wanted His people as a whole to be His dwelling place (see Ezekiel 37:27), and that change is significant. Ezekiel 34–37 reveals clearly how God developed a pattern that moved from the I-leadership to the We-ideal of whole-body lifestyle, the heart of God's economy—His executing of Kingdom purpose and direction through the community of believers.

Even as I stood in front of those seven hundred vibrant Christians in Soroti, Uganda, the new truth was ever-present before me: *What if it is not about the right kind of leader but rather how we watch for, listen to, and steward the purposes God has already prepared through the whole of His people?*

What if it is not about the right kind of leader but rather how we watch for, listen to, and steward the purposes God has already prepared through the whole of His people?

Shepherd Leaders — You're Fired!

So often today we think of the word *economy* only in terms of the money-managing business. But God's economy is the people-stewardship business. You may be surprised to know that historically, from the biblical era, the word *economy* was not primarily a financial term. Rather, it described the managing of relationships and resources in any given household.[4] A healthy economy actually meant a household of healthy relationships and well-managed resources. The days of Ezekiel were bleak economic times for God's people because His relationship with His people had been broken by their desire for a king.

Now, though, God's investment level increased dramatically so that He might make His people rich in relationship with Him. In this new arrangement, *He was taking over the stewardship of His own household; that is, the actual oversight, management, and care for His people.* Watch His new system of leading and caring for His sheep emerge in Ezekiel 34, 36, and 37.

In Ezekiel 34:1-10, the table was set for God to address His anger issues. In the midst of a broken economy—that is, broken relationships—God called out the major relational stockholders of the day, His shepherd leaders:

> The word of the LORD came to me: "Son of man, prophesy against the shepherds of Israel; prophesy, and say to them, even to the shepherds, Thus says the Lord GOD: Ah, shepherds of Israel who have been feeding yourselves! Should not shepherds feed the sheep?" (verses 1-2)

The representation of kings and subjects, of leaders and followers using the words "shepherd" and "sheep" was common language well known throughout the ancient Near East.[5] People understood shepherd language as descriptive of those who were to care for their spiritual, physical, and material well-being. To understate the issues, it appears that the shepherd leaders were not fulfilling their job descriptions—their "due diligence" was greatly lacking.[6]

Using language we established earlier, the shepherds understood I-thinking and I-acting, as captured in verse 2 in the New International Version: "Woe to the shepherds of Israel who only take care of themselves! Should not shepherds take care of the flock?" The shepherds' behavior was self-centered and self-serving. Ezekiel then revealed the more specific issues that were upsetting to the Lord:

> You eat the fat, you clothe yourselves with the wool, you slaughter the fat ones, but you do not feed the sheep. The weak you have not strengthened, the sick you have not healed, the injured you have not bound up, the strayed you have not brought back, the lost you have not sought, and with force and harshness you have ruled them. (verses 3-4)

The bottom line? The shepherds intended to meet their own needs and not the needs of the people. We also hear God's clear expectation for His leaders. He wanted them to tend and feed the sheep, since the sheep and not the shepherds were His primary concern. He directed them to move vigorously from I-focused actions to We-focused behavior.

Through some exciting relationships, I've seen this "I to We" difference played out. I work with a group of Christians who help run an engineering firm, and we have learned something together in the midst of a leadership transition at the company. As considerations were made for who should be the key leaders in the next generation of this company, I expected such people to be revealed by their area of expertise. Or I assumed it would center on their ability to attract business for the company. While those qualities have value, one intriguing and unexpected quality rose to the top of the charts as essential in next-generation leadership.

We discovered that those vice presidents, managers, and team leaders most noticed are those able to think beyond their own working group. Their ability to make decisions that are for the good of the whole company was the one unique quality discovered. That is, those who are able to think for the corporate good show greater capacity than those who think and act for the I-benefits for themselves or their own working group. Stewarding people for the sake of the whole is so much different than being effective within just your own group. We now realize that steward leadership is an essential trait for next-generation leadership at this firm.

The same could not be said for the shepherds of Ezekiel. God was not concerned that His leaders be warm and well fed—an I-focus. Instead, He demanded they give top priority to caring for His people—a We-attentiveness and stewardship responsibility. This movement was not optional. It had to be addressed, and the Lord of the universe was calling them out.

In the survey referenced earlier, take note of some of the primary characteristics seen in Christian—not secular, but Christian—leaders:

- Prideful, always right, always the big boss
- Harsh, uncaring, refused to listen
- Lack of integrity, not trustworthy[7]

Clearly the very issues among Israel's leaders still characterize some Christian leaders today. Self-centered, self-serving leadership apparently still rises up. Such issues in those of us called to shepherd His people are an affront to the Lord. We can certainly identify with tensions experienced in Ezekiel's day. Led astray by these self-focused, entitled shepherd leaders whose greed and self-serving attitudes put the people at risk, His precious sheep were clearly the focus of God's concern:

> They were scattered, because there was no shepherd, and they became food for all the wild beasts. My sheep were scattered; they wandered over all the mountains and on every high hill. My sheep were scattered over all the face of the earth, with none to search or seek for them. (verses 5-6)

The Israelites were in such disrepair as a people that other nations were ridiculing Yahweh's name, the God who no longer seemed to care for His people.[8] No wonder God's anger was heating up. His people were scattered and lost, wandering all over the place—like sheep without a shepherd. When I-driven leaders dominate, the We-flock simply falls apart. A majority of God's people were hurting, scattered, and without a place to fit in during this season. I have been overwhelmed as I have discovered so many Christian leaders who have "risen up" to assume major leadership roles, yet are struggling because they still do not find a place where they fit into community.

Many years ago while working in Alexandria, Egypt, I witnessed a whole people's powerful sense of abandonment and loss. During a serious financial crisis in the late seventies, the Egyptian government removed price subsidies on basic foodstuffs for the average Egyptian: flour, bread, and sugar. In all three cases, the new price was more than double the previously subsidized charge. This created a frenzy among a people already living close to or under the poverty level.

Many poor families did not know how they could continue to feed their families. The fathers and brothers in this male-dominated culture took to the streets, and madness and mayhem took over so that martial law was declared in many cities, including Alexandria. As an American living there, I was told to stay put and not leave the villa in which I was living. Great advice can sometimes go unheeded. I ventured out with an Egyptian friend to see what was happening. It turned into an afternoon I will never forget.

Though this happened more than thirty years ago, the emotions of that day still overwhelm me. We ventured down a small side street and onto one of the city's major thoroughfares. Suddenly, people were everywhere, running in the streets and overturning cars. Just down the street, I saw people torching the bus station. Yet, while the activity was frenetic, it was the emotion that I cannot forget even to this day. A sense of chaos, even madness, filled the air. I had heard of mob frenzy before, but this was the only time I have ever experienced it. It was a sense of fear and absolute brokenness all around, as people did not seem to know how to cope with their new reality.

Consider that, in their minds, their leaders had let them down. They were lost and had nowhere to turn, no one who would address their needs. Everyone was swept up with emotion somewhere between panic and terror. It was so thick that you could cut it with a knife. I was lost, clearly a sheep without a shepherd, among a people who were lost, scattered, and afraid for their very lives. The fear was truly horrifying.

The sheep of Ezekiel's day faced not only this type of terror, but also the work of active agents of destruction unleashed among them, wolves feeding on the frenzy, purposefully leading others astray. These wolves were calling others to join them in acts of destruction. Most people in such situations follow. Many followed the zealots who were burning down buildings and overturning cars in Egypt. In the midst of the chaos, we were confronted by a man leading a group bent on destruction. He realized that I was a blue-jeaned American and called his "friends" to encircle me. In what was a tense fifteen or twenty minutes that seemed like hours, my Egyptian friend slowly but surely talked us out of that dangerous situation. The small mob decided to let us go. I vividly remember walking casually back to the side street, then running breathlessly for several minutes to the safety of our villa. I sat down and wept. The wild beasts had not devoured us and we were secure.

The Israelites were scattered, alone, scared, and susceptible to all the wild beasts around them because they were sheep without their shepherds. God's economy of relationships at that point was in its own great depression with a people lost, alone, and afraid. And God was furious, as we see in verses 8-10:

> Since there was no shepherd, and because my shepherds have not searched for my sheep, but the shepherds have fed themselves, and have not fed my sheep, therefore, you shepherds, hear the word of the LORD: Thus says the Lord GOD, Behold, I am against the shepherds, and I will require my sheep at their hand and put a stop to their feeding the sheep. No longer shall the shepherds feed themselves. I will rescue my sheep from their mouths, that they may not be food for them.

The shepherds, who fleeced the people and fattened themselves, showed none of the shepherding qualities essential in their oversight. They not only did not keep the people safe, but rather caused them to be scattered across the nations. God's dramatic, no-nonsense response was simple: "I am against the shepherds!" As commentator John Taylor explained, "Having failed their responsibilities, they would not be allowed to rule anymore; the flock would be taken out of their care and they would be deposed from office."[9] The services of the shepherd leaders of Israel were no longer required.

Action Step 1: Remove I-Focused Leaders

The absolute bleakness of God's economy—broken relationships, broken culture, purposelessness—was beyond repair by human leaders, so God removed the leaders. In the language of chapter 1, you might say that the head of the spider was cut off. The leaders were removed and the scattered people continued into further despair, even destruction and death. Thankfully, their Father stepped in and provided the remedy for His wandering sheep. Something of substance had to replace the I-driven shepherd leaders. The people needed protection or the small mob would not be as gracious as ours on that horrifying day in Egypt.

Action Step 2: A New Shepherd for the Sheep

Beyond God's righteous anger and related action, His second deliberate act toward these woeful shepherd leaders was equally spectacular and certainly not expected. He revealed a new dynamic of His Kingdom plan. The same God who had provided vision, clear guidance, counsel, and care through Abraham, Isaac, Jacob, Joseph, Moses, and Joshua—as well as countless judges, priests, and kings for so many generations—stepped in anew. His economy of relationship needed a major stimulus package, and our Lord did not disappoint. Stated plainly, God took over the shepherding of the sheep and promised to search, rescue, and restore His people. Remember, this is the very people who emphatically told Him they wanted an earthly king; someone else to lead them, *not* Him. However, He would not, could not, abandon His sheep now strewn and lost across the nations.[10] Continuing in the words of Ezekiel:

> Thus says the Lord GOD: Behold, I, I myself will search for my
> sheep and will seek them out. As a shepherd seeks out his flock
> when he is among his sheep that have been scattered, so will I

seek out my sheep, and I will rescue them from all places
where they have been scattered. . . .

I myself will be the shepherd of my sheep, and I myself will
make them lie down, declares the Lord GOD. I will seek the lost,
and I will bring back the strayed, and I will bind up the injured,
and I will strengthen the weak, and the fat and the strong I will
destroy. I will feed them in justice. (34:11-12,15-16)

The Lord promised that He would inaugurate a new economy for His sheep; He would assume the role of shepherd. He
was prepared to perform the functions neglected by those self-
serving earthly leaders just removed.[11] This new order meant
God was steward of His household, overseeing the care for His
family, and reaching out to restore those who had been lost and
scattered. This is God's economy of relationship, and this new
reality may change the way you understand spiritual leadership
and whole-body life function in the Church.

Remarkably, though, God's promise to shepherd His people
personally also included the promise to bring the one shepherd.
In Ezekiel 37:24, Ezekiel detailed how God would provide His
servant David to care for the people. For now, God's care of and
stewardship for His sheep would remain in His hands. He had
abolished kingship and was creating what one writer called a
"theocratically organized community"—a God-framed fellowship.[12] We have a Spirit-formed starfish with its supernatural
Creator still very much involved. God was preparing a new kind
of God-centered community and a prophesied "David" would
be the one to lead it. But if God had removed the spiritual
leaders of Israel—kings included—what was His intent in these
prophetic words about a new king?

At this point, we can be certain of two things: First, that by
the Holy Spirit He was preparing a new way to live with His
people. Second, that He was leading this new economy of

relationships. Who would this earthly counterpart be, and how would He reflect the Father's care for His sheep? I see Jesus, from the family line of David, coming into focus: "When he went ashore he saw a great crowd, and he had compassion on them, because they were like sheep without a shepherd" (Mark 6:34). More will be shared about this in the next chapter.

What's so important for us to grasp here is that God's economy is not driven by dollars, numbers, or size but by relationships. He desires intimacy with His people, and to live in and through them. So far, He has removed the shepherd leaders because of their I-focused lifestyle and dominating, insensitive leadership. He now places all of His premium shepherding assets into one We-account: a people of His own choosing, through whom He will reveal His glory to all the nations and extend His Kingdom.

What's so important for us to grasp here is that God's economy is not driven by dollars, numbers, or size but by relationships.

Following this major transition of power and shepherding oversight, Ezekiel 34:25-31 provides additional language for the major renovation in process. God's covenant of promised peace through His servant David would bring safety, security, and showers of blessing. It would release the yoke of bondage that had become a normal part of life for His sheep. He would bring increase because it suited His purposes. His heart was to extend His Kingdom, not because of the greatness and faithfulness of His people, but because He longed for His lost sheep — the very people who had profaned His name and chosen an earthly leader over Him.

His people would no longer be the prey of these other nations. All of this confirmed this issue of strategic importance to God the Father: His glory would be restored from the ridicule and profaning of all the nations. This is stated emphatically in 34:30-31 and in 36:15:

> They shall know that I am the LORD their God with them, and that they, the house of Israel, are my people, declares the Lord GOD. And you are my sheep, human sheep of my pasture, and I am your God, declares the Lord GOD. . . .
>
> And I will not let you hear anymore the reproach of the nations, and you shall no longer bear the disgrace of the peoples and no longer cause your nation to stumble, declares the Lord GOD.

The house of Israel was under new management in God's economy, and the groundwork of change had only just begun.

Action Step 3: God's Holy Spirit Revolution

In the midst of all this transition, a new wineskin was under construction for the new wine of His Spirit. In chapter 36, we discover God was nowhere near completion in this transformative adventure. In fact, this was no longer just a major renovation project but rather an entirely new beginning. God had removed the shepherd leaders (step 1), made Himself shepherd over all the sheep, and promised a future Davidic king to carry on this essential shepherding care and oversight (step 2). Now it was time for something with further dramatic impact. Consider the verses depicting the beginning of the Spirit-breathed winds of transformation, Ezekiel 36:25-28:

> I will sprinkle clean water on you, and you shall be clean from all your uncleanness, and from all your idols I will cleanse you. And I will give you a new heart, and a new spirit I will put

within you. And I will remove the heart of stone from your flesh and give you a heart of flesh. And I will put my Spirit within you, and cause you to walk in my statutes and be careful to obey my rules. You shall dwell in the land that I gave to your fathers, and you shall be my people, and I will be your God.

It was not only for the shepherd leaders, but for every one of His lost, broken, and even self-indulgent sheep. God was doing this for the sake of His holy name among the very people who had profaned Him (see Ezekiel 36:22-23). The God of Abraham, Isaac, and Jacob now changed the way His presence would be experienced by the Israelites. He intended to move out from behind the curtain of the Holy of Holies in the temple and personally into the life of every one of His people. And unlike when He spoke through the prophets before Ezekiel, He now spoke openly about the role of the Holy Spirit. He disclosed how His Spirit would move.[13]

God's new We-economy developed as an "inside job" through the touch of His Spirit, person to person, that would radicalize His Kingdom people. No longer would His people have to seek Him only in the temple. He now would reveal Himself personally to each one. What would result ultimately was not simply a heart transplant, but a spiritual revitalization of the whole person. God promises not a general touch of the Spirit, as happened with the judges, but a transforming of the very heart of humankind through the infilling presence of the Holy Spirit. Note here that this "heart" includes the mind, will, and emotions, as well as the spirit of man—the impulses that drive the thoughts, desires, and conduct.[14] Such intimate, personal companionship with the Father gives opportunity for total transformation in every individual who has wandered away. He begins to move His people from "I to We" by promising to transform each individual's heart, mind, soul, and spirit from the inside out.

You may remember the story of Ernest Shackleton's voyage on the *Endurance* into Antarctica. You read of how the crew's one long year stuck in ice and snow surprisingly drew forth teamwork, self-sacrifice, and good cheer that characterized their lives together. The quality of their shared relationships amid incredible suffering seems unreal. Likewise, Ezekiel 36 confirms that God had opened up a new world of hope for His people. It was a whole new source of being for each of His sheep. It was not an economy dominated by wealth, status, personal significance, or earthly power. Rather, it was one empowered by the Spirit's dynamic entry into every person. The Good Shepherd had made His people intimately rich in relationship by pouring out His Spirit into their hearts and spirits. He created an internal safety and security that knew no bounds — one that could not be taken away. At this point we may wonder . . .

Will the experience of God's people be like what occurred unexpectedly among Shackleton's shipmates on their voyage?

Will there be a minimizing of status differences, a sharing of leadership and team responsibilities?

Will all share both in the work and the blessings?

Will the hierarchy of shepherd leadership that had been removed truly stay removed?

Will high trust and closeness between the Good Shepherd and His sheep — and among the sheep themselves — be developed?

Will there be less self-indulgence and self-seeking?

What we know for certain is that God's new economy is based on relationship. God the Holy Spirit is deepening the interconnectedness of His people for an even greater depth of connection. Any question about His Kingdom still focusing on the greatness of cities or kings has been removed. The grand organization of God's people grew into majestic splendor, then was ripped into two disparate kingdoms. Those kingdoms ebbed and flowed for centuries with godly and then corrupt leaders.

The kingdom of His chosen people finally folded into such brokenness and disrepair that they were scattered to the winds. They were the laughingstock of the nations. Now God seeks to redeem and restore His lost people through relationship—and He does so with an internal touch of His life-giving Spirit.

God's existence with His people has become much more about organic connections—relationships—than any kingly system or organizational structure. Remember our starfish? It has millions of life-giving cells that live and work together, forming a decentralized network. The cells adapt to their context and whatever needs or opportunities come their way. The only major difference between the starfish and these Spirit-filled people is that the Lord of the universe has unleashed His Spirit into every one of those human cells. There are so many active body parts to fulfill so much of what God desires among His people. A new vision is emerging.

To remove any question about His intent to live and move and have His way among His people, He goes one step further.

Action Step 4: God's Powerful Army

We return to Ezekiel 37, coming full circle to where we began. Now we can understand the movement of God's Spirit in the valley of dry bones in the clear perspective of the bigger picture. The people of the house of Israel have been scattered, lying about as dry bones, and now their God is breathing Holy Spirit life into them, enabling Him to live among them in a new and fresh way.[15] Finally we come to the last step of God's new economy. Ezekiel 37:1-14, from the first verse, sheds light on the miraculous change God is enacting in and among His people. A mighty roar fills the valley of dry bones as God calls the winds of His Spirit from the four corners of the earth to breathe life into His lifeless people, creating a great army. Stop for a moment and read this section again in Ezekiel 37. Think about God's removing the shepherd leaders and inserting the Holy Spirit in every believer as your new framework. Did you notice a different word used to describe God's people? No longer are they described as sheep. Look at Ezekiel 37:10, where Ezekiel again speaks the words of the Lord: "So I prophesied as he commanded me, and the breath came into them, and they lived and stood on their feet, an exceedingly great army."

No more are they a wandering, separated, individualized bunch of lost sheep, each left to fend for himself. They have become a commanding, We-army of God by the power of the Holy Spirit. We have watched very closely how He transformed a model of human-centered leadership to Spirit-driven body life. The focus is no longer on the I-leaders, but on the We-people as a whole. They are now an army prepared to execute His Spirit-breathed plans, a powerful, spiritual force that will change the face of the Church worldwide.

God's new economy was designed for all His people — not just the right kind of leaders or church planters where the rest are just sheepish observers. God's design from two thousand years ago remains His cutting-edge blueprint for today. It is an organic design, rich in relationship. The focus is on the life-giving work of the One who will live and move and have His way among His people. As my friend and publisher, David Wetzler, said to me,

> It is a helpful reminder that the church is not a business, but a living organism. The church has a different understanding and definition for profitability and market share than the world and is governed by different principles found in the Bible. This should cause us to reflect on the guiding principles and core values to which we adhere as we consider the role of leadership in the church.[16]

Simply stated, we have a new economy, and it is time to become that We-army He has destined us to become together.

Think of that organic, life-multiplying starfish again for a moment: "The absence of structure, leadership, and formal organization, once considered a weakness, has become a major asset. . . . The rules of the game have changed."[17] God will lead and multiply the many cells of His Spirit-driven body life. We see the foundation of an incredible kinetic force that will move through cultures worldwide, through the richness of normal, everyday relationships. Here we see a new level of importance for every soldier in this new army. It is an internal transformation of the individual that will create a powerful force unlike anything the world has ever seen.[18]

Summary

Setting the context for Ezekiel 37 through chapters 34 and 36, we discover God's profound anger at the shepherd leaders because they stopped caring for the sheep. In addressing this problem, He removed the leaders and became His people's very own shepherd leader. He promised to fill every one of His people with His Spirit, and then moved them from wandering sheep into a unified, powerful army—a new body-life design of His own choosing. We soon see a whole new Kingdom of priests, manifested by full participation in a living body, preceded by the coming of the Great Shepherd.

Application Steps

1. Find something in your life that you commonly do alone, and invite someone to join you. This could be anything from building a model airplane, hiking or climbing, taking a walk, to having a quiet cup of coffee or tea. After

the experience together, compare and contrast the value of having someone with you while doing something you have always thought you would prefer to do alone.

2. For those of you in a small group that meets regularly, stop your curriculum or study material for two months and instead have a time of worship, prayer, and sharing. In the spirit of 1 Corinthians 14:26, be prayerfully attentive through the week about what God would have each of you share with your community when you gather. When you meet, allow the Spirit to guide your time—ask Him to—as each shares as he or she is so led. Include children if your group has any. At the end of the two months, have a group meeting during which you reflect on the fresh ways you have seen God at work both leading and moving your community.

3. Do a Google search for "Business Principles." On a chart, sort the terms you find under the headers business, Bible, or both. For the business terms, discuss how we have translated them into the Church, appropriately or inappropriately. For those under Bible, find Scripture to support your belief.

4. God removed Ezekiel's false shepherds. Make a list of how this would positively and negatively affect your local church or ministry. Give three adjectives that would describe the possibilities of such a new culture.

Questions for Discussion

1. How would you envision your small group, your church, your ministry, or your organization being different if you viewed it as a starfish rather than a spider?

2. Have you ever had an "Alexandria" experience like the one described early in the chapter, where the author was in the middle of a frenzied group of broken, lost people? What did you learn from that experience?

3. Which of the four steps God took with His people is most
    striking to you:

    • Removing the shepherd leaders?
    • Becoming the shepherd leader for His people?
    • Filling each individual with His Holy Spirit?
    • Pouring out His Spirit on all the people together, making
      them into an exceedingly great army?

4. Related to Action Step 4, what if God really did remove the
    leaders and did not replace them in the sense that we have
    leaders today? What would be different about body life in
    the Church and world if this were the case?

---

1. Jane Overstreet, "Defining Christ-like Leadership, and Describing Best
   Practices in Leadership Development" (paper, Lausanne Movement,
   Leadership Working Group, May 2009), 1.
2. Overstreet, 2.
3. Overstreet, 9.
4. Paul R. Ford, *Knocking Over the Leadership Ladder* (St. Charles, IL:
   ChurchSmart Resources, 2008), 93.
5. Walther Eichrodt, *Ezekiel: A Commentary* (Philadelphia: Westminster, 1970),
   469.
6. Samuel L. Adams, "Between Text and Sermon," *Interpretation* 62 (January
   2008): 304.
7. Overstreet, 3.
8. Walther Zimmerli, *Ezekiel 2* (Philadelphia: Fortress, 1983), 153.
9. John Taylor, *Ezekiel: An Introduction and Commentary* (Leicester, England:
   InterVarsity, 1969), 220.
10. Adams, 305.
11. Willliam H. Brownlee, "Ezekiel's Poetic Indictment of the Shepherds," *Harvard
    Theological Review* 51, no. 4 (October 1958): 191.
12. Karin Schopflin, "The Composition of Metaphysical Oracles with the Book
    of Ezekiel," *Vetus Testamentum* (January 2005): 113.
13. Zimmerli, 135, 153.
14. Taylor, 232.
15. Carl Freidrich Keil, *Prophecies of Ezekiel* (Grand Rapids, MI: Eerdmans,
    1970), 119.
16. David Wetzler, personal note to author, 2008.
17. Ori Brafman and Rod A. Beckstrom, *The Starfish and the Spider* (New York:
    Penguin, 2006), 7.
18. Eichrodt, 499.

Chapter 3

Kingdom Clarity

God Comes to Live Among Us

My servant David shall be king over them, and they shall all have one shepherd. . . . My dwelling place shall be with them, and I will be their God, and they shall be my people. Then the nations will know that I am the LORD who sanctifies Israel, *when my sanctuary is in their midst* forevermore.

— EZEKIEL 37:24,27-28, EMPHASIS ADDED

In [Christ Jesus] you also are being built together into a dwelling place for God by the Spirit.

— EPHESIANS 2:22

Jesus Christ sent apostles and teachers for this very purpose — that the corporate Person of Christ and His church, made up of many members, might be brought into being and made known. . . . We are here to have the full realization of Jesus Christ, for the purpose of building His body.

— OSWALD CHAMBERS[1]

The real voyage of discovery is seeing with new eyes.

— MARCEL PROUST[2]

As we move from "I to We," we begin to see God's dwelling place — the beautiful place where He desires to live and move and have His way among us — with fresh eyes as we discover His purposes among us. From Ezekiel to the New Testament, God makes His move, and we take hold of its fresh meaning as revealed, step-by-step.

My experience among the formerly nomadic tribal groups of central Asia provides a striking illustration. Over the past twenty years, God has opened the door for the gospel and His presence to take root among the Kazakhs, Kyrgyz, Uzbeks, and other distinct people groups of that region. Many of us from the West have had the opportunity to work with these new brothers and sisters in Christ. Our friends worked hard to do evangelism and build pastor-led churches similar to what we have done in the West. They did what they were taught — by us Westerners. We evangelized them, saw many respond, and then trained many nationals to be pastors. We trained them — in newly formed Western-style seminaries there — to be leaders in a model similar to what we have been doing in the West over the past twenty years. We taught them to evangelize, lead with vision, and seek to grow big churches where people would meet for worship in buildings rather than in their homes. But things did not click for these more relationally focused friends who graciously acted out the strategies we truly believed would work for them.

They trusted us, their Western counterparts who had shared the gospel and discipled them. What they did not realize was that many of us who came to spread the gospel were from very different cultures than theirs. They did not realize that perhaps we had not done our cultural homework. Truthfully, we did not think through some of the differences between Western cultures and these highly relational, We-tribal cultures and the related implications. We failed to contextualize our teaching about church and failed in helping them determine what form of body-life fellowship would fit their relational setting.

As noted, we did not recognize that central Asians naturally live a more relationally centered, We-based lifestyle. We also did not realize how much more casual and slower-paced central

Asians live. They were not able to identify with our strategic thinking, fast acting, and often more task-oriented or results-driven style of ministry. Everything centered around relationships, all the way down to the way they followed a schedule. If a Kazakh comes to a meeting at 11:30 a.m. instead of the appointed time of 10 a.m., he is not late but rather was honoring his friends with whom he had just spent extra time. It is all about the relationship. So often, Kyrgyz or Uzbeks are amazed when they hear of an American who moved a long distance from his extended family to take a job with increased pay. Their approach to life revolves around healthy stewardship of their households. This is the closest most central Asians would get to a strategic plan: plan around extended family.

Secondly, from our Western worldview, we did not grasp how Christian body life would more naturally develop through those relationships as the gospel took root culturally in this context. Literally, the gospel was ready to move from household to household just as in the book of Acts. I picture the house church of three central Asian families in the foothills of the Tien Shan mountains. All Muslim converts, together they were experiencing that love and unity through the extension of family life in Christ. Their friends were watching, and dropped by often, only to be enveloped in God's love expressed through these Spirit-filled relationships. Households, by their very welcoming presence, revealed the love of Christ naturally. But we were not prepared to consider this in our training models because most of our values and methods were designed for the reaching and training of individuals and not groups of people. We were excellent at training the I-leaders in our own Western style but were perplexed by what it means to work among people who live a We-relational lifestyle. We had no idea how much the individualism of the West affects the way we develop ministries and encourage believers.

One final issue was a shocking surprise. Our "body life in a building" model found almost no acceptance in central Asia. For most Kazakhs, church buildings are a foreign concept as a place for friends to gather. The few churches that grew to any size were pastored by foreigners, in fact. You might say we picked the wrong model for the dwelling place in which God desired to reveal Himself among our believing friends. We had tried to lead from *our* perspective on *their* behalf. Much of our training simply did not take hold. Thankfully, though, our central Asian partners realized that God desired to live and move naturally among their extended families and friends. God's Spirit began to find a home in the households of Kazakhs, Kyrgyz, and others in this region. We will save the rest of this story for later, but the issues are relevant to the pressing subject of this chapter, God's dwelling place.

From our study of Ezekiel 34, 36, and 37, we understand now that God wants to build His people into a unique, life-giving community. Why? So that He can live among them and lead them into His purposes. Ephesians 2:22 shows the apostle Paul using the same language of our being God's "dwelling place" that Ezekiel used in his prophecy more than seven hundred years before. What happened between Ezekiel's promise of a Spirit-breathed army and Paul's sharing about body life among believers? Who was this Davidic king prophetically promised by Ezekiel and how will he model God's desire to live and move among His people?

Jesus: The Shepherd King Revealed

We look now for the Davidic king that God promised through Ezekiel. God the Father, the new shepherd leader, promised a new shepherd king, referenced earlier: "My servant David shall be king over them, and they shall all have one shepherd" (Ezekiel 37:24). God removed the shepherd leaders and took sole responsibility for the care, oversight, and direction of His people. As we move to the New Testament, we can see how He now passes that role onto God the Son: "When he [Jesus] went ashore [in Galilee] he saw a great crowd, and he had compassion on them, because they were like sheep without a shepherd. And he began to teach them many things" (Mark 6:34).

Earthly shepherds for Israel had not been seen since God removed them at least six hundred years earlier, but now one stood in their presence. The people were scattered in Ezekiel's day. Jesus saw those same lost sheep. God had not relinquished His shepherding role, but rather released it to the Word who became flesh, His Son.

As we seek understanding about the shepherd king promised in Ezekiel, consider one key prophesy fulfilled at Jesus' birth in Matthew 2:6. The wise men came searching for the promised king, following His star. The scribes and the Pharisees informed the wise men that the Messiah would be born in Bethlehem, using a reference from Micah 5:2-4:

> You, O Bethlehem, in the land of Judah,
>> are by no means least among the rulers of Judah;
> for from you shall come a ruler
>> who will shepherd my people Israel. (Matthew 2:6)

Jesus was indeed the shepherd of God who came to usher in His Kingdom for the people of Israel—and beyond. John 10 reveals four strategic insights about Jesus as the promised shepherd leader prophesied in Ezekiel. These perceptions also help us understand the We-nature and unity between the Father and Son. This supernatural, intrinsic unity would soon be given to the disciples through the Holy Spirit.

Insight #1

"He who enters by the door is the shepherd of the sheep. To him the gatekeeper opens. The sheep hear his voice, and he calls his own sheep by name and leads them out. When he has brought out all his own, he goes before them, and the sheep follow him, for they know his voice" (John 10:2-4).

God resumed the leadership of His people. The shepherd Jesus claims the same role. He calls them by name and leads them—and they know His voice, the one true Shepherd's voice.

Insight #2

"I am the good shepherd. I know my own and my own know me, just as the Father knows me and I know the Father; and I lay down my life for the sheep" (John 10:14-15).

The intimate relationship of the Father and the Son is highlighted. Just as the Father removed the shepherds in Ezekiel 34 and became the shepherd, the Son now becomes that shepherd, with the expressed purpose of laying down His life for the sheep.

Insight #3

"I have other sheep that are not of this fold. I must bring them also, and they will listen to my voice. So there will be one flock, one shepherd" (John 10:16).

The promise of the Father's (and now the Son's) care and leadership will now extend beyond just His chosen people to the Gentiles who are beyond the fold. But there will still be only one flock and one shepherd to gather, care for, and direct His people. Jesus will do this, expanding the Kingdom of God to the whole world.

Insight #4

"For this reason the Father loves me, because I lay down my life that I may take it up again" (John 10:17). "For it is written, 'I will strike the shepherd, and the sheep of the flock will be scattered.' But after I am raised up, I will go before you to Galilee" (Matthew 26:31-32).

The Son, the new shepherd leader of His people, will lay down His life. We also learn of this last critical factor in Matthew 26. His death will not be the end, but rather the beginning of something very important in the Kingdom. The shepherd leader of Israel will continue into the future in ways yet to be determined.

Imagine that you live in central Asia, and that your father and your grandfather were nomadic shepherds in the high steppe country. As you read the words above, you realize just how deeply Jesus the Great Shepherd loved you by laying down His life for you. He became the blood sacrifice for your sins and all of your believing family members. No longer will you have to kill the sheep in the Muslim ritual cleansing style. In Christ, by His shed blood, you are free from sin and forgiven without any further rituals required. This gift is so great you cannot help but sharing in joy-filled worship in your house church, singing loudly even for the neighbors to hear. You want to share the love of Christ with them as well, both in word and action, and to welcome them into your home for *plafth*, a traditional meat and rice dish. You long for them to come to a saving understanding of Jesus so that their households may become another extension of the love of Jesus in your village—and to other villages in your *oblast* (district).

In summary, Jesus is the promised Davidic king, the one who comes to shepherd His people on earth. He takes the role that God the Father had assumed in Ezekiel 34 when the shepherd leaders were removed. The sheep know His voice and He begins to lead them. His intimate relationship with the Father is a critical factor in this. He will lay down His life for the sheep, and even for those beyond the fold of Israel. Lastly, He will be raised up again for Kingdom purposes that will become clear.

Jesus is God the Son, carrying on the role of shepherd leader from His Father and continuing His Father's Kingdom purposes on earth in a visible and fresh manner.

The Unity Factor

Jesus provides us with one last scenario that further confirms His unity with the Father but takes us to a surprising next step in the We-process as His sheep. It is an important section of the puzzle coming together piece by piece. We move to John 17 in the Upper Room, where we witness Jesus' and the Twelve's last fellowship before His death.

Envision yourself there and reflect on Jesus' prayer in John 17:20-23:

> I do not ask for these only, but also for those who will believe in me through their word, that they may all be one, just as you, Father, are in me, and I in you, that they also may be in us, so that the world may believe that you have sent me. The glory that you have given me I have given to them, that they may be one even as we are one, I in them and you in me, that they may become perfectly one, so that the world may know that you sent me and loved them even as you loved me.

The unity between the Father and the Son is one fundamental dynamic we seldom consider in moving from God the Father as shepherd to Jesus the Good Shepherd who cares for, calls out to, and then dies for the sheep. Now we actually see unity and community—the We-factor—playing out as Jesus prepares His disciples for His death and resurrection.

What is so unusual here? First, He prays for us to experience the same unity that He and the Father have experienced. Why? So that the world may believe.

Consider our current strategies for evangelism, our tactics for establishing church-planting movements. Reflect on our procedures for training certain types of strategic, visionary leaders who lead well and multiply other new believers that are enfolded into God's household. When do we even utter the word "unity" in our plan of attack for such great Kingdom ventures? When is the last time you heard a discussion that suggested how we live together in unity may be more important than our present evangelistic strategies for reaching the world?[3]

Why is living in the unity of the Father and Son so strategically important? Because He said so. Jesus also tells the Father that He has given His followers the glory that the Father gave Him. Why? So that we who are followers of Jesus may be one—even as They are one. Something very important is going on here. Something more intentional than human strategy is happening.

The reason that God first filled each individual with the Holy Spirit in Ezekiel 36 before filling all the sheep together in chapter 37 is significant. The fullness of the Spirit in Christ individually is not sufficient. Our completeness in the Spirit together means much more than any of us would care to realize today. Unity in the Spirit, driven by the model of the Father and Son, moves us from "I to We" in ways that we have not yet considered.

These thoughts bring me back to something to which I referred in *Knocking Over the Leadership Ladder* four years ago. A new Russian believer came to one of our CoMission ministry team leaders in the midnineties and said, "We praise God that you have come from America to share the gospel with us. But please, would you tell your team members to go home until they like each other, and then come back and share the gospel." Sometimes the message gets lost in the midst of broken or weak community. This is especially true if the unity of those relationships does not portray the grace-filled, life-giving message of Jesus the Good Shepherd. *We may have missed the central, strategic role of unified, solid relationships that reveal the bond of God the Father and Jesus the Son.* Therein is the very glory of the Father and therein lies the model that will cause many in the world to believe. God's plan is centered in the unity and power in the body of Christ, His major strategy.

Consider my friend Rick's words about five years after he and his family moved from the United States to Mexico to invest in needy Mexicans for the sake of the gospel:

> After being away from the American church, I am beginning to think more and more about the "organic" nature of the church—natural, spontaneous growth that comes from healthy relationships as its foundation rather than from good systems and visionary leadership. You understand that I know systems and vision are not bad things, but without healthy relationships and releasing others to their ministries, the church looks and feels like a business with a good CEO as leader even as it preaches Jesus.[4]

In the Upper Room, Jesus did not pray for great Kingdom leaders. He did not pray for brilliant, world-winning strategies to be fashioned in the minds and actions of His followers. Perhaps our single-minded pattern of constantly focused concentration on training leaders and church planters is misplaced in this season of ministry. Rather, Jesus' single-minded prayer was for our unity to be like His with the Father. He prayed that the glory of the Father—that which He does not share—be given for the sake of the priceless gift of unity so that many will venture into the household of God.

There are things embedded in the way we love each other, share our spiritual gifts, and live out God's purposes together that we may just now begin to grasp. A group of strong, independent-minded, strategic-thinking individuals is just not enough. The Son prays for our unity to be like His and God the Father's. Do not miss this critically placed message. Something very important began in the Upper Room in Jesus' prayer, immediately before He went to Gethsemane, was arrested, and was crucified.

Consider the depths of this We-principle as we continue forward. In our present I-world, never forget that God has designed His economy—His relational means of managing and fulfilling His purposes—to function as a We-community. That is the heart of Jesus' prayer in the Upper Room, a core piece of God's relational design to reach the ends of the earth.

The Body of Christ: The Place Where God Lives

His Kingdom vision continues as the risen Lord sends His disciples into the world. The mission to reach the lost, ever expanding beyond the lost sheep of Israel, continues.[5] Jesus leaves no question as to the continuity of the mission into the next generation in Acts 1:8: "But you will receive power when the Holy Spirit has come upon you, and you will be my witnesses in Jerusalem and in all Judea and Samaria, and to the end of the earth."

It was the same Holy Spirit whom God promised would fill every sheep and place a new heart in each one. It was the same breath of God who shook the dry bones, restored lost sheep, and molded them together into a powerful army. God the Spirit would continue the presence and power of Jesus on earth. The same Jesus of Nazareth who stood in His synagogue and said, "The Spirit of the Lord is upon me" (Luke 4:18), now prepares the disciples for the next dynamic spiritual movement toward the creation of that army prophesied in Ezekiel 37.

We see and hear the power of the Holy Spirit that arrived during Pentecost in Acts 2:14-41 through Peter's commanding message. So often the strategy taken for reaching the world is understood as preaching the way Peter did. That is, individuals sharing the gospel so that people can respond. This is indeed one important function in body-life ministry, but Peter was actually just one among many full of the Holy Spirit. Interestingly, in Acts 2:1-12, many others spoke first. The work of Jesus is immediately fulfilled in a multiplicity of people revealing a multiplicity of gifts.[6] The Spirit was poured out as tongues of fire, given so that outsiders who had come to Jerusalem could hear words in their own language. It was this very movement of God's people toward an organic-We that set the context for one man named Peter to speak boldly in the power of the Holy Spirit.

The same Spirit drew the people together into profoundly deep relationships immediately after Peter's message. Acts 2:42-47 reflects a community that is overwhelmingly inclusive and exceptionally practical. Fundamentally, the community was addressing the basic level of personal needs. The Word of God shared, fellowship, the breaking of bread, praying, and generous sharing marked the Spirit's moving among the people in their response to the message. To say that people felt that they belonged would be an understatement. Not surprisingly, the next statement reports that people were being saved day by day. The Spirit of God has drawn people together so powerfully that their community becomes the focal point of their lives. It started with supernaturally gifted believers filled with tongues of fire, moved to Peter's powerful preaching and calling thousands to salvation, and then continued into life-giving, resource-sharing body life. *This* is the Church!

We often focus on what happened and so lose sight of *how* it happened. All the Acts 2 events are immersed in the Spirit of God's work:

- *Through people's gifts* enacted in tongues of fire and Peter's preaching
- *In people's response* to the message of salvation
- *Among people's lives* through community, prayer, and sharing

God, as promised, is making His home—His sanctuary—among the people from the start of the Spirit's coming in power, already revealed in these three specific ways.[7] We will look more deeply at this Acts 2 pattern in the next chapter.

It is so easy at times to think of the elements of Christian body life in Acts 2:42 and following as essential tasks to be done together. But do not lose sight of a foundational point here: Relationships and community provided the framework for all of these activities. God designed us to live out our lives together, not in an individual, independent pursuit. From the beginning of the move of God's Spirit upon all of His people, the Christian life was primarily a We-process, where individuals found their fit within the body of Christ.

That is why the Kazakhs and Kyrgyz adapted so quickly to a house-church model: They made a sincere effort to adopt a Western style of church, but such a model seemed foreign and impersonal because God's house did not seem as warm, friendly, and personal as each of their homes. The household setting fit their natural, cultural style of extended family living as the norm.[8] Once they grasped that God's presence could be experienced together in their homes, they readily caught on to this more naturally relational "worship center."

As I watched my east African and central Asian tribal friends train other national believers in their own settings, I immediately noticed something different. By the very nature of their We-cultural style, they discussed biblical principles in a very relational way. As principles were presented, people would interact in the group until it got quiet, which was a cue to move on to the next principle or biblical theme.

People watched and listened to each other. Even the teacher modeled a posture that valued all that was being shared. In my Western thinking, I would have been on the next page of my outline, needing to finish what I had prepared. What a fascinating change in approach. It will not surprise you that in cross-cultural settings I have not finished an outline now in over six years. Such an emphasis on belonging and including others communally is the nature of relational cultures. I have learned to value the We-process of learning that includes strengthening relationships even while training concepts and applications. It is no longer an I-training, it is a We-engagement in learning together in the Spirit and from one another. If you want biblical principles to be multiplied into the lives of people around you, this is the way.

A new life was beginning among the people of God, but it was more than just a sense of closeness and belonging. These people were becoming the body of Jesus Christ on earth. The indwelling Spirit not only was cleansing people and giving them a new heart (see Ezekiel 36:26-27), but also making them into the place where God will live in and with His people.[9] Put simply by Paul in 1 Corinthians 12:27: "You are the body of Christ and individually members of it." There is a dramatic change in the dynamic of friendship and community. The community that has been established by the fellowship of the Father, Son, and Holy Spirit cannot be fully revealed through organization. It has to become a life-giving organism.[10] It is now an interwoven, life-giving interdependence that thrives and multiplies through relationship.

God's Household

Perhaps the clearest passage in the New Testament that reflects this new reality of the body of Christ is Paul's words in Ephesians

2:19-22. Here he talks about the nature of this body life in the Spirit:

> You are no longer strangers and aliens, but you are fellow citizens with the saints and members of the household of God, built on the foundation of the apostles and prophets, Christ Jesus himself being the cornerstone, in whom the whole structure, being joined together, grows into a holy temple in the Lord. In him you also are being built together into a dwelling place for God by the Spirit.

Paul highlights three particulars crucial to our understanding of the We-context. He identifies this process as a part of "God's economy" in Ephesians 3:2. The nature of God's economy is the "stewardship of God's grace that was given to me for you." Paul is identifying how the mystery of the gospel is revealed. He makes very clear the vital, central role of organic, body-life relationships.

We have joined a new household as the people of God, strangers no more. In calling people to their identity in Christ and to one another, Paul used imagery that people of his day understood in their cultural setting. To be a member of a house and its household was standard in the first century. So much so that Jesus stayed with Peter in Capernaum and used that setting as His base of operation. This fact is noted in Mark's gospel at least five times.[11] The depth of relationship grew between Jesus and Peter not only because Jesus called him alongside, but because Jesus also shared in Peter's family's care. Jesus' usual missional approach, as well as the apostle Paul's, was to find a house and household willing to commit themselves to Jesus' Kingdom message. The Philippian jailer and Lydia from Thyatira are examples of people whose households responded to the gospel.

In this extended spiritual family:

- God is the Father
- Jesus is the head of the household
- The Spirit provides the power and energy for the community
- The disciples are members of the household
- Men and women in Christ become brothers and sisters[12]

This innovative community provides the place of belonging and also the opportunity for living interdependently in Christ.[13] All of us are responsible participants—investors in this body life together. It is a community invested with powerful spiritual gifts in each individual and sewn together by love relationships.

God's Building, God's Temple

Worship is always at the center of our relationship with God. Look at the second image Paul used to describe our new community in Ephesians 2:21: "In whom the whole structure, being joined together, grows into a holy temple in the Lord." With Christ Jesus as the cornerstone and the apostles and prophets as key building blocks, the structure takes shape as all the pieces come together. Peter added a superb metaphor in 1 Peter 2:5, playing off of Jesus as the cornerstone of this new and growing house of worship: "You yourselves like living stones are being built up as a spiritual house, to be a holy priesthood, to offer spiritual sacrifices acceptable to God through Jesus Christ."

Langdon Reinke, a friend in ministry, made this comment as he edited this section:

If the new structure in which God dwells is made up of people who become a priesthood, why would anyone want to go back to previous models—the tabernacle, the temple—which were only a foreshadowing of things to come? In 1 Peter 2 and Ephesians 2:19-22, *we* actually become that temple of God!

We are living stones, joined together person by person, equally important in fusing the whole building together in concert with one another. In fact, we are the building! What an amazing message for us today at a time when we are separated from one another by so many realities of life.

In his book *Community: The Structure of Belonging*, Peter Block spoke to this issue: "Our isolation occurs because western culture, our individualistic narrative, the inward attention of our institutions and professions, and the messages from our media fragment us. We are broken into pieces."[14] By the very nature of being in Christ, a part of God's household, each one of us is intrinsically built together with one another. We are built together, inextricably framed together, as a place of worship for God the Father.

We form the very walls of His sanctuary, each precious stone in place as one who is bound to the next. This is not an optional-participation model. We are construction material in the hands of the Father. The "I to We" process through which the Spirit of God takes us actually creates the very design of living stones. We are the ones who discover our life together in Christ, to the praise and glory of God.

> This is not an optional-participation model. We are construction material in the hands of the Father.

It is fascinating that we are not only building blocks for God's temple, but Peter also called us all living stones, a holy priesthood.

The new model of spiritual leadership in the Kingdom does not allow for a select few being the priests of God as was true for the people of Israel and Judah. Rather, it includes every one of us as priests. Consider this: Together we are not only the framework of God's temple but also the gathered priests who lead and participate in worship day after day in His Kingdom, crying, "O Lord, how majestic is Your name in all the earth! We praise You, we honor You, we glorify You! We lift You up! We, the body of Christ, form the very house of worship where You have chosen to live."

Being Built Together

Simply stated, we are not a building already completed. We are not a temple that has already been built into its final form. We are organic: very much alive, very much in process, and very much adjusting and changing to the purposes of God being lived out among us. God continues to create new life and new forms through Spirit-led initiatives. But even more importantly, this new life and these new forms come through the people whom God brings together in this "Jesus' body-life-in-the-making" building project.

God reveals His purposes through the written Word, the Bible, with so much clear vision and direction. But He also reveals His purposes through the spiritual gifts and passions of people He brings to every church, ministry, or missional situation. Peter Block uses two helpful phrases here: collective transformation and collective possibilities.[15] While we focus so much in the West on individual transformation, imagine the possibilities when the Spirit of God has access to our collective transformation. Try to grasp the creativity available in the collective possibilities through the Holy Spirit of God in us.

How dynamic it is when, by God's design, we live and move as one organic body, adapting to situations and shifting focus here or there. Like the starfish, we can split off and multiply. The house-church movement in central Asia again comes to mind, where the gospel is moving from household to household. Or seeing men's accountability groups sprout up and multiply when men find a safe, accountable place to encourage each other. Such events happen because we are an organization that is much more organic and free-flowing than any human-driven operation. Making the decision to be accountable to the whole body of Christ through your relationships sets in motion an astonishing process. Within this organic context of hospitality and collective possibility, new and varied gifts are accessible through the participants.

A community is created that brings in many from the fringes into their appropriate, "living stone," priestly status among the whole. It is not always simple. God can change direction in body life through new building blocks He brings into any situation, and this is all to His praise and glory and for His purposes. It is, after all, His building, and we are His building blocks together for His glory and praise. And it is His Holy Spirit driving the "being built together" process. Again, like a starfish supernaturally led by the Spirit in all of its organic parts, we can adapt and multiply in new ways and new settings.

Eighteen months ago I joined a group of Lutheran pastors and lay leaders from one region of the United States in a body-life team. We are meeting and talking by phone regularly. They graciously invited me to come and share about our new Body Life Design process. As a group of about twelve, we are seeking to be open to the Spirit for what He wants to do among us in concert. To be honest, Lutherans are not actually the first place I would go looking for a vibrant, Spirit-led process—our Pentecostal partners in Uganda would likely top that list. But something very unusual is happening in this group. For most of the participants, it is a first pursuit in seeking the Spirit's leading. Consider the words from two men involved with this "experiment."

The value of fellow Christians and ministry leaders wanting to join together in a common pursuit because the Spirit of the Lord is leading them to want to is powerful. I have never experienced such camaraderie and fellowship this side of heaven. But I believe that such experiences give us a foretaste of the heavenly community that we will all someday enjoy because of Christ.[16]

There is a joint wisdom in the body of Christ through the activity of the Holy Spirit which is active in this group. Sometimes I just like to sit back, listen, and pray.[17]

For these Christian leaders, this experience has been as much about risking in deeper, body-life relationship as it has been about pursuing the Spirit together. But it is a wonderful starting point for brothers and sisters who are learning to listen to the Lord collectively and learning to trust each other in the process. The ownership of shared life together among these leaders has been key to the Spirit's speaking about a number of areas where He is challenging us. When such ownership is shared, no one leader carries the torch of leadership — a life-changing insight for many pastors. Along the lines of that shared ownership, consider these words from Janet Williams, a friend and partner in ministry:

Everybody has a part to play, and is gifted to play it. No one person is supposed to be responsible for knowing everything and being able to do everything. That is why other people are there. It frees all of us to use our God-given gifts. It also makes all of us responsible for using our gifts. It is not about reading the New Testament to find the one way of doing evangelism. It is all about the people God has called for this place and time. I like that.

It is His economy, His purposes envisioned and enacted, discovered in and through His "being built together" fellowship of believers. Individuals find joy, fulfillment, purpose, and mission clarity in the process of joining with what God is doing. I like that too. And, I agree, it changes things.

Body-Life Examples: Changing Our Perspective

First Corinthians 12:12 provides a helpful overview of the nature of the body of Christ, powered by the Holy Spirit: "For just as the body is one and has many members, and all the members of the body, though many, are one body, so it is with Christ." If you have questioned whether we are truly the presence and power of Jesus in the world, question no more. Together, we are His living, breathing body. Every Christian is an organic, Spirit-filled part of the whole person of Jesus Christ in the world. We grow together in the power of the Spirit through the relationships God gives among the "members" of this life-giving body. We do not *do* body life, but rather body life happens in and around us as we function interdependently with our giftings and in relationship with those whom God brings.

Sherwood Lingenfelter, in his book *Leading Cross-Culturally*, told the story of Gerald and Joshua.[18] Gerald was a young missionary tasked with encouraging several churches on an island in the Pacific Ocean. He and his wife had come to work with youth. Four years into their tenure, however, the senior missionary left. Gerald, following the model of ministry of his organization, was given the lead role in spite of his youth and lack of cultural experience with the local people.

He found the weekly preaching particularly difficult in this new role, given his ongoing struggle with the language and feeling less gifted at speaking than his predecessor. So Gerald asked the Lord to show him how best to serve this community of believers.

His first step was to invite several local men who could help him with the preaching. Out of his honest need and his desire to build the local fellowship from within, body life began to rise up.

Joshua, one of the young men who came forward to help, and Gerald established a relationship over one year. As Sherwood told this story:

> One man, Joshua, had an alcohol problem and was struggling in Christ to be free. Gerald and Joshua agreed to work together, each knowing that they could not go on without the other. They agreed to call each other "fifty-fifty," knowing that neither could do the work alone. Gerald would prepare his weekly sermon in English and then meet with Joshua on Saturday. . . . Together they discussed the meaning and implications of each aspect of the message. Through such conversations, Gerald and Joshua prepared their messages for Sunday morning worship services.[19]

They spent three years doing this and Joshua grew tremendously in understanding and living the Word. He helped Gerald grasp many local illustrations that readily fit the Word into his culture. Gerald finally realized what God was doing through this meaningful friendship and partnership. He asked Joshua if he would consider preaching alone one Sunday — with the same preparation together. So Joshua preached to his friends and acquaintances. The people were overjoyed, excited by how God used their own Joshua to share the Scriptures among them.

From that point forward, Gerald assisted Joshua and others in several local congregations. He gradually stepped aside completely from this upfront role. Consistently, the Holy Spirit raised up appropriate body-life players within their own culture to fulfill this preaching role in body life. Out of Gerald's need, Joshua stepped up long before he realized what was happening. Preaching, which so often is considered a true I-ministry in church life, became a We-process of relationship that deeply impacted not only the two of them, but eventually the whole island.

Gerald's struggle with the local language was a weakness that actually revealed a window in God's economy for him to work with local believers. In our Body Life Design process, we often ask three questions for the very reason and body-building result that occurred in Gerald and Joshua's friendship:

- How are you powerful in your spiritual gifts?
- Where are you weak, or not powerful in the Spirit?
- Whom do you need to bring alongside so that God can strengthen and extend body life?

Once I really grasp that I am—and each of us is—only one member of the body, it opens the door for God to do so much more than He could through any one individual. I do not need to be impressive and go to seminars or graduate school to learn things where I may not be powerful in the Spirit. Consider the opportunities this brings to friendships in the Kingdom. It is the very fabric of how God has designed His economy of relationships to build and grow.

The Common Good

Moving back to 1 Corinthians 12, we are now able to grasp more clearly that God's economy is so often revealed relationally. It is through the Spirit-empowered body of Jesus Christ that He prepares each of us to function together for the common good. We go back to the text, verses 4-11:

There are varieties of gifts, but the same Spirit; and there are varieties of service, but the same Lord; and there are varieties of activities, but it is the same God who empowers them all in everyone [note: *not* just a few, select ones]. To each is given the manifestation of the Spirit for the common good. For to one is given through the Spirit the utterance of wisdom, and to another the utterance of knowledge according to the same Spirit, to another faith by the same Spirit, to another gifts of healing by the one Spirit, to another the working of miracles, to another prophecy, to another the ability to distinguish between spirits, to another various kinds of tongues, to another the interpretation of tongues. All these are empowered by one and the same Spirit, who apportions to each one individually as he wills.

Each individual is essential to this process of living out life together. Each one has the Holy Spirit allocating him specific gifts that God has determined, as noted in verse 18 of the same chapter. But their purpose—for all of us—is for the common good. Why? Since we are Jesus' body, living and active in the world through His Spirit, each one of us is organically building and extending His Kingdom. We do this from our place in His relational fabric of the Kingdom. We are created for the common good of the Spirit-breathed body of Christ.

I recently heard from a long-time friend in ministry, John Laster, who wrote of an intriguing change in his life. I had written recently about the amazing house-church movement I was observing firsthand in central Asia, and he responded with vigor. He and his wife, Lisa, are experiencing "the common good" in a new way in their local fellowship. He wrote,

Paul, we are experiencing these body life dynamics in amazing, humbling and new ways for us. We are in a house church where we have been enveloped and sustained over the past ten months. What is awesome is the "one-anothering" and the

amazing Spirit-led stuff that goes on. As you taught me years
ago, in different words, fellowship is the nucleus around
which Spirit-led transformation grows.[20]

Hear the essence of John's heart: He and his wife are partici-
pating in a relational context of church where the Spirit is working dynamically for the common good. Needs and sustenance
are being found in the midst of the "one-anothering" of body
life. The body of Christ is designed to build itself up in love, the
very foundation upon which people can be healed, new lives
drawn to Jesus, and new churches planted as new relationships
are established. Such love does not get in the way of the task of
world evangelization. It is the very heart and foundation of God's
economy for doing so.

All Parts Working Together
Paul continued in 1 Corinthians 12:14-20:

> The body does not consist of one member but of many. If the
> foot should say, "Because I am not a hand, I do not belong to
> the body," that would not make it any less a part of the body.
> And if the ear should say, "Because I am not an eye, I do not
> belong to the body," that would not make it any less a part of
> the body. If the whole body were an eye, where would be the
> sense of hearing? If the whole body were an ear, where would
> be the sense of smell? But as it is, God arranged the members
> in the body, each one of them, as he chose. If all were a single
> member, where would the body be? As it is, there are many
> parts, yet one body.

It appears that one or two parts applying themselves individually do not constitute a whole body. Hearing, speaking, and

smelling are all critical senses in the body—all are invaluable and needed. No one can easily be thrown aside because of his or her lack of value to others. What happens if we do overemphasize certain parts of the body as more needed or more valuable than other parts? Whether it is the leader, the preacher, the teacher, the pastoral caregiver, the church planter, or the missional consultant, certain gifts and certain roles are often raised up. We seem to give higher honor or importance to them. These verses clearly speak against this.

I have had the privilege of working with many ministries and denominations in the worldwide body of Christ over the past twenty years. One of the most disturbing trends has been the many organizations who have determined to train toward one distinctive style of person or set of ministry skills. For some it's the visionary leader/CEO, for others it's the strategic church planter or multiplying missional leader, and still others the strong lead teacher.

A recent comment from a leader in one of those ministries took me aback, given the reality of the passage just referenced. He said, "Paul, please understand that we are not trying to be the whole church, the whole body of Christ. We are focusing on particular ministry tasks and a certain type of individual in our ministry, because we want to reach the world." But while reaching the world may sound noble, the body of Christ, in the whole or in its parts, was not designed to function with just eyes and mouths. We can try as hard as we want, but there is no one style or spiritual-gift combination in a leader that will fulfill such churchplanting movement objectives, especially over a long time.

Please do not misunderstand my intent here. There is a critical need for a variety of gifts and a variety of ministries. Evangelists, coaches, mercy ministries, visionary leaders, mentors, trainers, and pastor-teachers are all designed so by the Father. The issue I am identifying here is the possibility that, at times, we unwittingly give favor or honor to one specific gift or role such that the rest of the body is either not validated or simply underused. God wants the whole body present around those church planters, pastors, evangelists, trainers, and more. In fact He has purposefully designed those alongside the specialists to play essential parts in the body-life ministry. He enfolds His purposes in the combination of gifted people and their relationships. We have the opportunity to steward the wider and deeper process He has prepared beyond just the lead gifts or specialized roles we highlight.

There actually is One who can lead with a wide range of gifts, meeting every need and fulfilling every strategic Kingdom purpose; His name is Jesus. Given this, since we are His Spirit-empowered, life-giving body on earth, the only way we can provide that one model of leadership or pastoring or church planting is by doing it as the body. We can fulfill His call to be witnesses, make disciples, and multiply new believers and churches. But we must do this by stewarding the whole body of Christ, which varies in every setting according to God's prepared intent. It varies each place in each country because God's economy brings different people with different gift sets and ministry passions to every situation on earth.

God did not prepare the body of Christ to
meet our intentions but to fulfill His.

You all are the body of Christ, not just a certain few who have the right stuff for what it takes to fulfill the task of reaching the world. To lead like Jesus we do so through a body-life combination of giftings, because that is how Jesus lives and moves and has His way. That, my friends, is a new way of thinking for most of us.

God did not prepare the body of Christ to meet our intentions but to fulfill His.

Body-Life Stewardship

God has prepared the body of Christ to provide a strategic variety of gifts and passions for every context in any culture. This truly opens up a whole new world of opportunity. Our focus becomes more about body-life stewardship than simply identifying and calling out a special breed of ministry leader or teams. The movement from "I to We" in ministry and leadership creates the possibility of dynamic change. God's army has been prepared by its leader and empowered by His Spirit, so a strategic design is already in place.

Let's now go back to the "rest of the story" about our Kazakh and Kyrgyz friends. After twenty years of false starts with the "body life in a building" model, the gospel is now taking root in new ways that fit these relational central Asian tribal cultures. They are adapting to a house-church model of Christian fellowship, since so much of their lives centers on extended family life. The gospel is shared, and individuals respond; but most commonly that response happens within the broader context of their household of extended family and close friends. You may remember in Acts 16:29-34, not only was the Philippian jailor converted—but also his whole family. This is also happening in central Asia. Recently, during my annual trip, I was staying with believers and sharing in a number of the house churches in a movement that has grown to more than sixty churches strong over the past two years. I was amazed at a number of things, three of which I will highlight.

Equipping and Releasing

The first thing that struck me is how young Christians have the opportunity to mature in the context of such a relational body-life process. In one group I attended, a fourteen-year-old young man was leading the house church's study in the Word. This followed the normal, extended time of worship together with all family members present, young and old, plus both believing and unbelieving visitors. In the room were at least three adults who were gifted teachers of the Word—one of them the teenager's father. But the young man—we will call him James—did not seem the least bit intimidated. He led out from the text to be covered and taught some of the time, then asked questions and facilitated discussion at other times. I was dumbfounded. How could he be so comfortable with this group of twenty or so people, especially with three "expert" teachers in the room?

In reality, James was doing nothing more than what he had learned by observation as a regular part of the group. Everyone shares in corporate worship and time in the Word, and this week he just happened to be the one leading the Bible study time. So he was released to do what he had been equipped to do by observation in the context of safe relationships. Why should he be uptight or nervous? He was just playing his part as a member of the household of faith, as a member of body life in a local setting. As stated earlier, everyone is responsible for using his or her gifts in the body. James may have a nascent gift of teaching, and it showed in his powerful sharing of the Word that evening.

In a natural setting of relationships, everyone understands the opportunity to play his or her part. People feel equipped by watching others model various gifts and roles. Others can then step out and risk trying different serving opportunities. In the process, God raises up equippers, teachers, servers, administrators, leaders, and other critical body-life roles.

Functional Body-Life Training

Further reflection brought me a second, more dynamic realization: Why must we limit our thinking to leadership training models? What if this is not just about leadership training? Body-life ministry training should be where leadership is merely one of a variety of distinctive, powerful ministry roles critical to overall spiritual health.

Equipping others, showing hospitality, teaching as James modeled, pastoring, and intercession are examples of other types of body-life gifting to be observed in others and shared. This is a natural body process that we can learn to do together. It is the essence of what happens in living together in an organic, relational setting where the Spirit of God is at work. God will raise up leaders to share the leadership functions and for us to follow. We all must learn submission to the Lord in following those who lead, yet that is but one facet of a wide range of body functions. Whole body stewardship breeds a wider, more creative world of multiple gifts and passions acting together.

As people discern, exercise, and grow in their spiritual gifts, they begin to minister through the power of the Holy Spirit. That is, after all, what using your spiritual gifts means—allowing the power of the Holy Spirit to work through you for the common good. This is not really about leadership training, but rather about stewarding various gifts and roles. We limit body-life growth because we want to train only leaders. In doing so, we actually miss out on a number of body-life applications going on in the midst of shared life. As the Spirit of God is manifested in the gathering of believers and speaks through some to encourage others, a dynamic dimension is added. The body truly grows and builds itself up in love.

Shared Leadership

The third insight I have gained from watching my Kazakh and Kyrgyz friends is how they are applying Ephesians 4:11-13 to spiritual leadership as a shared process:

> [Christ] gave the apostles, the prophets, the evangelists, the shepherds and teachers, to equip the saints for the work of ministry, for building up the body of Christ, until we all attain to the unity of the faith and of the knowledge of the Son of God, to mature manhood, to the measure of the stature of the fullness of Christ.

An apostolic band of leaders, using this passage as a guide, has formed to provide oversight for this fledgling group of house churches throughout their country. All four brothers have one or more confirmed gifts from among the five gifts listed in the passage, and are seeking to use those gifts to extend the gospel into new villages and cities throughout their country. Each one is also leading his family, showing proven character, and is actively involved with one or more house churches in his community. They are encouraging other house churches and leaders as a part of their oversight. The goal, though, is for them to have more freedom to minister at large, sharing local leadership with other brothers and sisters whom God raises up. They may soon be bringing on a fifth brother who is a gifted administrator-pastor and much needed to share in the detail part of the work.

They understand their calling, as described in Ephesians 4:12, is to equip the saints and thus build up and extend the body of Christ. They understand the core values of both submitting to spiritual leadership on their team and functioning with a servant heart. Their prime purpose is not to grow big churches, but rather to build up the body of Christ in its many and multiplying local settings. Their commitment here is revealed in how hard they work for unity among the believers in their house churches and in the broader movement of house-church leaders. Relationships and unity deeply matter to central Asians, and so they work hard to encourage one another, address conflicts, and reconcile issues as needed. They understand Paul's call to unity of relationship as essential to body-life health both locally and in the broader contexts in house churches.

What is most intriguing and exciting in this process, though, is that they are functioning as a band of brothers who truly *need* each other. They are actively sharing equipping, leading, evangelistic, administrative, and pastoral functions because each has realized that he has weaknesses—and needs the gifted strengths of the others. Given their tribal and communist leadership models of the past, both I-control styles, this is an amazing development. And scores of house-church leaders are learning as they watch this.

Their model of shared leadership on this team is culturally groundbreaking as they seek to steward their multiplicity of gifts and as their mobile ministry team travels to various places. They admit need, rely on each other, and therein provide an authentic model for all the house churches under their care and oversight. Body-life shared ministry breeds body-life shared ministry, creating a nearly unstoppable organic multiplication among the house churches and leaders. This is especially true when priority focus is given to the Word of God and to unity in Christ.

Imagine the opportunity to work together with three or four others in a shared leadership process. It is less about becoming a great Kingdom leader and more about ebbing and flowing together as a powerful team. Members share in the overall leadership and equipping of those whom God has placed in their care, including one another. One brother leads, but he is acutely aware of his own weaknesses. He knows he needs the four others with

him to provide the full range of equipping and supporting necessary to multiply the body of house churches. It is not about one
leader, but about a leader who shares ministry so openly that at
times you cannot tell who is in charge.

Stewarding a Team of Rivals

One other role model comes to mind as we creatively think about
body-life stewardship. Abraham Lincoln is remembered as one of
the greatest leaders in our country's history. He is certainly one
of those great people to whom many look as a role model for
steady, wise, directive leadership during one of our country's
most difficult periods. Author Doris Kearns Goodwin, in her
book *Team of Rivals: The Political Genius of Abraham Lincoln*,
highlighted aspects of Lincoln's wisdom that many have missed.
As history tells us, Lincoln stunningly defeated William Seward,
Salmon Chase, and several other more qualified candidates for
the Republican nomination for the presidency in 1860. He
followed that with a victory over Democrat Stephen Douglas for
the presidency. What happened next is where the intrigue
begins—and becomes pertinent to our body-life discussion.

Much to the dismay of many around him, Abraham Lincoln
chose a team of political rivals to make up his cabinet. In doing
so, he shocked the country. His cabinet selection rationale was
uncomplicated. For the good of the country, he would pick men
who would be the best for the country. Each would bring particular strengths that addressed very real, developmental needs for
the United States in 1860. Selections were made by Lincoln,
despite the fact that these were men who would dissent with him
on critical issues. These men were his competitors. They struggled with much of Lincoln's style. They even would tussle with
each other. This, his first and perhaps most strategic decision,
was to pick the right "iron sharpening iron" relationships, for the

very purpose of keeping the country honest.

Lincoln knew his weaknesses and knew he needed help. Consider his words to William Seward, asking him to become his Secretary of State: "Governor Seward, there is one part of my work that I shall have to leave largely to you. I shall have to depend upon you for taking care of these matters of foreign affairs, of which I know so little, and with which I reckon you are familiar."[21] People were dumbfounded that he would bring in Seward, but for the sake of the country's unity and direction, both men conceded to this necessary union. Amazingly, Seward became one of Lincoln's closest friends, and they spent many evenings together over the next four years of Lincoln's presidency. These competitors, for the unity of the whole, chose partnership and became dear friends and companions. It was not about becoming a great leader. Rather, it was about addressing the needs of the country, filling strength where he had it, and seeking others to fill key roles where he was weak or inexperienced.

The president, because of his decision to bring in others like Chase, Stanton, and Bates to his team, understood that he would spend a great deal of time as intermediary among these often contentious personalities. He would repeatedly have to fight for the relationships. Yet he defended these men with whom he often and vehemently disagreed. He held his tongue, mended fences between cabinet members with regularity, and did not react in kind when treated with contempt or dishonesty by men whom he had hand selected. In many ways, love covered over a multitude of sins, and Lincoln's gracious style always bore him good favor, for the sake of unity in a divided country about to explode.

Abraham Lincoln was a true steward of his team of rivals. He sought out and got the best from each man's unique qualities. From Kearns Goodwin:

By calling these men to his side, Lincoln had afforded them an opportunity to exercise their talents to the fullest and to share in the labor and the glory of the struggle that would reunite and transform their country and secure their own places in posterity.[22]

The country gained incredibly in the arenas of foreign affairs and the national banking system, to name just two. Lincoln was able to focus on his powerful strengths as well, because these teammates were covering his weaknesses with their strong suits. The stewardship of unique qualities in those around him, and the stewardship of healthy, unified relations all around him, provided what the country needed through his team of rivals. What a helpful model we see for the stewarding of body-life giftings and body-life relationships.

Summary

God had liberated His people from the self-serving shepherd leaders and began to gather, feed, and lead His flock. His promised Davidic king came in the form of His Son Jesus, the Good Shepherd of the sheep. This shepherd leader will lay down His life for those sheep. Before He did, Jesus revealed His desire for His followers, including those who believe today, to become one as He and God the Father are one. He also asks His Father to share His glory with us, the same glory that the Father and Son share. His heart is that we all might be one so that the world may know Him. Unity in body life is an essential and foundational piece to reaching out with the gospel.

The unity we share with the Father, Son, and Holy Spirit was completed when the Spirit was poured out on Pentecost. The Spirit moved through people with tongues of fire and through Peter in his preaching. He moved in people as they responded to the Word preached by Peter. And He moved among people through community, prayer, and sharing that resulted in further thousands coming to Christ. Something unique happened among the people where God lived, whom Paul called the body of Christ. The process of believers being built together has begun, becoming that place where God lives by His Spirit. He desires to continually live and move and have His way among us, giving each one gifts and drawing each one into the fellowship of the Holy Spirit.

Changes will come in how we live out body life together as we grasp the implications of this paradigm. Everyone has powerful spiritual gifts to offer, intrinsic weaknesses to admit, and true need for others in the body. Together we truly are the organic body of Jesus on earth, living out His purposes in community. Even leadership in the church and missions will be affected as we address the implications of this body-life change. Apostolic teams, shared leadership, and a multiplicity of gifts will bring a new kind of body-life freedom to leaders who choose to steward what God has given to the people whom He has brought around them.

Application Steps

1. Using the image of Lincoln's cabinet sharing the workload as your model, pick a project you wish to complete. Identify three to five people with whom you could fulfill this set of tasks. Define five key tasks to be done. Have each person focus on one area of personal strength.
2. Design a training program to prepare others for shared leadership. To model the core idea, have at least one other person share in developing the training. Find a group where you can share your teaching and see how it flies.
3. Discover a "James," like the one I watched in central Asia. Spend the next week searching for a brother or sister in

Christ who needs to be given an opportunity to minister. Create time, space, and opportunity for this individual to engage in finding his or her fit in the body of Christ.

4. Invite a friend to your home. This can be a lost art in our culture. Spend time simply experiencing a relationship in your home. After the evening, reflect on the experience. Make a decision about whether to be more intentional about doing this more often.

Questions for Discussion

1. What does unity look like on your team or in your small group? What enables your group to go deeper in sharing? What hinders going deeper?

2. What prevents people from using their gifts as a part of your team or group ministry?

3. In John 17:20-26, why did Jesus pray for unity?

4. What does it mean that, together, we are the living, breathing body of Jesus on earth? How could you apply this in one of your We-settings?

---

1. Oswald Chambers, "The Spiritually Seeking Church," *My Utmost for His Highest*, http://utmost.org/the-spiritually-self-seeking-church.
2. Marcel Proust, 1871–1922.
3. Be aware that Phill Butler is one person in the global missions arena who has been talking about Kingdom "partnerships" for a number of years. He remains one trainer and collaborator who is deeply committed to unity in harvest outreach among Christian churches and organizations. Take note of his book *Well Connected: Releasing Power, Restoring Hope Through Kingdom Partnerships* (Colorado Springs, CO: Authentic Books, 2005), as well as of his organization, VisionSynergy.
4. Ric Lehman, personal note to author, March 2004.
5. Sherwood G. Lingenfelter, *Leading Cross-Culturally* (Grand Rapids, MI: Baker, 2008), 33.
6. Lingenfelter, 30.
7. John Skinner, *Ezekiel* (Whitefish, MT: Kessinger, 2010), 336–337.
8. Roger W. Gehring, *House Church and Mission* (Peabody, MA: Hendrickson, 2004), 79.

9. Walther Zimmerli, *Ezekiel 2* (Philadelphia: Fortress, 1983), 266.
10. Ralph Neighbour Jr., *Christ's Basic Bodies* (Houston: Touch Ministries, 2010), 11.
11. Gehring, 32, 46, 121, 123.
12. Gehring, 47.
13. Peter Block, *Community: The Structure of Belonging* (San Francisco: Berrett-Koehler Publishing, 2008), 3.
14. Block, 2.
15. Block, 4.
16. Langdon Reinke, personal correspondence among LCMS Body Life team, July 12, 2012.
17. Reinke, by unnamed person in the LCMS Body Life team.
18. Lingenfelter, 120–121.
19. Lingenfelter, 121.
20. John Laster, personal correspondence to author, June 2011.
21. Doris Kearns Goodwin, *Team of Rivals: The Political Genius of Abraham Lincoln* (New York: Simon & Schuster, 2005), 316.
22. Goodwin, 747.

Part 2

Royally Getting Off Track

Trust God from the bottom of your heart; don't try to figure out everything on your own. Listen for God's voice in everything you do, everywhere you go; he's the one who will keep you on track. Don't assume that you know it all. Run to God! Run from evil!

— PROVERBS 3:5-7, msg

Now you are the body of Christ and individually members of it.

— 1 CORINTHIANS 12:27

We have learned to make a living, but not a life. We have added years to our life, but not life to our years. We have been all the way to the moon and back, but have trouble crossing the street to meet a new neighbor. . . . These are the times of fast foods and slow digestion, big men and small character, steep profits and shallow relationships.

— GEORGE CARLIN

In him you also are being built together into a dwelling place for God by the Spirit.

— EPHESIANS 2:22

This dynamic army of God's people, prophesied in Ezekiel 37, comes into full form in the New Testament. Jesus, the promised shepherd king in David's line, ushered in that Kingdom and revealed God as the Word made flesh. Then, as described in 1 Corinthians 12, the promised Spirit-enlivened dry bones become the living, Spirit-empowered, witness-bearing body of Jesus Christ on earth. Every part of this living body would be endowed with supernatural gifts to reveal God's grace in its various forms. Grace-filled love now enables healthy, life-giving relationships.

Though we have been given this opportunity to live out Spirit-breathed life together, it seems that most of us are at best stumbling along in our We-Kingdom life as believers. There is Spirit-breathed life in many places worldwide, but there remain the dry bones of spiritual deadness, broken relationships, and scores of ministries, with tens of thousands of leaders, lukewarm or struggling. What happened? What has blocked the fresh, consistent, powerful moving of God's Spirit among us? What happened to slow down this army of God?

To find out, we will look at three areas of misguided tendencies. Each inhibits the organic movement of God's Spirit among His people. In chapter 4 we will look at the "Cult of Rightness," our cultural tendencies that focus on right theology but not always on right actions. Identifying the background influences of the Greeks and Hebrews will shed light on why we believe and act — or do not act — the way we do in regard to truth. We will discover how the Word of truth consistently embraces Spirit-empowered body-life activity and grace-filled community. Living out truth as the body of Christ, the step beyond right thinking, is what captivates the world. How is truth understood in the context of body life?

In chapter 5, we will grapple with our cultural tendency to place individuals in the spotlight. It may be exhibited in our glorifying certain kinds of leaders who, like Jesus on the mount of temptation, have opportunity to be lifted up into a position of unusual self-importance or authority. We will consider how that can cause leaders to separate themselves from the body and steal focus from releasing different players from the body. We will also identify the new reality of people's choosing to highlight themselves in the quickly growing Internet world of social networking. What are the implications of this cult of the spotlight? Who ends up getting the glory in these new digital contexts?

Chapter 6 looks into the world of organizational goals and strategies that have become an increasingly significant part of our corporate and Christian world over the past three decades. Historical influences have given us systems that affect how we plan. Given this, what does goal setting and strategizing look like for Christians and Christian organizations? How much strategy is appropriate? How do we allow goal- and system-driven strategies to lead and direct the Spirit-led body of Christ? We will observe strategic models of excellence that drive the corporate world and evaluate the impact of these principles on many Christian organizations' cultural DNA. How do we handle the increasing "corporate" expectations and the related pressures to grow ministries and multiply churches? We will then consider the nature of "Kingdom organics" and how God's strategy works in and through relationships that make up our organizations. Ephesians 4:11-16 will provide a simple roadmap of God's practical strategy for enacting His purposes through His people.

Chapter 4

The Cult of Rightness

Once more I will astound these people with wonder upon wonder; the wisdom of the wise will perish, the intelligence of the intelligent will vanish.

— ISAIAH 29:14, NIV

Though by this time you ought to be teachers, you need someone to teach you again the basic principles of the oracles of God. You need milk, not solid food, for everyone who lives on milk is unskilled in the word of righteousness [right living], since he is a child. But solid food is for the mature, for those who have their powers of discernment trained by constant practice to distinguish good from evil.

— HEBREWS 5:12-14

Believe the Word? YES! Live the Word together? Not so much.

— ANONYMOUS

The Word became flesh and dwelt among us, and we have seen his glory, glory as of the only Son from the Father, full of grace and truth. . . . His fullness we have all received, grace upon grace.

— JOHN 1:14,16

There is nothing wrong with being biblically right. It is genuinely important that we understand the Word of truth, the Scriptures of the Bible, as foundational in each of our lives, our churches, and our outreach. But our actions — and involvement with others in the body — reveal our need to pursue more than biblical correctness. Truth be told, how we are connected to the Lord and to one another in daily life is what exposes the heart of our theology. When we believe the truth, our actions and relationships will reflect it.

Right Theology and the Good Samaritan

In Luke 10:25-37, a lawyer wanted to know how to receive eternal life. Jesus' initial response was to ask the man what was written in the book of the Law. The lawyer knew his Scriptures, as he recited: "You shall love the Lord your God with all your heart and with all your soul and with all you strength and with all your mind, and your neighbor as yourself" (verse 27). Jesus told him he was indeed right: "Do this, and you will live" (verse 28). But the lawyer wanted to justify himself—to be right in his own eyes—and pressed the issue by posing that ageless question, "Who is my neighbor?" (verse 29). Jesus proceeded to tell the story that has come to be known as that of the Good Samaritan.

> "A man was going down from Jerusalem to Jericho, when he fell into the hands of robbers. They stripped him of his clothes, beat him and went away, leaving him half dead. A priest happened to be going down the same road, and when he saw the man, he passed by on the other side. So too, a Levite, when he came to the place and saw him, passed by on the other side. But a Samaritan, as he traveled, came where the man was; and when he saw him, he took pity on him. He went to him and bandaged his wounds, pouring on oil and wine. Then he put the man on his own donkey, took him to an inn and took care of him. The next day he took out two silver coins and gave them to the innkeeper. 'Look after him,' he said, 'and when I return, I will reimburse you for any extra expense you may have.'
>
> "Which of these three do you think was a neighbor to the man who fell into the hands of robbers?"

The expert in the law replied, "The one who had mercy on him."

Jesus told him, "Go and do likewise." (Luke 10:30-37, NIV)

Three people pass by—two Jewish religious leaders and then a non-Jew, a Samaritan. The two leaders do not stop as they are able to justify—in their own theological eyes—why they did not have to help the man felled by robbers. They are "right" in passing on the other side for reasons of spiritual purity, but they show no compassion. You might say, in fact, that they love God, but did not love their neighbor as they would themselves. Coming along later, the Samaritan has no particularly religious reason to stop and help the stripped and beaten man, yet he does. It is only compassion that moves his heart to action. He mercifully does all that he can that day and for days to come to provide what the man needs to return to health. He is the true neighbor.

Loving God and loving others are inextricably tied together. The challenge of living out the integrity of the Scriptures is confirmed or denied in the laboratory of life and relationships.

Interestingly, though, we live in an evangelical era that places great emphasis on preaching, believing, and receiving the Word of God. "I know the truth, and I will go anywhere to hear it," I heard a churchgoer proclaim recently. Our churches are full of people who pride themselves in believing correctly. In fact, many of us claim to believe rightly in our own hearts and speak boldly about how "on target" our theology is. We challenge others about truth and their understanding of it. Yet many of us do not portray the grace and truth of the Word in action.

Often our love of God is not visible in how we love our neighbor. What happens when our beliefs are not matched by the way we act in relationship to other Christians and to the world? It brings us back to that adage: "What you do speaks so loudly that I cannot hear a word you are saying." Truth without action breeds the cult of rightness.

What kind of impact does knowledge without compassion usually bring? The true meaning of biblical correctness is found in the authentic practice of day-to-day relationships. Right theology will reflect itself in kind deeds, training, encouragement, and even challenging others toward responsible action. However, when they are absent, the cult of rightness takes root.

Life and Death Relationships

High altitude mountaineers will tell you that doing your homework is essential for effective climbing on the world's big mountains. Knowledge precedes successful action, especially in the fourteen mountain peaks over 8,000 meters in altitude (26,250 feet). Learning how to tie the climber's knots and fix the oxygen equipment is imperative. You have to know your stuff when it comes to carabineers, fixed ropes, bergschrunds, and crevasses. Understanding warning signs for altitude sicknesses like pulmonary edema (lung congestion) or cerebral edema (brain congestion) are a must, or you will lose your life amid poor decision making on the mountain. Understanding the "word" on the practicalities of mountain climbing is vital, but there is something more: your partnerships matter. The commitments among climbers cannot be casual or fair-weather in nature, or everyone involved is at risk. Knowledge alone is not sufficient. Smart individualists *die* on mountains no matter how correct their information on climbing because they have no one to help. Being right without right relationships is a problem.

When you get on the mountain, and into the so-called "danger zone" over 8,000 meters, you become utterly dependent upon your climbing mates. All the knowledge in the world comes to naught when you lose your footing or are struck with illness.

The issue then becomes how well connected you are with those around you in the danger zone. You never know what is around the corner, so how you are linked together—both in relationship and physically via an array of critical equipment—creates an unusual need for the utmost trust.

Never was this more real than for the group of climbers on the second-highest mountain in the world, Pakistan's K2, in 1953.

> Led by Charles Houston, a mainly American team attempted the mountain's South-East Spur (commonly known as the Abruzzi Spur) in a style which was unusually lightweight for the time. The team reached a high point of 7750 meters [25,427 feet], but were trapped by a storm in their high camp, where a team member, Art Gilkey, became seriously ill. A desperate retreat down the mountain followed, during which all but one of the climbers were nearly killed in a fall arrested by Pete Schoening. . . . The expedition has been widely praised for the courage shown by the climbers in their attempt to save Gilkey, and for the team spirit and the bonds of friendship it fostered.[1]

If the team had not been roped up together, it is likely that most would have been killed that day on K2. And Pete Schoening's belay—that is, fastening the rope to one's ice ax stuck in the ground on the edge of a very steep slope—was practically miraculous. He held the weight of six men, all of whom had begun sliding down the mountain. They knew the facts—that they were safer by being tied directly one to another—and their actions proved this truth to be correct. The fact that they were inextricably tied together literally saved their lives.

All the mountaineering knowledge in the world will not help you if you are alone on the mountain or are untied from your teammates. You will not last long in the mountains on your own if your knowledge is not a shared process as you climb together. The same could be said for our lives as believers in the body of Christ, people interwoven together in the fellowship of the Holy Spirit. We were designed to be together as one body. We are in the process of being built together. It is the very nature of being Christian. Truth, then, is designed to be lived out in the midst of those relationships.

How well connected are you to other believers, regardless of how solid your knowledge of Scripture? Understanding and applying truth depends upon your body-life connections. In the "iron sharpening iron" process and the steps lived out in relationship, we must traverse the paths of life and work together.[2] Are you full of answers, but not well tied into others who can train, counsel, and encourage you with that Bible you know so well?

How are we, the body of Jesus, living out the Scriptures both individually and collectively? While holding tightly to what we believe, how do we reveal Jesus, as the body of Christ, in how we love our neighbors? There is more to truth than just being right.

Greeks and Hebrews

Historical background from the two cultures that most affected the Old and New Testaments of the Bible provides important insight here. While the New Testament was written in Greek, many of those who experienced the gospel of Jesus and the early church lived an Old Testament Hebrew mindset in their approach to life. How do both cultures affect us?

In today's Western world we are much more affected by the Hellenistic (Greek) culture than the Hebrew culture. As Brian Knowles explained, "We relentlessly attempt to organize everything into manageable intellectual blocks and structures. We want all questions answered, all problems solved." Like the

Greeks, we often want a religion of utility, with techniques that we can apply in various situations. We tend to turn the Scriptures into a systematized textbook of answers, a step-by-step blueprint or guide to life.[3]

Apparently, like the Greeks, we want to be right. For them, the Word of God was something primarily to be learned and understood. Biblical knowledge was information to be contemplated, mastered, and then passed along to the next generation. The Greek word for disciple, *mathetes*, is a learner—a pupil.[4] Younger men would move into a circle of disciples around a learned master. Each one would study largely by responding to his master's teaching, showing comprehension, and after a number of years being released as one with authority to teach. In turn, they would gather others around themselves and disciple them in a similar model.[5]

The Greeks established schools to pass along culture as information, believing that knowledge well-learned was stored in the mind and thus would affect daily life. Greek education clearly focused on content and meaning, gathering learners around ideas. Knowledge was king. It established a process for growth in understanding core concepts. As you may recognize, institutional learning in the West has been similarly developed. Christian Bible schools and seminaries follow such systematized models of learning. Gathering information about biblical and theological topics from teachers and books is assumed to allow students to grow spiritually. The purpose is to gain more biblical knowledge, which undoubtedly will provide the framework for teaching others essential truth.

The Greek influence in the West also explains why so many churches and schools are focused on information about doctrinal orthodoxy.[6] The information one believes is assumed to determine how one lives. Thus, for us in the West, the emphasis tends to be on correct information—and believing that information properly. Yet that information may or may not be reflected in spiritual living. Or, equally challenging at times, it is actually what leads to legalism. If I believe correctly, I am set—even if my life portrays no real spiritual change or increasing fruit of the Spirit in relationships.

Nonetheless, underpinning all of the New Testament is a Hebrew understanding of God, life, and relationships that warrants additional reflection—and action. For the Greek, the Word was information to be learned. The Hebrew was much more concerned about getting beyond mere information and focusing on the consequences of that learned knowledge. You do not pass God's test until you show the consequences of putting knowledge into action. For the Hebrew the learning process was much more dynamic than memorizing information.

The Hebrew concept of wisdom was ultimate: Wisdom was truth lived out, truth in action. It involved encountering truth as the foundation for moving into the dynamic arena of life and relationships.[7] Greek education focused primarily on content and meaning. Hebrew education focused on the impact of such learning in life and relationships. Greek teachers wanted to shape their students' minds. Hebrew teachers sought to shape their students' hearts and lives as the outcome of what they learned.[8]

I began to grasp this distinction through my Ugandan tribal friends over the past five years. In my first several years of training, the content was excellently presented and the evaluations testified that new truth was learned. But we saw little change in the way these pastors and church planters carried out their leadership responsibilities and shared ministry. Intriguingly, beginning in year three and dramatically more noticeably in year four, our relationships with these brothers began to grow deeper. As this took place, real change began to happen among them. They began to equip and truly release others around them into significant ministry, breaking from their tribal chief model of I-leadership and stewarding others more intentionally.

It was here that our team also passed off the primary training responsibilities to a team of twelve pastors, all highly credible as spiritual leaders with healthy relationships. Realize the critical point here: We did *not* transition training responsibility when they learned the principles. Rather, it happened when their lifestyle revealed a stewarding of others to the point of multiplying themselves. They moved from Greek understanding to Hebrew truth revealed in relationships. We also inherited the treasure chest of deep, lifelong friendships with these brothers.

The Hebrew life was about a relationship with one's Creator God, pursuing life and godliness to the fullest. It was less about trying to define God.[9] In that pursuit comes the understanding and the relationship between God and His people. It is an outlook that is more open and expansive and allows God to surprise His people. If, as Ephesians 2:22 suggests, we are indeed being built together in Christ to become a place where God lives continually, He certainly can come in and surprise us. So it is in the dynamic, energetic mind of the Hebrew. In historian Abraham Heschel's words, "To try and distill the Bible, which is bursting with life, drama, and tension, to a series of principles is like trying to reduce a living person to a diagram."[10] Such ordered thinking may never have entered the Hebrew mind.

To the Hebrew, truth was not an idea to be considered. It was much more a life to be experienced together.[11] If God's desire is to live among us and do as He pleases, we make this difficult by spending most of our time looking for the right answers. We do need solid, biblical theology. Of that there is no question. But how each of us participates in the dynamic process that goes alongside right thinking—right relationships and actions—makes all the difference in moving from "I to We" in God's economy.

If God's desire is to live among us and do as He pleases,
we make this difficult by spending most of our time
looking for the right answers.

Did you know that it is much easier to follow the lead of a strong, biblically based teaching leader than it is to participate actively in life-changing, church-multiplying body life?

Through modern invention and outright apathy, our Western world has grown more and more passive. We have developed a TV [and now technology]-obsessed, entertainment-prone and spectator-minded generation which seems largely content to watch life rather than live it. The typical church [pick your age demographic] has become a spectator sport with chairs arranged theatre style facing a stage where often paid professional performers titillate emotions and tickle ears of their fans for an hour or two each week.[12]

The speaker who is regularly preaching and/or teaching is presenting what he believes to be a right theology. He went to school, got it right, and now is helping others get it right. In listening to that hoped-for accurate biblical understanding, the listeners participate primarily as observers, unless they put it into practice in relationships and lifestyle.

But where do we live out our "right theology"? For the Hebrew, reality was found in the God who makes Himself known in the ebb and flow of both nature and historical events by His acts and words. God comes to men and women in their earthly experiences of relationship—with Him and with one another.[13] Truth begins with an I-understanding that becomes a We-reality when lived out in body life with others. God's economy is one of dynamic impact in and through the relationships where truth is lived out in the day-to-day of life. In fact, we have opportunity to daily live out the Word of truth in action and in relationships. It is so much more than just believing the information.

God's Schoolhouse

I vividly remember my parents talking about their one-room schoolhouse experiences. It brings the reality of Hebrew learning front and center. The school's one teacher was responsible for all the grades. All the students, representing a wide range of ages, were in the same room. Without question, the learning process was quite different from most educational settings of today. The teacher would teach, as right knowledge and understanding were essential for every student. But that teacher shared the responsibility for teaching with certain older students nearly every day. Learning immediately became a knowledge-to-application process and a shared, relational interaction for them. They would take the new content and application for a certain age group and guide a group of younger students in their learning and application of the knowledge. And the younger students—the next generation—were watching their teacher share the training process with their older brothers and sisters while they themselves were learning. They caught the learning as it was applied before their very eyes. This style of learning was similar to the life that many of them lived outside the schoolhouse. Many learned skills as apprentices by watching and then applying what was modeled. You learned, but you also applied very quickly, turning that knowledge into action.

The process of learning was a shared practice, with very few experts in the room. The older students not only learned content but were immediately given responsibility to apply their learning with others. On those days when the teacher needed to focus on just a few students, the learning process would continue—again, very much like the community life in which the students lived outside the classroom. It was community lifestyle, with shared work done for the common good across families.

> The one-room schoolhouse gives insight to the Hebrew model of shared learning revealed in immediate application through relationships.

Remember the central Asian house church where James, our fourteen-year-old Bible study leader, simply did what he saw modeled by others? Right content, correct understanding, and thorough comprehension were highly valued in that group. But there was no time to claim rightness and develop his own learning system. He had to take what he was learning and share it with others—immediate application for all involved. Obedience in action means gaining a dynamic, applicable understanding of the knowledge learned, and then acting upon it. Life change takes place, both personally and in body life—a reality far beyond knowledge or insight.

The one-room schoolhouse gives insight into the Hebrew model of shared learning revealed in immediate application through relationships. It gives practical insight into the organic nature of the breadth and depth of *knowing* biblical truth. We can learn the living and active Scriptures together and translate them into life and relationships—as one dynamic process. To see and feel the power of the Word is to live it out in relationships. It is in the moral sphere of life where Jesus wants to live and move and have His way.

The Word Made Authentic in Life and Relationships

Right believing, correct theology, or accurate doctrine — pick your phrase — is absolutely essential. Paul commanded Titus to teach sound doctrine in Titus 2:1-3, even as he called elders to hold firm to "the trustworthy word as taught" (Titus 1:9). In this Titus may be able to give instruction in sound doctrine and also to rebuke those who contradict it. Paul challenged Timothy to take what he had heard from Paul and entrust it to others able to teach others (see 2 Timothy 2:2). A core qualification for overseers in 1 Timothy 3:2 is the ability to teach. Much more could be said on this, but you have heard this before. Books have been written on the centrality of knowing what we believe, why we believe it, and how we can transfer such understanding to others in leadership and in the Church. It is where we start the process of the Word of God becoming alive and lived out in us and among us.

The Balance Needed

In the West, though, we have to be very careful, given our Hellenistic influences toward structured, efficient, systems-type learning. As Catholic mystic Richard Rohr suggested, "Rightness allows for an amazing arrogance that allows Christians to so readily believe that their mental understanding of things is anywhere close to that of Jesus. . . . Jesus never said 'This is my commandment, thou shalt be right.'"[14] Our call to sound doctrine is not optional, but our propensity to overplay sound doctrine against its needed balance of right relationships is an issue of concern.

I became dramatically aware of our Western emphasis on expertise at the expense of relationship when I was uniquely introduced to a central Asian audience. In the first encounter,

I noticed it most dramatically. We arrived very late in the southernmost part of a central Asian country, and Azul and his family were waiting to greet us outside the door. We arrived at 9 p.m., so I anticipated a short get-to-know-people time and then off to bed for the next full day of training. But, to my amazement, the place we entered was full of excited people. Azul stood at the front of that overcrowded room — people were even seated on the windowsills — and spoke two powerful sentences: "This is my friend, Paul Ford. Listen to him."

It became immediately apparent that my credibility in this central Asian tribal setting was not based on my knowledge or theological degrees. It was in my trusted friendship with Azul. They would listen because Azul knew me and knew my family. From the time we had spent together, he knew how I treated my wife and our son. He knew my love for the Word of God and my solid theology, and how it affected the way I lived. The fact that I was his friend meant people anticipated my arrival. We went until 2 a.m. and quit only because I was too tired to continue. Thankfully no one sitting on a windowsill fell asleep and out the window!

As you might expect, when I am introduced in the West, it is my theological pedigree and writings that are always the first things highlighted. My doctoral degree and my published works appear to be what make me credible to this Greek-influenced audience. About half the time my wife, Julie, is mentioned and maybe 10 percent of the time our son is mentioned. What I have accomplished in my education is more important, apparently, than my capacity as a husband or father. It appears that the Greeks have won the "introductions" race over the Hebrews by a landslide. Yet, it is not my I-biblical prowess or my I-accomplishments that are of substance. It is my We-capacity in relationship, my We-friendships that have given me credibility with our friends in central Asia.

In my recent trip to this region, I asked an American partner in our work there whether or not I was fooling myself by coming halfway around the world to invest in our national friends. He looked at me with a thoughtful smile, laughed, and said,

> These people know you and love you. They trust you, and you now have long-term established relationships over ten years even though you do not live in the country. They are using the biblical principles you have trained since the beginning, and now your continuity of friendship has revealed those principles to be true. They love when you come and are even disappointed when Julie does not come along.[15]

By the way, we work on solid, practical, biblical theology every time I visit. In fact, I am doing a regular Skype call with one brother from this ministry on developing a theology of spiritual gifts and body life. But it is the relationship that gives context for the depth of impact in both training and support of their multiplying house-church network.

Right believing by the individual believer, leader, or layperson is a foundational part of Christian church doctrine, life, and multiplication. But it is not the I-believing that makes us strong and allows the Spirit of God access to effect change in us and others—it is the We-process of life and relationships that grows from our shared experiences in the Word and life. It is how our theology is enfolded into our lives and our life together as the body of Christ that makes the real difference. It is very difficult for God to live in our midst and powerfully move among us if we are only looking for right answers.

It is how our theology is enfolded into our lives and our life together as the body of Christ that makes the real difference.

The Word became flesh and dwelt among us, as John 1:14 states. In the West, we often think of the Word only in the sense of the Bible. The Word *is* truth, but therein is one of the most pivotal paradigm shifts to address. The Word of the Lord came to earth in the flesh through Jesus, and the written Word that remains in the Scriptures is imperative to our spiritual growth and multiplication. But there is also the embodied Word, the body of Christ continuing on earth through the Holy Spirit. It is our unity and community in Jesus that reveals the Father's glory in us and His Son to the world.[16] We have become the very sanctuary where He lives by His Spirit. He desires to have His way among us, both today and tomorrow.

We reveal the Word through our lives in community as the body of Christ. The Bible is enfolded into the lives of believers with dramatic results. Phill Butler, a veteran of building ministry partnerships across scores of cultures worldwide, gives us perspective here. He wrote, "The body of Christ becomes a powerful, unified community, demonstrating real love, committed to each other, to growing in Christ, and witnessing to the world around us."[17] In truth, there is no way we can have a holistic and healthy picture of sound doctrine—of right believing—without an equal investment in body life. Phill continued, "The God design of whole relationships is actually central to the Christian life or Kingdom work."[18]

The Parable of the Cream-Filled Cookie

Pentecost gives great insight on the practical ways the Bible is to come alive through how God puts His Word into action. Acts 2 clearly reveals the critical correlation between the Word in truth, the Word in power, and the Word in love. Pentecost was not simply an event for the powerful I-speaking of Peter from the Scriptures. Rather, it was a coronation of the dynamic

Spirit-empowered We-life of the body of Jesus Christ alive on earth.

In the previous chapter, I noted the importance of Acts 2 and the impact of the Spirit's work in three ways: (1) *through people* applying their spiritual gifts, demonstrated by tongues of fire and Peter's preaching, (2) *in people* as they responded to Peter's message of salvation, and (3) *among people* through the community, prayer, and sharing that followed. We now move to deeper insight and application of those core issues through an illustration I call the parable of the cream-filled cookie.

Think of an Oreo or your favorite cream-filled cookie as your tasty model for this illustration. The best part of the treat, the cream, is delivered between two cookies, or sandwich pieces. Yes, it is a sweet sandwich! In the same way, God's Word—the cream—is experienced most dynamically when it is delivered sandwiched between two essential sections that hold it together: powerful We-gifts and loving We-relationships. Watch closely as we see this dynamic illustrated in Acts 2.

The Cream Center

Peter preached one of the most powerful messages in Christian history at Pentecost in Acts 2:14-41. He spoke to the prophetic promise of the Holy Spirit's outpouring and the role of Jesus, David's descendant. He reminded his audience of the foretold crucifixion and resurrection of Jesus, which they all witnessed. Then Peter called the crowd to repentance and baptism in the name of Jesus. People were powerfully moved and cut to the heart. He offered the forgiveness of sins and the gift of the Holy Spirit to all who repented. More than three thousand people responded to the message. It is difficult to grasp how dynamically the Spirit of God was at work among the people that day.

In our parable of the cream-filled cookie, the cream is the Word of God, the Scriptures. The Word always has been and always will be the cream—the focal point. The Word of the Lord is and always will be at the center of our lives, even as it was in the Old Testament. God spoke clearly through Abraham, Isaac, Jacob, Joseph, Joshua, the judges, the prophets, and the priests. In this new Kingdom economy, though, He fills all believers and lives among them by His Holy Spirit. God spoke in the power of the Holy Spirit through Peter, and the Word of God was again revealed. The cream is rich and central to all that God is doing.

The Two Cookies

By the Maker's design, two cookies hold the cream of the Word in place, two new and dynamic pieces that reveal the vibrancy and energy of the promised Holy Spirit. These two cookie pieces are clearly portrayed in Acts 2, just before and just after Peter's dynamic, Spirit-led message. Together, they secure the precious cream and reveal its message in two profoundly life-giving ways.

The first cookie represents the gifts of the Holy Spirit. This is the body of Christ soon to be dynamically reflected in every believer, body part by body part. Many people miss the importance of the tongues of fire that were poured out in Acts 2:1-12. But this move of the Spirit through many believers reveals the Word of God in power. Why were the different tongues given at this point? Because the Spirit provided words to each in his or her own language to make sure they understood the cream of the message. In this way the Holy Spirit revealed to all that the Lord of the universe was present and speaking personally to each of them in their own tongue, revealing the Word.

But rather than speaking in a loud and booming voice from the heavens, God spoke through His people. Now that He had begun to live and move and have His way in them—as promised in Ezekiel 36–37—His new Kingdom economy was active and working through body life. Then one brother, Peter, stood up and spoke the cream-filled message of repentance, baptism, forgiveness of sins, and the coming of the Holy Spirit. Peter continued to reveal the power of the Spirit at work in his anointed preaching.

From this point forward, the body of Christ personified the power, grace, and love of Jesus to the world through these gifted believers. From this first dramatic, energizing move of the Spirit, God's body-life design will change ministry forever. The We-body of Christ is taking form before our eyes. A full range of spiritual gifts will make up this work of Jesus, many more than just tongues and powerful teaching. This cookie reveals the Word in power through these many and varied portions of grace: mercy, service, encouragement, shepherding, words of wisdom, giving, administration, leading, prophecy, and many more.

The other cookie piece in the cream-filled cookie is grace-filled relationships. We see these clearly in Acts 2:42-47 as the response to God's Word. The early church saw an explosion of grace-filled relationships. The move of the Spirit was so great that people devoted themselves to one another, the apostles' teaching, the breaking of bread, and prayer. God revealed Himself through the Word spoken—the cream. The Word is understood through the energizing, multifaceted gifts of the Spirit in the people, through the gifts of tongues, and Peter's evangelistic preaching. God was now revealing Himself in life-giving relationships, a level of community that is transformational for all involved. Paul used names such as the household of God, the body of Christ, and the fellowship of the Holy Spirit in his writing. This signifies the fellowship of the Trinity now modeled in this new community of faith.[19]

If we remove or crush either cookie, the cream of the Word is broken. Frankly, you get the picture of disunity that dominates much of the Western Christian world. Broken and unresolved relationships and lack of relational depth on ministry teams just break the surface of what happens when body unity is damaged. Jesus prayed for unity in John 17:21-23 because He knew that these soon-to-be-Spirit-enfolded love relationships were the most powerful revelation of the Word made flesh on earth. But in reality, the greatest sadness here is the loss of the sanctuary of God's presence among us. He chose to live with us, and disunity often blocks the work of His presence among us. We are no longer being built together because . . . we are no longer together.

I will never forget the first time I used this illustration in a group of ministry leaders in southeast Asia. As I took apart the Oreo cookie, holding just one of the cookie pieces, I began to ask, "What would happen to the Word, the cream, if the range of powerful gifts were not used, or if body-life relationships were broken apart in disunity?" As I asked the question, the cookie piece in my hand slipped out and crashed to the table. It broke into many pieces, and there was a unified gasp in the room. Not only was the cookie piece shattered, but the cream was broken apart.

Without energizing body-life ministry through the gifts, and without loving, life-giving relationships, the Word's impact is shattered and diminished. Satan loves our lack of focus on stewarding all the gifts. He is thrilled with our specialized skills training that moves people away from their supernatural empowerments. He loves to see Christians powerless and in disarray. He cherishes broken relationships and Christians separating as individuals, living apart from Christian fellowship. Why? Because it breaks down the love and power of the Word in relationships and shared ministry. He knows that Jesus lives where two or three are gathered, so he wants to keep them apart to limit the dynamic power and grace-filled love that is the heart of authentic body life. Sadly, when this happens the body of Christ stops being the body, fragmenting into little pieces of truth, power, and love here and there.

Let's review the three parts of the cream-filled cookie and consider some points of application:

The Word of God
1. Know the Word, as it is of central importance.
2. Grow deeper in knowing Jesus through understanding what you believe and why you believe it.

Body-Life Gifts
1. Discover and steward your body-life role through the powerful spiritual gifts given to you by the Father and empowered by the Holy Spirit.
2. Use your gifts to reflect Jesus through equipping, supporting, and multiplying body-life ministry.

Body-Life Relationships
1. Become a good steward of the relationships God gives you by living a life of character, grace, and love.
2. Work for unity and ongoing health in those relationships and new ones He brings in the multiplication process of body life.

Paul's Body of Work Confirms God's New Economy of Relationship

The development of Christ's Church from Pentecost forward highlights distinctive patterns in Paul's writings about these vital body-life realities. As we survey and attempt to summarize Paul's writings about body-life gifting and body-life relationships, you will note the incredible breadth and depth of his understanding and appreciation of the ways God wants to continue to move among His people after Pentecost.

It may be hard to absorb all the details that follow, but it is important to share them all to confirm the central role of these organic, body-life principles. I want you to sense the gravity and significance of the cream-filled cookie realities of Kingdom life. More than anything else, this will reveal how essential it was to Paul's understanding that the Word be made flesh through the body of Christ—in concrete, everyday terms. The stewardship given to every body member, and the grace-filled love and unity that is to dominate those gifted players, exposes God's We-strategy for working through His people.

Steward the Spiritual Gifts

Regarding the move of the Spirit into every believer through powerful spiritual gifts, we already examined 1 Corinthians 12:4-12, in which we see how Jesus' life fills His body in specific, energizing ways. Every Christian is now an active body-life partner in ministry, critical to the organic power and growth of the whole body. Paul continued in detail with the Corinthians through the rest of chapters 12 and 14 as he brought understanding and correction to some dynamic challenges with certain gifts. As Phill Butler noted, "When the church, the body of Christ, began to emerge, it was another illustration of God's penchant for parceling out different roles to different people."[20]

Take stock and steward the whole body of believers around you, and not a select few who can fulfill a certain type of ministry.

It is still difficult to grasp this amazing truth: We are the organs, eyes and ears, hands and feet, and together the mouthpiece of Jesus in the world. Romans 12:3-12 reflects the need for individuals to soberly estimate their fit in the body through each one's specific gifting. Ephesians 4:11-16 identifies the nature of certain gifts given by Jesus to equip others in the body to fulfill their work of ministry, to build up and unify the body. Every ligament supports, each part does its work. Peter, in 1 Peter 4:10-11, added that the stewarding of one's spiritual gifts reflects a portion of God's multifaceted grace, bringing glory to the Giver of the gifts and revealing His power in words and in actions.

Steward the Grace-Filled Relationships

In the realm of relationships, where God lives among His people, Paul's coverage is even more extensive. There is a reason the love chapter, 1 Corinthians 13, is placed between two spiritual-gifts chapters, 12 and 14, where Paul addressed critical body issues. Gifts and love are also paired inextricably in Acts 2. Angelic words without love sound like clanging cymbals; dramatic prophetic insight without love is absolutely empty. One cannot use the gifts of the Spirit effectively apart from the fruit of the Spirit. The Word was to be made real in everyday life and relationships. When certain gifts created community problems, Paul immediately spoke to the issues.

Consider as well our earlier references to Timothy and Titus. Remember that Paul was committed to sound doctrine. He was committed to training others to teach sound theology as he had taught them, to entrust it to others who would do likewise. He emphasized the need for overseers to be able to teach the Word, giving instruction in sound doctrine. But in both the Titus 2 and

1 Timothy passages, Paul also communicated the imperative of elders having a lifestyle that is high in character and healthy in relationships. Take a look at each passage and consider the number of relational imperatives linked to spiritual leadership. The people who had healthy relationships were the ones selected to lead.

In Romans 12:9-21 and Ephesians 4:17-32, both immediately following spiritual-gifts passages, Paul promoted the need for love, unity, and reconciled relationships. In both Philippians 2:1-11 and 3:12-17, the call to unity, like-mindedness, compassion, and forbearance is clear. Love and unity must function in tandem with the power of spiritual gifts in the ministry of the body.

Paul wasn't yet finished in providing guidance for right relationships. He added a comprehensive set of relational guidelines for the new Kingdom economy. In Christ, believers are called to a higher level of accountability in the household of God. All key relationships are addressed in Ephesians 5:21–6:9 and Colossians 3:18–4:6. (Also, compare Peter's similar exhortations in 1 Peter 2:10–3:7.) Specific behavioral guidance is provided for husbands and wives, parents and children, masters and slaves, and believers and unbelievers. Paul was exhaustive in calling the household of faith to a quality of relationship that will reflect what began at Pentecost in Acts 2:42-47 and 4:31-37. I give significant focus to these issues in chapters 5 and 6 of my book *Knocking Over the Leadership Ladder*, if you want to go deeper.

God's people have moved from lost, I-driven shepherds
and lost sheep to a powerful, grace-filled body of
life-giving We-relationships, where God Himself now lives
in the midst of their community.

God is serious about His mighty army in its new "house-hold" frame with the authentic fellowship of His Holy Spirit. He wants all members released in power and brimming over with love for one another. So it is in God's new economy. His people have moved from lost, I-driven shepherds and lost sheep to a powerful, grace-filled body of life-giving We-relationships, where God Himself now lives in the midst of their community.

Hope Amid Challenges

The balance of solid doctrine with body-life gifting and healthy relationships brings us back to the core of a biblical lifestyle: We must rediscover those cookie pieces that surround the cream or we will continue to miss God's deeper and wider body-life approach for winning the world. Reengineering the proper balance between the Word of truth and effective stewardship of body power and relationships is critical for Western cultures. We are at a crisis point. The cult of rightness can be corrected if we encourage and enable truth to be lived out in authentic relation-ships and with spiritual power.

Phill Butler, a veteran of thirty years with Christian minis-tries all over the world, offered this concern about the need to restore and empower body life:

> I am convinced of one thing. The brokenness in the church, the divisions that abound, and our consistent resistance to the God design of restored relationships and practical unity is our [the church's] greatest sin. *It is the world's roadblock of all road-blocks to belief.* On the outside it is the greatest single road-block to power and credibility in our engagement in the world. *Inside the church, it is the greatest impediment to the joy, refresh-ment and fulfillment God intends for us.*[21]

Part of our challenge, and one major reason why issues of body unity and power are so in need of returning to central focus, relates to the change in most of our households. Ray Simpson, the leader of a Christian community in northeast England, offered this thoughtful perspective:

> At first sight, no two things have less in common than home life in biblical times and home life today. A Jewish or Celtic home was a long-established household around which the basic things of life revolved. A modern family has been described as a temporary arrangement of beds around a fridge and a micro-wave oven; the important things happen elsewhere.[22]

This is not fresh news, but it further demonstrates why we need to rediscover God's desire for true body life in Christ. The issues range far beyond an overt cultural focus on right believing or correct theology.

But there is hope. Changes are happening in ministries moving toward a body-life design for their leadership and teams. I have seen thousands of pastors, missionaries, church planters, and other active Christians begin anew to intentionally steward both their powerful spiritual gifts and their relationships. Body-life power has been released and many strongholds broken in the midst of renewed team, church, ministry, and family relation-ships. I see people being restored in this season of right believing when believers have a tendency to "shoot their wounded." Gayle Haggard, wife of fallen Christian leader Ted Haggard, gave a concise guide for stewarding body-life relationships—in this case, her choice to stay married to husband Ted, a high-profile pastor who had a moral failure.

> I believe what the Scripture says, that when a brother sins, those who are spiritual should gently restore him. And I

think restore means to restore to health, so that a person can fulfill their gifts and callings in God. I would liken it to the story of the Prodigal Son; even though he thought he deserved second-class status, the father didn't respond that way. The father threw a robe around him and restored him as his son.[23]

Such straightforward actions exemplify part of our need to steward grace-filled relationships over the long run. Long-time Christian counselor and author Larry Crabb sees the possibilities in terms of revolution:

I envision a revolution that creates a community of broken people united not by their problems or diagnoses but by their hunger for God. I envision a revolution that frees people to fully participate in that community because they feel the safety of the gospel that embraces people . . . that supernaturally equips people to pour life into one another.[24]

Lord, make it so.

Summary

Living out the Word in relationship is not always popular. The two religious men who bypassed the man hurt on the side of the road understood right thinking, but it did not translate into loving action. The cult of rightness creates an environment where we value right biblical thinking over actively living the biblical ideal. Part of this has come out of Greek influence in Western culture. Biblical knowledge was information to be contemplated, mastered, and then passed along to the next generation. But the Hebrews understood truth as something to be translated into life and relationships, where the head *and* the heart were affected.

Such insight affected how they lived day-to-day relationships.

When people overvalue knowledge and understanding, their thoughts become disconnected from their actions. Such truth believed without action can breed the cult of rightness.

But God desires that truth be communicated and then lived out. Acts 2 and the parable of the cream-filled cookie give us a simple framework for how God intends His Word to be experienced. The Word of God will always be the center of His purposes, the cream. However, the Word is profoundly embodied in two dramatic ways that reveal the very body life where God lives by His Spirit. The Word is revealed in dynamic spiritual gifts given to every believer. The Word is also reflected in grace-filled community, where love and fellowship are the norm. Without the Word embodied in body-life power and portrayed in loving relationships, as 1 Corinthians 13 states, even tongues of angels can be like a noisy gong. Jesus came as the Word in the flesh, and we now carry His life-giving ministry as His body on earth employing spiritual gifts and living out healthy, unified relationships.

A friend of mine once said that it is easier to witness with your words than be a witness with your words *and* your life. Being a witness takes the whole of your life and the whole of your relationships, where words cannot be cheap or easy. We have a chance in this season to move from brokenness and powerlessness to again become a people who live together in love and truth, and become energized, gifted players who fit together and breathe the life of His Spirit to the world around us.

Application Steps

1. Find a ropes course or some kind of trust-building exercise that your group or team can experience together. Afterward, let each person share what he or she learned,

along with one new insight gained about another person in the group.

2. As a group, complete a gifts survey workbook such as *Discovering Your Ministry Identity* (available at www .churchsmart.com) or another similar tool. After all have completed the workbook, break into pairs and give each partner thirty minutes to share what he believes his spiritual gifts to be. As one person shares, the other person listens, asks questions, and looks to see if the person has the characteristics and liabilities of his identified gifts. At your next group meeting, ask these questions and let everyone share:

   - Where are you powerful through your spiritual gifts?
   - How are you weak?
   - Whom do you need?

3. Ask the Spirit to show you what this could mean for your group as you consider ministry ideas together.
4. Find another image for the parable of the cream-filled cookie. Bring it to the group and share how you understand the spiritual gifts and the grace-filled relationships impacting the Word.
5. Select a simple disagreement that could happen in your ministry or group. Role-play two scenarios: the cult of rightness and grace-filled relationships. Debrief the experience.

Questions for Discussion

1. What ideas come to mind, from the one-room schoolhouse example, about growing a group of young disciples?
2. In your own words, what is the cult of rightness? How do you see its effects around you in church and ministries?

3. Define the difference between Greek thinking and Hebrew thinking. What would the balance look like?
4. What insights into the relationship between spiritual gifts, community, and the Word does the cream-filled cookie illustration provide?

1. "1953 American Karakoram Expedition," Wikipedia, summarizing Charles S. Houston and Robert Bates, *K2: The Savage Mountain* (New York: McGraw-Hill, 1954).
2. The very essence of this book has been affected by brothers like John Blake and Steve Hoke, partners in my work who speak truth into my personal life, marriage, and all aspects of my work. They sharpen me, encourage me to be a better husband, force me to think deeper and wider, and always freshen what I develop with their thoughts and ideas. Brian Burnett brings so much to me as an iron-sharpening friend in many ways; the way he thinks in pictures about my ideas and concepts brings a new depth to those same ideas. Grip-Birkman global resource team founder and dear friend Hal Burke has taught me that co-training with another trainer in our Coaches Training Workshops models the very heart of the "I to We" process. He also dearly loves our son. The sharpening and stretching process goes on and on!
3. Brian Knowles, "The Hebrew Mind vs. the Western Mind," Association for Christian Development, http://www.godward.org/Hebrew%20Roots/hebrew_mind_vs__the_western_mind.htm.
4. Colin Brown, *Dictionary of New Testament Theology*, vol. 1 (Grand Rapids, MI: Eerdmans, 1975), 485.
5. Brown, 48.
6. Knowles.
7. Thorlief Boman, *Hebrew Thought Compared with Greek* (London: SCM Press, 1960), 67–68.
8. Paul and Monica Schutte, "Developing a Biblical Philosophy of Education," December 24, 2002, http://mysite.verizon.net/res1cii2/sitebuildercontent/sitebuilderfiles/developingabiblicalphilosophyofeducation.pdf.
9. N'Tan Lawrence, "Hebrew Thought Compared with Greek (Western) Thought—A Key to Understanding Scripture Through the Eyes of the Authors," Scribd, http://www.scribd.com/doc/102445374/heb-grk.
10. Abraham Heschel, *God in Search of Man* (New York: Farrar, Straus & Giroux, 1955), 20.
11. Marvin Wilson, *Our Father Abraham—Jewish Roots in the Christian Faith* (Grand Rapids, MI: Eerdmans, 1990), 136.
12. Wilson, 36.
13. George Eldon Ladd, *The Pattern of New Testament Truth* (Grand Rapids, MI: Eerdmans, 1968), 22.
14. Richard Rohr, *The Naked Now: Learning to See as the Mystics See* (New York: Crossroad, 2009), 45.
15. Quote from an unnamed ministry partner in central Asia, March 2012.
16. Geoffrey W. Bromiley, *A Theology of the New Testament* (Grand Rapids, MI: Eerdmans, 1974), 509.

17. Phill Butler, *Well Connected: Releasing Power, Restoring Hope Through Kingdom Partnerships* (Colorado Springs, CO: Authentic Publishers, 2005), 30.
18. Butler, 54.
19. See Ephesians 2:22; 1 Corinthians 12:27; Philippians 2:1-5.
20. Butler, 57.
21. Butler, 6–7.
22. Ray Simpson, *Church of the Isles* (Suffolk, UK: Kevin Mayhew, 2003), 72–73.
23. Sarah Pulliam Bailey, "Why Gayle Haggard Stayed," *Christianity Today*, February 2010, 63.
24. Larry Crabb, *Shattered Dreams* (Colorado Springs, CO: Waterbrook, 2001), 187.

Chapter 5

The Cult of the Spotlight

We're an overconfident species. Ninety-four percent of college professors believe they have above-average teaching skills. A survey of high school students found that 70 percent of them have above-average leadership skills and only 2 percent are below average. . . . Some argue that today's child-rearing and educational techniques have produced praise addicts. . . . I wonder if there is a link between a possible magnification of self and declining saliency [importance] of the virtues associated with citizenship. Citizenship, after all, is built on an awareness that we are all not that special but are, instead, enmeshed in a common enterprise.

— DAVID BROOKS[1]

God chose what is foolish in the world to shame the wise; God chose what is weak in the world to shame the strong.

— 1 CORINTHIANS 1:27

Paul, I have stopped texting, already checked my Facebook page, put down my *Investment Weekly* magazine, and have put away my daily planner that scopes out exactly how I will spend my time each day. I have turned off ESPN's *SportsCenter* in the background. . . . I even turned off Rachael Ray on the Food Network. You have my full attention — wait a minute, I have a call. Oh, never mind, I will let them leave a message. Go ahead. Now, where were we, Paul?

— CONVERSATION WITH A FRIEND

We live in a country that glorifies movie stars, sports heroes, business success, and "bigger is better" approaches. We are some-times fooled into believing that being in the spotlight is both important and strategic — if not essential — in life. Websites such as Facebook and YouTube, along with texting and Twitter, enhance one's chances to shine, be noticed, or "discovered" amid hope of renewed or new friendships in such social networking settings. The cult of the spotlight often seeks attention or even glory for the individual, and leads away from the heart of real community.

> The cult of the spotlight often seeks attention or even glory for the individual, and leads away from the heart of real community.

The cult of the spotlight rings a bell from the past. The great kings of old were raised up and glorified among their followers. People hung on their every word and sometimes were actually hanged if they didn't. Those kings are still around. They are wearing different clothes, wielding a different kind of power, speaking to many audiences, seated in various kinds of throne rooms, or playing assorted instruments or sports. These new kings and queens are lording it over their subjects, and thoroughly enjoying the pandering affections of these devoted, loyal supporters.

With Warren Buffett, Lady Gaga, Peyton Manning, Muse, Mark Zuckerberg, Hope Solo, Mark Harmon — or your personal favorite — the kings and queens of the spotlight abound. And with the fast-moving, ever-changing spotlight, you may not recognize some of these names as others now shine brighter. But now many "common" people are talking up their every action on Twitter or Facebook. A new world is rising: No longer must I be a king or a great leader to find affirmation and admiration in the in the eyes of others. A great website or Facebook page gives everyone the opportunity to see so much of who we are, and in picturesque or humorous ways.

How the world has changed! Yet, from the Garden of Eden to the World Wide Web, how the world has *not* changed. Where does the body of Christ fit into our world of the spotlight? To the ones who are called to offer all praise and adoration to God alone, how can we live in the world and not act like the world?

Finding My Place to Shine

There is tremendous value in wise, strong leadership in the world at large and in the body of Christ. There is a genuine need for outstanding, godly leadership. Yet cultural events in the West during the past thirty years have stunted our understanding of leadership's value. In fact, I wrote *Knocking Over the Leadership Ladder* several years ago to express my concerns about this unrecognized development. Being or becoming a leader is so important to people that we must spend some time addressing this "leadership spotlight" if we are to move from "I to We" as God's household today. We must stop and assess our cultural drive to create or become great leaders, both inside and outside the Kingdom of God.

High-quality leadership is crucial to success in business, community, and the Church. True. We need those among us who are willing to grasp the future and define a compelling vision for the rest of us. Calling others to join the cause and help establish new directions is equally important. We also hold in highest regard those who lead the way in creating needed trust relationships and brokering a climate of mutual cooperation that benefits the whole. Those who lead out in validating, empowering, and releasing others to play significant parts in the mission or project provide an essential service. It is hard to imagine where we would be without such visionaries, change agents, and partnership builders.

Leaders, more often than we realize, are the leverage point

in the building of community at every level of a process or a mission. That is, as they appear in the foreground, and they represent other citizens, players, employees, or ministry partners.[2] It is their position alongside those they lead that makes their role so strategically important. It is the "I representing the We" relationship. Yet the nature and responsibility of this role is sometimes missed or misunderstood in the cult of the spotlight.

A leader carries out the roles of planning, executing, and multiplying. This person represents the whole process and team or organization. But whether leading six or six thousand, it is not about the leader. Rather, it is about whom that spokesperson, CEO, or visionary represents. Put simply, it is about how leaders see themselves in relation to those they represent. The cult of the spotlight often diminishes this reality, shining brightest on the I-leaders at the head of the conference room table.

I in the Way

Several factors come into play as a leader directs his or her body of workers into the future. First, leaders are often searching to find their significance in something or someone. In what does he find his worth and value in daily life? How is her search for significance playing out in the spotlight of leadership? What if, while standing up front, he is tempted to think of himself as more important than those he represents? Suddenly, the whole picture begins to change. No longer do the values and priorities of the team or community drive the leader's actions. The phrases "self-serving" and "vested interest" come to mind.

We all at once find ourselves on the mount of temptation with Jesus, where He was offered all the kingdoms and glory in the world (see Matthew 4:1-11). All it took for Jesus to enjoy this wonderful spotlight was to sell out His soul to the Evil One. Warren Bennis offered the following observation on such temptation to go after one's own glory and benefit when asked what advice he would give to anyone who wants to be a CEO. The first thing he suggested is "to abandon your ego. You can't solve everything yourself, so you have to learn to build and work with a . . . team. If you don't have that, forget it."[3] The leader—no matter how impressive, powerful, or awe-inspiring—is but one of many who make up the community. He or she is not wired to do work that is supposed to be done by the whole body. When the individual I-leader raises herself up in self-importance, she loses perspective of the whole.

Individualism and Authoritarianism

Second, cultural issues come to the fore. In the West, individualism raises itself up very quickly, being intimately tied in many of us to the search for significance. *New York Times* columnist David Brooks wrote about the difference between cultures with an individualist mindset and ones with a collectivist mindset:

> If you show an American an image of a fish tank, the American will usually pick out the biggest fish in the tank and what it is doing. If you ask a Chinese to describe a fish tank, the Chinese will usually describe the context in which the fish swim. These sorts of experiments have been done over and over again, and the results reveal the same underlying pattern. Americans usually see individuals; Chinese and other Asians see context.[4]

But regardless of cultural background, we must begin to see ourselves not as isolated individuals, but rather as one in the context of relationships, an integrated part of the whole. You define much of how you see yourself in the setting of your relationships. If you choose to spotlight yourself and raise yourself above others as more important, then the dynamics change dramatically for the whole group.

Brooks identified a natural outcome when the focus is on the individual. He described how "people in these societies tend to overvalue their own skills and overestimate their own importance to any group effort."[5] If you tie this to our earlier issue of searching for your personal worth or significance through your role or accomplishments, it is easy to see why so many leaders get blinded in the spotlight of leadership. The impact of individualism and the related sense of entitlement and dissatisfaction of Christians in the West is disturbingly real.[6]

Much to my surprise, I have found a different yet very similar issue in collective societies. In the tribal cultures of east Africa, this I-tension with leadership comes out in the form of an emphasis on authority. Each person knows that his or her identity and role is understood and lived out in family and community. Each must play his or her part in fulfilling family and tribal responsibilities. Every part of culture is understood and lived out in a We-context. That is, every part except for leadership. The one place where the individual rises into the spotlight here is in a position of authority. One Christian brother in Uganda with whom I worked wrote me an e-mail in which this one sentence identifies the cultural challenge: "As you may know, as a country, our biggest challenge is leadership that believes it is born to rule over others."[7]

I see this behavior modeled in ministry leaders throughout east Africa. Pastors act like tribal chiefs and lord it over the people in their churches, but often without seeing themselves as a servant representative of those people. They commonly do not share ministry functions with others for fear of losing authority, weakening their "rule" over them. In fact, many aspire to pastoral leadership because it can bring prestige and power. To be a pastor is to be a person of significance in the community. One of the reasons we spend much time alongside a number of ministries working on our Body-Life Team principles is to address this very issue. The body of Christ does not effectively multiply through strong, authoritative leaders who do not allow others to share in the work. This approach short-circuits the process of equipping and releasing or multiplying oneself through others before it even begins. Many of these pastors and church planters struggle with their own search for significance, believing they may find it only in the spotlight.

Add up these issues and cultural tendencies in the body of Christ, and you begin to see the obstacles preventing the expansion of God's spiritual We-household. I have watched this cancerous reality, stemming from an undue focus on the leadership or leader, steal the life from the body of Christ for many years now in multiple cultures. The following are some of the symptoms and warning signs:

- Body-life growth and health take a backseat to the leader's life of enjoying — and remaining in — the spotlight.
- The leader's dominance and desired safety in his or her position limit spiritual growth in others; people are not equipped and released.
- The need for recognition and affirmation may be deterred by the "rise" of others. It becomes difficult to allow others to share in the functions of ministry.
- The leader values the trappings of title, prestige, power, influence, and honor so much that those things begin to affect his or her judgment in areas of spiritual oversight.

- The leader may step away from encouragement and/or accountability from the body of people around him or her, and stumble into sin.[8]

When we live by God's design, I-leaders are equipped and released to serve the We-body. Christian leaders must see themselves with clear vision — that is, as one among the whole body of Christ, a priest among the priesthood of all believers. David Platt stated the issue well:

I believe in the people of God. Or more specifically, I believe in the work of God's Spirit through God's Word in God's people. The last thing I want to do is rob Christians of the joy of making disciples by telling them that I or anyone or anything else can take care of that for them.

Someone might ask, "But if a church has a gifted communicator or a gifted leader, wouldn't we want as many people [as possible] to hear that person?" The answer is "not necessarily." The goal of the church is never for one person to be equipped and empowered to lead as many people as possible to Christ. The goal is always for all of God's people to be equipped and empowered to lead . . . people to Christ.[9]

Let us get back to focusing on all the citizens of the Kingdom, because God lives there and desires to live and move and have His way.[10] He desires to raise up into the spotlight the whole household and not just a few Christian leaders. The spotlight, in fact, is not one of the tools God has designed for character development and spiritual maturation.

He desires to raise up into the spotlight the whole household
and not just a few Christian leaders.

Welcome to the iWorld

There is another issue of citizenship in the body of Christ we must address. It is from another kingdom called the World Wide Web. With more than 955 million users on Facebook alone and growing daily, it is the new millennium marquee for connecting people all over the world.[11] Welcome to the sphere of social networking, a truly unique blend of independence and interdependence. Welcome to the spotlight of a very different kind, one that combines the arena of human relationships with sophisticated marketing hustle.

The Internet world began the public side of its usage about the same time the leadership movement gained momentum: the mid- to late-1980s. The phenomenon of social networking, though, has picked up steam with the onset of the cell phone and its amazing technological advances since the turn of the century. Internet, media, and photo access via cell phones has grown exponentially during this period, feeding already explosive cell-phone usage around the planet. Such handheld devices, and now iPads and other tablets, have become a safety net for families, a lifeline for relationships that cross the earth, and a most amazing communication tool for doing business remotely.

These technologies bring us to the forefront of a new frontier so vast and different that we struggle to grasp the full implications. The level of connection between people is at an all-time high, as is the amount of information that can be accessed and shared.[12] Yet what remains in question is how much — and what kind — of a sense of belonging is created or negatively impacted by all of this. How does it help or hinder people emotionally, spiritually, and psychologically? And, in our discussion, what is the upshot for those seeking authentic Christian community? Is this yet another, and perhaps the ultimate, opportunity for individuals to move into the spotlight?

Facebook, at this writing, outdistances competitors MySpace, Google+, and Twitter in the race for interactivity among friends. Richard Stengel, in a *Time* magazine article, noted, "Facebook has merged with the social fabric of American life, and not just American but human life: nearly half of all Americans have a Facebook account, but 70% of Facebook users live outside the U.S. It's a permanent fact of our global social reality."[13] Remarkably, "one of every dozen people on the planet has a Facebook account. They speak 75 languages and collectively lavish more than 700 billion minutes on Facebook every month. . . . Its membership is currently growing at 700,000 people a day."[14] Even when I travel to rural Uganda, many of our friends there have Facebook pages and are online regularly.

I remember my first attempt at communicating meaningfully with others after setting up my Facebook page. A number of friends, peers of mine ranging in ages from early forties to late fifties, had told me it was a wonderful way to connect with old friends. They said it was imperative that I "connect" on this medium. I was beginning to see that this Facebook community has some aspects that would indeed lend to the forming, reforming, or deepening of friendships old and new. Hey, this has possibilities!

After more than twenty photos suddenly showed up "tagged" on my Facebook page—in less than two months—I decided to give it a try. I was beginning to discover that this kingdom of digital connectivity has its own language and value set that drive the communication. People can acknowledge you in their pictures and the link comes to your page unless you "block" it—which is another rather essential concept on Facebook. And, just as in texting and Twitter, you can abbreviate words and be understood. Our son, Stephen, actually trained me in the world of texting. I text regularly with him, and it has been a great gift in our friendship.

I set out on my first foray into the world of Facebook, aka fb. I confirmed "friend requests" and invited people I know to be my friends. After fattening my friend list by thirty or forty people, I was on the road to connecting! I was set up to watch the news feed on my "wall" of friends who were writing comments. I began reading my wall of comments that friends were making—not to me, but general comments. Another new fb cultural insight: People think and talk out loud to their "audience" of friends on Facebook. Intriguing.

I finally came to my first real "interaction." Interestingly, just as I started reading posts on my wall, someone made a really snide, mean-spirited post about a very dear friend. The writer did not do this personally in a private message to me. It was a message posted on the wall for all of our mutual friends and family to see. I was stunned. Rather than writing a direct comment back, I wrote a personal message and said, "Hey, please do not do that. Talk to this person directly and personally if you are frustrated. This is not fair to write such things publicly."

Then I learned my first truly difficult lesson on Facebook kingdom lifestyle. I got a public post back from a friend who somehow had read my personal message to the person who had blasted my friend. It was really nasty, including language not normally a part of my vocabulary.

I was learning another Facebook kingdom reality, one not nearly as exciting as all I had learned to date: People can criticize you publicly on your wall—even condemn you—and it is there for all your wall of friends and family to see. Stunned, I wrote back to this person, again in a private message not on the public "friends" wall, and quickly signed out of fb. No further need for details. I suddenly felt emotions I had not experienced since middle school. It was as if I had walked back into the season of my life where I was lambasted often and without any true recourse. Now I check Facebook at least two or three times a month, slowly warming back to this unusual, unique "community" process.

For the record, my early experience is not the norm for many Facebook kingdom participants. I have seen hundreds of gracious, interactive, meaningful posts unlike the ones I just described. With interaction with friends from around the world, I do realize the distinct and positive possibilities. And I enjoy some of the fun-loving banter that is cherished among friends. For many it obviously provides tremendous opportunity for meaningful communication and, in many cases, deeper relationships can and do result.

While the ubiquity of Facebook certainly speaks to the pursuit of community and friendships for many people, the reality of so many mixed messages can be confusing. And it appears that I am not alone. Maybe it is Facebook's attempt to map out people's "trusted relationships"[15] while at the same time providing a platform for advertisers using the data gathered on nearly a billion people. "It is unclear how those hundreds of millions of people will feel when they realize they've been permanently joined on the site by advertisers who are not all that interested in friendship."[16] A recent addition to Facebook's growing advertising staff, David Fischer, brings his expertise from—surprise!—Google and offers another revealing remark: "We very much have the view that this [Facebook] product has only just begun."[17]

What happens when you mix friendships and business in such a dynamic environment? How does posting open comments for your world of friends to see affect intimacy in friendships? Or does it provide a substitute for communication that is much easier because you are more in control? How does an increase in quick, short-form communication affect relationships? What drives so many to put up their "page" and portray their lives in photos, "likes," and short blurbs about their daily existence? Is fb actually about connection or perhaps is it more about information and surface-level acquaintance for many participants?

One thing is already certain: Facebook and other means of social networking give the individual a unique opportunity to shine a spotlight on his or her life in a way that has never before been possible. It was a personal note from a twenty-something friend that finally helped me better grasp this part of our electron-speed digital world. It turns out that it may have something to do with the spotlight. I was getting input on the outline for this book from a range of friends and partners in ministry, and what came from this female friend is very telling:

> Love that you are mentioning Facebook. You'll be with us in the hip crowd soon and simply writing "fb" in no time! I think that fb is not so much about having relationships. It's about being connected — that word seems to be in the current hip vocabulary a lot these days. It is all about connecting to the right people or always being connected, another way to say "I want a lot of people to know about me so that I can think I'm popular, but I don't want them to actually KNOW me."[18]

In a world where isolation and separateness is also a wider condition of modern life, people are searching for ways to be known.[19] If I can shine in my own spotlight on Facebook, maybe people will catch more of who I really am. They can comment on my photos, laugh at my links, and search through my list of friends. But while I am in that spotlight, I had better be careful to stay in control, in case people were to discover things about me that they do not like or would use to discredit me. Therein lies part of the tension when your stuff is "out there" in social media.

Welcome to the world of *Alone Together*, a book by Sherry Turkle. Sherry has written several books on the ways technology can enhance life. Out of that research, though, the last half of this book addresses concerns that she has discovered in the process. It seems that staying in control, even while in the spotlight of our own lives, is important for self-protection. Maybe we are fearful of being known, especially within the incredible busyness and disconnectedness of our lives in the new millennium. Consider the following comments by Turkle:

> These days, insecure in our relationships and anxious about our intimacy, we can look to technology for ways to be in relationships and protect ourselves from them at the same time.[20]
>
> Digital connecting may offer the illusion of companionship without the demands of friendship.[21]
>
> We discovered the network, the world of connectivity, to be uniquely suited to the overworked and overscheduled life it makes possible. And now we look to the network to defend us against loneliness even as we use it to control the intensity of our connections. . . . The world is now full of modern Goldilockses, people who take comfort in being in touch with a lot of people whom they also keep at bay.[22]

And what about the impact technology is having on old-fashioned face-to-face communication? If part of the desire is to find oneself in the context of safe and genuine relationships, maybe there are some mixed messages here. Turkle continued:

> Today, our machine dream is to be never alone but always in control. This can't happen when one is face-to-face with a person.[23]
>
> In the new etiquette, turning away from those in front of you to answer a mobile phone or respond to a text has become close to the norm. When someone holds a phone, it can be hard to know if you have that person's attention. A parent, partner or child glances down and is lost to another place, often without realizing that they have taken leave.[24]

Rather than giving ourselves away to others at the level of face-to-face communication, we are choosing to cater to ourselves.[25] "Oh, I'm sorry, Paul, were you talking to me? I got a text and got lost in my own communication." Perhaps oftentimes we simply get lost in the new technology and lose focus, but the result is a denigration of community. As people attempt to shine in their spotlights and find their place in their networks, many may not find any fit whatsoever as they search.

Given this model of such tentative, distracted "friendships," many twenty-first-century churches tend to welcome seekers or new believers into their large gathering room on Saturday night or Sunday, but so often they do not receive them into other, more personal "rooms" of their lives during the week.[26] The hope in many—and reality in some—churches is that we invite them in as true neighbors in the household of God. That is our opportunity, whether we network online or relate face-to-face. What chances has God given us to invite people into our lives, moving them from I-isolation and searching into a context in which they can experience genuine We-hospitality?

Stepping into the We-Life

Regardless of the unique challenges technology presents, Romans 12 provides clear guidelines on how to handle life when the spotlight gets perhaps too close to the center of self and stays there. Going all the way back to Ezekiel 34–37, we have seen that God's design is to move believers into both community and personal joy in the context of the Spirit-led body of Christ. In chapter 12, the apostle Paul offered readers a chance to practice what he had been preaching throughout the great book to the Romans.[27] He answered the question, How do you and I live in Him, for Him, and with others to fulfill this virtuous way of life empowered by the Holy Spirit? Paul's practical steps begin in Romans 12:1-2:

> I appeal to you therefore, brothers, by the mercies of God, to present your bodies as a living sacrifice, holy and acceptable to God, which is your spiritual worship. Do not be conformed to this world, but be transformed by the renewal of your mind, that by testing you may discern what is the will of God, what is good and acceptable and perfect.

The apostle Paul's first exhortation was to "present your bodies as a living sacrifice, holy and acceptable to God." He was not stepping out on his own here, but simply following the words of Jesus regarding the cost of discipleship:

> If anyone would come after me, let him deny himself and take up his cross daily and follow me. For whoever would save his life will lose it, but whoever loses his life for my sake will save it. For what does it profit a [person] if he gains the whole world and loses or forfeits himself? (Luke 9:23-25)

The movement from the I-world to the transformed We-realm of the body requires sacrifice.

Several years ago, Marshall, a Jewish friend, and I were talking about how many people in the West have turned inward toward self. Narcissism, entitlement, dissatisfaction, and ladder climbing have dominated Western culture since the late 1980s. How close are we to becoming this "living sacrifice" in Christ, with a mindset that prepares each one of us for our active roles in His body life? Marshall and I came up with five steps that will help us visualize and comprehend this process. Where do you fit in the "I to We" spectrum that follows?

Step 1: The Self-Indulgent I

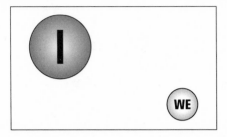

- Everything is for and about me.
- People are there to fulfill my wants and my needs.
- It is all about me, and I do not care about your needs or wants.
- I find safety and security in my things, in my success, and in my comfort areas.

Step 2: The Self-Serving I

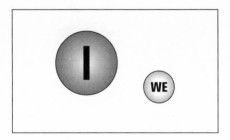

- I am aware of the needs of others but unwilling to help them.
- I will help them if it serves me to do so but am not likely to do so otherwise.
- I may surprise you and meet a need, but it is only to make me look good.
- I am still mostly stuck in my success or my leisurely comforts.

Step 3:The Serving but Irritated I, with a Touch of We

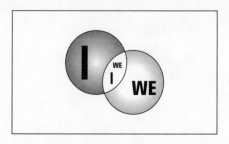

- I consider the needs of others and sometimes serve them but am often irritated in doing so.
- I will do it if I have to, though sometimes it actually feels good.
- It is still mostly about me, though I am tempted to help now and again.
- My success and comforts do not seem to satisfy to the same level as before. Something is changing.

Step 4: The Others-Aware I Moving to We

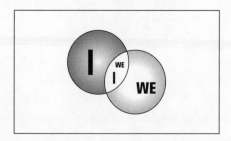

- I am aware of and sometimes choose to serve the needs of others.
- I often realize that it is not just about me anymore. I may still act like a benevolent dictator, but my heart is open.

- My success and/or comforts are losing their hold over me at times; they are not bringing the happiness they once did.

Step 5: The Self-Sacrificial I Committed to the We

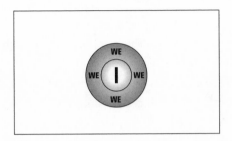

- I choose to sacrifice for others as a lifestyle.
- It is not about you and me—it is about We.
- I have a healthy sense of admitting my need for Jesus, you, and others.
- I still have to be careful to not fall back into allowing comforts or leisurely pursuits to steal from the We.

Marshall and I decided that step 5 is simply not possible without Jesus. Without His grace and love poured out for us on the cross, and His Holy Spirit inside us making us righteous, we are unable to live a daily life that consistently moves from "I to We." Ever since Adam went to the first "apple store" in the book of Genesis, we have had to face the reality of our brokenness and desperation apart from God. We have spent centuries trying to make Him into our own image—"idolatry" by another word. Welcome to the age of technology and our newest efforts to create a world of our own. I rejoice that in Christ we have the spiritual power through the Holy Spirit to manifest a self-sacrificial lifestyle.

It should be noted that several partners in ministry who reviewed these diagrams suggested a sixth category—the "rescuer," who sacrifices for others out of his or her own need for acceptance and personal significance. Codependence is the name commonly given to such a need, and it is worth noting—and addressing, if it fits you. The search for significance certainly can play itself out in this way for many in or outside the body of Christ, and such codependent rescuing is both unhealthy and even dangerous at times.

With I-focused realities abounding all around us, even believers can act like those described in steps 1 through 4 on the diagram if they get too caught up in the spotlight on Facebook, World of Warcraft, or elsewhere. The same destruction can happen if we get caught up in the kingdoms of material stuff, power, or popularity; or of climbing the work or ministry ladder; or other addictive behaviors such as sex, alcohol, or greed. We could pray: "Jesus, we ask You to cleanse us and bring our iWorldly affections under Your care and Holy Spirit control."

Step back into Romans 12, the beginning of discerning His will in verse 2: "Do not be conformed to this world, but be transformed by the renewal of your mind, that by testing you may discern what is the will of God, what is good and acceptable and perfect." Our minds are renewed by the Scriptures, the ultimate guide for faith and service. We are back to the center of the parable of the cream-filled cookie: "Your word is a lamp to my feet and a light to my path" (Psalm 119:105). Through it we test the thoughts, attitudes, and values that drive our daily actions. The written Word is still the center, the starting point, and the guide in all that we do and say, think or write, enact or complete.

So many daily arrows in life constantly shoot I-attitudes and self-serving options directly at us. Seeking Him in His Word to change our minds day to day is imperative. It is no wonder that we have a hard time keeping our minds clear on His priorities.

The I-temptations to lust and pornography, power, popularity, ladder climbing, or alcohol are ever present. These addictions thrive on the availability of an undisciplined mind and body. Sadly, these are the very patterns of the world that Paul talked about in verse 2.

As one who physically exercises regularly, I find that if I miss two or three days in a row of bike riding or weight lifting, a subtle loss of strength is noticeable. If I take a week or ten days off, when I resume I have to ride at a slower pace and lower the weights to rebuild my capacity. For example, when returning from an overseas trip of sixteen days, I go back to about one-third the level of a normal workout and build back up. Otherwise I will hurt myself because of the loss of rhythm and strength. Such is the truth of the Word and the Spirit's guidance. Daily supplements from the Bible provide strength, wisdom, joy, and clarity of discernment that come through the Scriptures. Frankly, without this spiritual cover and strength, the pressing in of the world around us will be harder to discern and more difficult to fight off. Satan has opportunities to take you to the desert of temptation with his sweet offers of worldly options.

Paul's guidance for discerning the will of God has actually only just begun. What follows Romans 12:2 is wisdom beyond learning self-sacrifice and conforming our minds to His Word. Romans 12:3-8 recalibrates and expands our perspective to body life. Initially, the spotlight returns to ourselves, and we learn quickly the reason why:

> By the grace given to me I say to everyone among you not to think of himself more highly than he ought to think, but to think with sober judgment, each according to the measure of faith that God has assigned. For as in one body we have many members, and the members do not all have the same function, so we, though many, are one body in Christ, and individually

members one of another. Having gifts that differ according to the grace given to us, let us use them: if prophecy, in proportion to our faith; if service, in our serving; the one who teaches, in his teaching; the one who exhorts, in his exhortation; the one who contributes, in generosity; the one who leads, with zeal; the one who does acts of mercy, with cheerfulness.

Notice here the dramatic shift that moves the spotlight from the individual to the whole body. Paul spotlighted the orchestration of individual spiritual gifts into body ministry as the next essential piece of discerning God's will. His setup is fascinating, as two aspects for understanding Romans 12:3 are often missed. To "think of himself more highly than he ought to think" certainly sounds like a pride issue, most often the central issue focused on in this verse. But those of us who live in I-thinking/ I-acting cultures may miss several critical insights. The concern here is not that someone thinks pridefully about himself, but it's more that he chooses to position himself apart from others in the body. Paul was actually addressing a We-body-life issue. He was calling every player to account, to see himself and his actions as a vital part of the unified body—the subject of verses 3-4. Unity is the focus, not individual pride. Put simply: See yourself properly as "one among" and not as one to be lifted up by the praises of people.

The other critical insight in verse 3 of this body-life passage is the phrase "think with sober judgment." Paul was not simply encouraging people to think about what causes them to have attitudes that separate themselves from other people. Rather, he was encouraging each one to soberly discern—that is, carefully, intentionally—their gifted fit in the body. The joy of our Kingdom life is that we are never alone. We always have a place to fit in the family and the purposes of God, just as He determines (see 1 Corinthians 12:18). He makes us His dwelling and therein creates a unique role fit for every one of us.

I am reminded here of watching the apostolic team that oversees the house-church movement in central Asia. Five men, equally strong and independently minded, find such joy in admitting need that allows their partners to cover those weak areas with their powerful strengths. God planned it to work that way. Each one is finding his fit in body life.

So much of the search for the spotlight is to understand who you are and what that means in your life. The search for significance is so often filled by material possessions, popularity (Facebook friend count, perhaps), position, or, more seriously, addictive behaviors. But the real underlying need may actually be one of finding your place. Paul's words here provide a strategic piece in the search for who you and I really are.

It is a body-life fit issue. Take a deeper look at who you are and how you fit in the body from a spiritual-gifts standpoint, as the continued flow of the passage advises (verses 6-8). You will begin to see yourself more clearly than ever before. If you are separate from others in the body, not only may pride be an issue, but you will never understand yourself clearly or fully from a Kingdom perspective.

> If you are separate from others in the body, not only may pride be an issue, but you will never understand yourself clearly or fully from a Kingdom perspective.

I think again of Abraham Lincoln and his risky strategy of filling his cabinet with rivals to his presidency. He knew himself to have particular strengths and very real weaknesses. He also knew that certain men could provide wisdom, experience, and expertise he did not have. To his most noteworthy opponent, William Seward, he said, "I now offer you a place, in the hope that you will accept it, and with the belief that your position in the public eye, your integrity, ability, learning, and great experience, all combine to render it an appointment pre-eminently fit to be made."[28] Lincoln had soberly estimated his own strengths and weaknesses. He knew that he needed others such as Seward, Bates, and Chase to share their unique skill sets on behalf of a nation in crisis. It was not about being the strong leader doing it all but rather stewarding all the players together into their best-fit positions, for the sake of unity and survival of the country.

So then, make a sober estimate of who you are and how you may fit among us. Why? Paul wrote, "For as in one body we have many members, and the members do not all have the same function, so we, though many, are one body in Christ, and individually members one of another. Having gifts that differ according to the grace given to us, let us use them" (Romans 12:4-6). The transformation of one's life and the renewing of one's mind are designed to take place in the framework of body-life relationships. That is God's design.

> The transformation of one's life and the renewing of one's mind are designed to take place in the framework of body-life relationships. That is God's design.

Finding how each of us fits together means taking a look at how we function in different roles for the common good. In the body of Christ this process begins with discovering and using your spiritual gifts as a key to your own fit. Paul continued in verses 6-8 and he encouraged faith-filled, generous, and zealous use of each one's particular gifts.

God has determined that you are in the Kingdom spotlight—along with the rest of us. The spotlight is actually on the whole body of Jesus, the place where God lives among us. Jesus died for your sins, forgave you, and in fullness of the Holy Spirit has a special fit for you. Play your part in the body of Christ, as Paul exhorted. It reminds me of a small plaque our friend Nancy Boecker gave me twenty years ago that still sits on my desk: "Always remember: you are absolutely unique—just like everyone else."

Notice, Paul had already challenged believers to never pridefully set themselves apart from others in the body. The whole body of Christ is highlighted, to the glory of God. There is no spotlight for anyone but Jesus.

Finding Your Fit Relationally in the Body

After focusing on conforming our minds to the Word and finding our gifted fit in the body of Christ, Paul covered a third major activity in discerning the good and perfect will of God. Remember the Acts 2 cream-filled cookie? The *Word* is the cream—the center—and always will be. *Check.* The first cookie piece that revealed the Word in power was *spiritual gifts.* Here in Romans 12, Paul challenged us to make a sober estimate and find our gifted place in the body and play that part. *Check.* The second cookie piece is the Word revealed in *grace-filled relationships.* Paul continued in Romans 12:9-21, focusing on the art of relationships:

> Let love be genuine. Abhor what is evil; hold fast to what is good. Love one another with brotherly affection. Outdo one another in showing honor. Do not be slothful in zeal, be fervent in spirit, serve the Lord. Rejoice in hope, be patient in tribulation, be constant in prayer. Contribute to the needs of the saints and seek to show hospitality.

Bless those who persecute you; bless and do not curse them. Rejoice with those who rejoice, weep with those who weep. Live in harmony with one another. Do not be haughty [prideful], but associate with the lowly. Never be wise in your own sight. Repay no one evil for evil, but give thought to do what is honorable in the sight of all. If possible, so far as it depends on you, live peaceably with all. Beloved, never avenge yourselves, but leave it to the wrath of God, for it is written, "Vengeance is mine, I will repay, says the Lord." To the contrary, "if your enemy is hungry, feed him; if he is thirsty, give him something to drink; for by so doing you will heap burning coals on his head." Do not be overcome by evil, but overcome evil with good.

Is it hard to live out the above verses? In the yearlong struggle for survival among Shackleton's twenty-seven men on the *Endurance*, he said that an "egalitarian spirit" came to dominate. That is, everyone did what it took to minimize resentments because there were not any "more equal" than the others.[29] This passage reveals the challenging choices we get to make, day in and day out, to build, strengthen, and even rebuild relationships in the body of Christ. Love is the lubricating oil that makes body-life relationships work smoothly and effectively—and that releases powerful, shared ministry among many players.

The content of these verses is so clear. Please reread this segment several times to deepen your grasp of the primacy of living out right relationships. Make it a checklist for relationships in your small group, house church, ministry team, leadership group, or board. Moving from "I to We" means a willingness to be accountable to one another in the specifics. Acts 2:42-47 shows what happened when the Spirit moved powerfully among relationships. Romans 12:9-21 gives us wise and practical specifics on how to continue in the same powerful love for one another as the driving force in our community of faith. *Lord, by Your*

Spirit empower us to reveal this fruit of Your Spirit!

Note one of William Seward's comments about his former political rival who became a deeply trusted friend, Abraham Lincoln: "Presidents and Kings are not apt to see flaws in their own arguments. But fortunately, for the Union, it had a President, at this critical juncture, who combined a logical intellect with an unselfish heart."[30] We hear so much about Lincoln the leader and Lincoln the orator. But we hear so little about Lincoln the effective steward of both unique qualities of those around him and the relationships among those rivals. His character, his sober estimate of who he was and was not, and his ability to honor and protect his cabinet members from the press and from one another were indeed unique. These godly qualities were truly the value-centered heart of the man. His relational focus, portrayed in his capacity to model and encourage healthy relationships, matched his intellect. Thank God that it did.

Summary

In a country that glorifies the personal spotlight, how does the individual Christian and the body of Christ fit in? One of the great options that the world provides in the search for significance is the chance to become a noteworthy leader of some kind. We place an excessively high value on leaders and leadership. Sometimes we forget that the leader actually represents so many others, one among those he or she represents. The leader sometimes forgets this as well and loses perspective on the critical role of standing on behalf of others and empowering them. Thus it becomes easy to fall into the temptation of highlighting the individual. This is also true in other, more collective-type cultures, where authority and control are the goal. The leader plays but one key part among many valuable roles, enabling others to share in those essential leadership functions.

God designed the whole body of believers to play their gifted parts so that He would get the glory. When the spotlight falls on the leader, problems arise. The same is true if one seeks the spotlight in the iWorld of social networking. What begins for the individual as a search to connect relationally may become a search for the spotlight of significance. The possibility for the Christian to lose sight of the call to steward one's gifts and relationships in the center of the community is real. The chance of becoming *Alone Together* with many others lurks in the background if this sense of calling and discerning one's soberly discerned fit is lost.

In Romans 12, Paul called us back to the life of self-sacrifice and drawing near to the Lord and away from the world. One essential part of this process is to discover and fulfill one's place in the body of Christ. He challenged us to make sober estimates of who we are and how we fit, addressing both issues of significance and function in the body. One of the action steps following gives specific plans for doing this sober estimation process. We have a place to belong and a place to play our unique parts. We also have a place where we commit to loving one another, and a place where we fit with one another.

Application Steps

1. Take a current newspaper, news magazine, or online magazine and search for the words "lead," "leader," or "leadership." What characteristics are they defining? How has the "cult of the spotlight" perhaps influenced this?
2. Review the diagrams in the steps of moving from "I to We." Share with the group one step you intend on taking to move toward a more We-centered life.
3. Analyze your personal social media presence. Track how long you spend on Facebook or Twitter for one week.

Discuss the importance of this to you—and its potential impact on your team.

4. Reread Romans 12:9-21 in your group. Answer the following questions in groups of two or three. Which of the exhortations is the easiest for you to do regularly? Hardest? How well do you handle blessing those who persecute you (see verse 14)? What one issue or relationship can we pray about for each other and offer to be specific in holding each other to account?

Questions for Discussion

1. How can you tell when someone is building a group or team so the spotlight is on himself? What could you or others do to encourage that person to move back from "I to We"?

2. What has been your experience with Facebook and other social media? How has this form of communication and information impacted community and relationships for you? What are the underlying differences (the pros and cons) of "posting on a wall" (public) versus "private messaging" a friend?

3. Review the problem described in cultures with authoritarian leadership. What unique challenges do these cultures pose to body life?

4. Reread Romans 12:1-3. Which phrase in these verses jumps out at you? Why? How does this idea of soberly discerning the I-fit as flowing into the We–body life strike you?

---

1. David Brooks, "The Modesty Manifesto," *New York Times*, March 10, 2011, http://www.nytimes.com/2011/03/11/opinion/11brooks.html?_r=0.

2. Peter Block, *Community: The Structure of Belonging* (San Francisco: Berrett-Koehler Publishing, 2008), 39, 41.

3. Warren Bennis, "Speed Dial Warren Bennis," *Bloomberg Businessweek*, September 27, 2010, 22.
4. David Brooks, "Harmony and the Dream," *New York Times*, August 11, 2008.
5. Brooks.
6. Paul R. Ford, *Knocking Over the Leadership Ladder* (St. Charles, IL: ChurchSmart Resources, 2007), 33–49.
7. Geogracious Ogwapit, e-mail correspondence to author, January 31, 2011.
8. R. Scott Rodin, "From the Field—Becoming a Leader of No Reputation," *Journal of Religious Leadership* 1, no. 2 (Fall 2002): 117.
9. David Platt, "The Genius of Wrong," *Mission Frontiers*, July–August 2011, http://www.missionfrontiers.org/issue/article/the-genius-of-wrong.
10. Block, 85.
11. Richard Stengel, "Only Connect: Person of the Year 2010," *Time*, December 27, 2010, 43. Number of active users was updated from 600 million to 955 million per "Facebook," *Wikipedia*, accessed on September 12, 2012, http://en.wikipedia.org/wiki/Facebook.
12. Stengel, 51.
13. Stengel, 51.
14. Stengel, 51.
15. Stengel, 60–61.
16. Brad Stone, "Sell Your Friends," *Bloomberg Businessweek*, September 27, 2010, 72.
17. Stone, 70.
18. Unnamed friend, e-mail to author re: outline for this book, February 15, 2011.
19. Block, 2.
20. Sherry Turkle, *Alone Together: Why We Expect More from Technology and Less from Each Other* (New York: Basic Books, 2011), xii.
21. Turkle, 1.
22. Turkle, 13, 15.
23. Turkle, 157.
24. Turkle, 164.
25. David Platt, *Radical* (Colorado Springs, CO: Multnomah, 2010), 7.
26. Ray Simpson, *Church of the Isles* (Suffolk, UK: Kevin Mayhew, 2003), 67.
27. John Calvin, *Romans*, xxv.
28. Doris Kearns Goodwin, *Team of Rivals: The Political Genius of Abraham Lincoln* (New York: Simon & Schuster, 2005), 285.
29. Dennis N. T. Perkins, *Leading at the Edge: Leadership Lessons from the Extraordinary Saga of Shackelton's Antarctic Expedition* (New York: American Management Association, 2000), 90.
30. Kearns Goodwin, 400–401.

Chapter 6

The Cult of Strategies and Tactics

The heart of man plans his way, but the Lord establishes his steps.

— PROVERBS 16:9

I will see where I really fit into a whole evangelism strategy so these wonderful people can come to know Jesus.

— A PASTOR

I was with you in weakness and in fear and much trembling, and my speech and my message were not in plausible words of wisdom, but in demonstration of the Spirit and of power, so that your faith might not rest in the wisdom of men but in the power of God.

— 1 CORINTHIANS 2:3-5

God places His saints where they will bring the most glory to Him, and we are totally incapable of judging where that may be.

— OSWALD CHAMBERS[1]

Robert Munger was one of my spiritual heroes in my early twenties. Dr. Munger wrote a small booklet, *My Heart, Christ's Home*, that deeply touched me and influenced tens of thousands of lives in my generation. I had the privilege of becoming his friend during my seminary years in Pasadena, California. During that season I wrote a short play adaptation of *My Heart, Christ's Home* and performed it with Dr. Munger present. What a thrill!

During the last year of my master's program, I led a team implementing a major missions conference at our school. Dr. Munger, who went back into the pastorate during the last year of my master's program, was invited to be our keynote speaker on the final night. We had planned and promoted the events well and had a large attendance throughout the week. We could hardly wait for our expected crowd of eight hundred to a thousand people to hear Dr. Bob.

As we waited that evening, only a few people sprinkled into the hall. By our starting time, fewer than one hundred people were present, and I was mortified. I went back to pray with Dr. Bob, and apologized profusely for what in my mind was a poorly attended event. I remember the look he gave me at that moment, a look of spiritual intensity seared deeply into my memory. He said, "I don't ever remember God promising to execute His plans according to our purposes. God always brings exactly whom He wants. He always fulfills what He intends." What an evening it was. God's desire to reach the world was communicated powerfully through Dr. Bob's message, with the Spirit moving deeply among those of us whom God brought.

It was one of my first major lessons in body-life "organics." We can plan well by earthly standards, but need to watch and wait in case God changes our purposes into His process of transformation and change. Those two dimensions—our plans and His purposes—can often be very different things.

The Good News About Organizational Goals and Strategies

Another economic meltdown has overtaken the West and—by virtue of our global economic connections—much of the world as well. Pick your season: from the Great Depression of the 1930s to the long gasoline lines of recession during the 1970s, to the Internet bubble bursting at the turn of the century, and even to the subprime mortgage financial meltdown in the last decade. Sometimes corporations' or people's plans for wealth and greatness result in shocking, often unplanned, outcomes. The best-laid growth strategies and tactics often turn south into a morass of lost income, broken relationships, and even personal depression. As Solomon stated in Proverbs 16:9, we indeed make our plans, but the Lord is the one who actually establishes what really happens. This allows for the distinct possibility that we may not be as wise or as strategic as we sometimes think we are. Our intent toward planning and executing our strategies may, in fact, cause us to stop watching for God and His purposes.

> Our intent toward planning and executing our strategies may, in fact, cause us to stop watching for God and His purposes.

Organized, Systems-Oriented Plans

We can agree that many positive results come from visionary planning, goal setting, and strategizing in organizations. Consider the many obvious ways well-thought-out approaches can effect healthy outcomes. As Christian anthropologist Paul Hiebert noted, "American culture places a premium on clear, well-bounded sets: well-defined roads with curbs and marked lanes, well-edged lawns with no weeds or flowers in the grass, paint and glass well separated in the window, and fixed prices."[2] We have followed our Greek and then European influences in making life around us look orderly and impressive structurally, aesthetically, and even organically in gardens and parks. We value that many things in our lives are laid out in an organized fashion, and feel good when our presentation impresses others with quality and organization. I remember the first time I walked into one of the many public parks in Moscow, Russia. It was shocking to me that the grass was not mowed and flowers appeared to be growing wild. I was stunned that everyone in the world did not have the same approach to clean lines and orderliness as we often do in the United States. Russians, with strong Eastern influences, do it differently.

Further, our systems orientation has revealed itself in the business and organizational management arenas. One brief historical side note may be of interest. Some of the European influences I mention here actually can be traced to the Reformation, as noted by Max Weber in *The Protestant Ethic and the Spirit of Capitalism*. What many have called the Protestant work ethic—a systemization of ethical conduct that grew up with Calvinistic Protestantism in the sixteenth century—has affected the way families live and work in very constructive ways.[3] We learned a system of behavior that was honorable, positive, hard-working, tolerant, and longsuffering. It provided the foundational work ethic for our now-common system of capitalism. People were encouraged to function with healthy motives in all they did, and to even maintain self-control and mental concentration.[4] Such values proved to be extremely beneficial when building a healthy, growing economy of goods and services. It served the people and provided meaningful income for families.

Such systematic encouragement—in part from spiritually rooted training—was widespread and infinitely influential. Diligent workers resulted, and communities of skilled laborers became productive centers for goods and services. My grandfather and my father were the two who most portrayed these influences to great effect in my own life. When I started my first job as a ninth grader at the *Fulda Free Press* print shop in southwestern Minnesota, I already understood the need to work hard, follow instructions, play fair, and "stick with it" even through difficulty. Little did I know that so much history was behind that work ethic and those heartfelt attitudes in my family's generations across the ocean, back to Scotland.

Personal Observations and Reflections. I have spent the last twenty years of my life working closely with nearly one hundred Christian denominations and mission agencies covering a wide theological spectrum. I can tell you that likely the least-used spiritual gift in the Church is the gift of administration. So many times, in fiscal and administrative arenas, churches or ministries and their respective leaders are left wanting. It may be a pastor or treasurer with no accountability who embezzles money or a lack of organized, consistent communication in a particular ministry. It may be a board seemingly unable to prepare and execute plans that relate to the ongoing mission of a ministry. These problems are legion from such lack of detail awareness, planning, or implementation.

I have learned the hard way that we need the wisdom and active support from believers who are supernaturally gifted with administration or have a natural systems orientation. I used to be threatened by those with such detail capacity because I was afraid they were out to steal my vision or derail my simplified plan of action. But so often it was just the opposite outcome desired by these careful partners. They did not want to steal my vision, but rather to enhance it by providing more depth and clarity. They wanted to enhance the vision and its direction by helping me think through some of the details that I had glossed over in my preparation, or had missed in my big-picture analysis.

My vision is often crystal clear, but my plans for getting there frequently do not have enough detail. I have learned to welcome such detailed input, especially from key partners who are more careful in thought and preparation than I. In fact, long before this book you are reading went to the publisher, eighteen friends in ministry gave me direct, detailed input on how to make every chapter better. Their contributions on clarity, flow of thoughts, sentence structure, and "that just does not make sense or fit" declarations were invaluable guides to my writing. You might say that this book was "written by the body," the organics of which we shall discuss soon.

One of the great blessings in my life in the systems and planning arena has been a man named Brian. A friend of twenty-five years, Brian leads a midsized engineering firm in the southwest part of the United States. His overall strengths are in planning, leading, and managing processes with excellence. As president, he guides the overall flow of business through regular meetings with all levels of management in the company. The owners' group trusts Brian's leadership. They reflect together and give feedback to Brian and one another. In the end, they consistently embrace his thorough plans. The company has successfully navigated a number of major upheavals in the economy while Brian has been at the helm.

I have had the joy of coaching Brian over the past six years, as well as coming alongside three lieutenants who likely will be a part of the company's future leadership when Brian and others step out of the company. Needless to say, Brian's systems thinking and planning have had tremendous influence on me as I watched him—and conversed with him—on many issues and action plans over these years. How blessed I am that he has helped me to think through processes and plans more intentionally in particular areas of my work. Even in the Christian world, many key strategies and systems, such as those of Christian leadership professor Bobby Clinton, prove valuable.[5] And those who have the gift to implement them are truly a blessing to any organization.

Systematized, orchestrated approaches seeking excellence, efficiency, and growth have forever changed the way we function organizationally. Given our calling to run the race with discipline to win the prize (see 1 Corinthians 9:24) and to estimate the cost of discipleship as one planning to build a tower (see Luke 14:27-30), we find genuine focus and help in many of the principles offered in these programs and their administrators. The Lord knows where we need such cover in administration, systems, and organizational development. Approaching leadership as a shared process by allowing gifted individuals to execute strategic plans can change everything a leader does, as you will more clearly see in part 3.

The Bad News About Organizational Goals and Strategies

While we continue to observe and learn from the many Christian organizations with whom we interact regularly, I confess sincere concern that many have fallen into some very dangerous patterns. As we assemble our ministry systems and organizational goals and strategies, the world's influences can quietly pressure Kingdom planning and implementation in ways that were not intended. In some cases, it may actually steal from the Great Shepherd's purposes that He prepared to be lived out among us in body life. As He seeks to live, move, and have His way among us as His dwelling place, Kingdom purposes may be obscured or glossed over in favor of ways that are seen as more efficient or effective for doing the business of ministry.

If there ever was a time when we must be watchful, that time is now.

A number of challenging issues are frequently in play. First, many ministries are under growing pressure to become more "corporate"—very much like secular companies. The temptation to adapt to best practices in management and administration without grappling with the implications of using such processes may be more problematic than perceived at first glance. The strain may come from the need to merge certain systems, roles, or departments because of dropping income. It may be further aggravated through the call for more efficiency or increased effectiveness by the board. It may come in the form of greater accountability demanded, with more specific measurements for evaluating both programs and personnel.[6]

The pressures to produce results that lead to growing and multiplying churches, church planters, and leaders are very real. That is part and parcel of our high producing, "expected to be the world leader" culture. This brings on a second challenge of increased expectations. Thus, in the growing and transforming of Christian organizations, there is considerable demand for larger systems, better leaders, clearer goals, and more detailed quality-control evaluations.[7] Various ministry organizations have become quite similar to corporate-world companies. Add to this the already-in-place cultural underpinnings of "more is better," "bigger is better," and "higher up the ladder is more important."[8] It is safe to say that we have some extremely high expectations making the rounds in many Christian organizations.

If a pattern of productive, upward mobility is established, a third challenging reality appears. It can be difficult to manage such a growth process and not mix motives in the process. Our way in Christ is the way of the cross, a road of "downward mobility." Such Christian "productivity" in an exciting growth season can easily move toward the opposite: the intent to control and direct growth in ways that God did not intend. Another problem may develop when the joy of God's bringing growth becomes the chance for a leader to move toward self-glorification. Did you hear the one about the Christian who was so humble that they gave him a badge, but then they took it away from him when he began to proudly wear it?

How careful each of us needs to be, especially if and when God brings growth to something in which we have a part. Author Scott Rodin addressed this issue with profound clarity: "Here we touch the most important part of Christian leadership in the future. It is not a leadership of power and control, but a leadership of powerlessness and humility in which the suffering servant of God, Jesus Christ, is made manifest."[9] It is difficult to keep a servant heart, a humble spirit, and a grasp of the truth that any success is God's doing—not a result of us or our well-developed systems and strategies.

The result of these three challenges? Phill Butler, with his broad experience of building healthy, collaborative partnerships in multiple cultures, wrote, "The combination of our desire for quick results and the Western tendency toward individualism has created frustration, ineffective strategies, and unrealistic expectations."[10] I listen to the leaders, middle managers, and those thousands of workers out in ministry across much of the world. I hear from so many that this season is a demanding and stressful time in their Christian service because of growing expectations from leadership.

I think of one ministry executive who recently discovered the level of unrealistic expectations that his ministry leadership has placed on the shoulders of its Christian workers. The vision, mission, and goals of that organization are godly, Kingdom-driven, and well-intended for building and extending the body of Christ worldwide. But the excitement and challenge of opportunities for workers in the organization are weighed down by the fear of being underqualified for or overwhelmed by the ministry's expectations. They are held accountable through an immense trail of paperwork.

Our son, Stephen, is an avid fan of Arsenal, historically one of the big soccer clubs in Great Britain. Pressure for the club to perform is constant. Recently, fans have been frustrated about personnel decisions and the club's direction. Suddenly, for a team that has had a tremendous decade of success—and made a lot of money—the sky is falling! Pundits everywhere are calling for someone's head. Pressure on the manager is growing, as are expectations of spending mountains of money to obtain more world-class players. One would never know that this has been a wildly successful team for more than a decade, likely the best-run organization in European football from a financial stand-point. Sometimes even the best plans and strategies still end up under a busload of impractical or unreasonable expectations.

As such expectations continue to increase, another allied distress is developing worldwide. Enhanced communication technology allows access to almost everywhere on earth these days. I am still amazed when I go to the remote parts of Uganda or central Asia and see cell-phone usage as common as in America. There is also an increase of economic, transportation, and human resources worldwide that is creating a more level playing field. Alliances and partnerships to complete large and diverse products like airplanes and broadband cell phones are becoming the norm. The amplified demand for higher perfor-mance with accountability stresses an already pressed—and often downsized—workforce.[11] These realities only reaffirm the concerns in the ministries already noted and deepen the chal-lenge to stay the course and on mission. Christians live in this world of heightened expectations. In fact, in many ways we *are* this world of expected high yield and growth-driven outlook.

Not surprisingly, those who work in Christian organizations and denominations are facing these very pressures. Ministries are expected to "grow" by creating the right strategy and tactics built on sound biblical vision and goals: "This is how we are going to reach the world." Or, "Our leadership has a clear plan to bring in the needed dollars to expand our mercy ministry to twelve more countries." The plan of action, often well designed, then becomes the norm—as do the pressures and expectations for making it work.

This can be exciting stuff, when the words of God in Scripture are matched to the power of the Holy Spirit at work among the board members, ministry leadership, and people in the field. But if plans are made apart from the work and activity of what God is already doing by His Spirit among those people, that ministry can quickly lose its power. As Scott Rodin said, "It becomes our words, our interpretation, our exegesis, and our proclamation."[12] It also becomes our plans, our strategies, and our schemes at that point. The result? "Slowly and naturally, these words of ours will seep into the ugly thoughts, mangled motivations, pretending, irrational fears and unfaithfulness."[13] The line between a Spirit-led and executed plan and human-driven goal setting and the resulting applications is extremely thin. Discerning motives, seeking spiritual wisdom, and pursuing body confirmation all play important parts in deciphering the difference between these two.

> Watching for whom God brings, and soberly estimating what each person brings to the team, may be more strategic than we imagine.

God never intended for us to put faith in well-developed systems or strategic plans. He never planned for us to set up training models that focus on one or two key skills and then to train the whole body of players as if they were each like everyone else in the body. Maybe we have adopted a cultural model that looks nothing like God's original design. He calls us to live out a healthy economy of relationships together as His very dwelling place, and reveals goals, directions, objectives, and actions flowing out from this environment. Perhaps we have been looking for the right organizational action strategies when God desires that we give priority to His organic strategy of right relationships in body life. Watching for whom God brings, and soberly estimating what each person brings to the team, may be more strategic than we imagine. Since God brings whom He wants to fulfill what He intends, maybe our attention initially should be more on the "who" than on the "what" and "how" of strategy.

Some Working Solutions

As Brian and I have discussed various challenges over the past several years—and how they affect his company and others with whom he consults—several things have become clear. Typically, corporate goals and strategy, and the skill-set training provided to fulfill those priorities, are focused primarily on task completion. The employees—the players who follow the mission and strategies—are there to fulfill those tasks. Even with the well-intended focus on team and project groups over the past fifteen years, the call for results is the trump card in corporate or small-business dynamics. Most often, people and whatever distinctive traits they bring to their roles are considered only after goals, strategies, and objectives are well-defined. They then implement those action plans. As Scott Rodin explained, "We . . . see people as means to an end and value the product over the process. We . . . see relationships as tools for our productivity and community as an asset only when it contributes to the bottom line."[14]

Realizing this, we developed stewardship concepts for use throughout Brian's company. One key element is that leaders are encouraged to identify the unique qualities in each member of their work group or teams within the group. This opened up the possibilities of identifying how people could share various roles in working together on a project team, given the respective strengths, weaknesses, and needs of each person. It also revealed unusual strength areas in which individuals could be used more in their broader work group and in the company at large.

Secondly, how people are valued became a more strategic and intentional priority. Identifying this additional area of need, we added a second focal point to *stewardship* principles. Brian has acknowledged that this growth area has been critical to his leadership effectiveness, given that his previous focus was mainly on organizational goals and strategic tasks to be completed. He encouraged his next-generation partners in leadership to steward relationships with people in their work groups. Establishing deeper trust among team members would, it was hoped, result in better communication and stronger camaraderie on projects. Brian began to model such stewardship by going to breakfast or lunch with all other leaders in the company. His words: "I began to coach leaders of three groups in the company, encouraging the same model: identifying unique skills and pursuing individuals personally to establish some degree of relationship." His model has been observed, accepted, and copied by others.

The positive impact was felt almost immediately in both areas for Brian and these three group leaders. Now, more than four years into the process, stewardship is affecting both areas. People's unique skills are being identified and used in various and new ways. In the person's own group and in the company as a whole, greater trust has been established in many work relationships. People are encouraged to ask for help in their weak areas, as Brian and the three are modeling. Many are doing so. Several of the groups are establishing mentoring relationships among team members as a result of the higher trust built into the work relationships. These principles can truly work in any setting.

Kingdom Organics: Principles of God's Strategy

It is valuable to see these stewardship principles enacted like this in the workplace, but there is a different way in God's economy.

It is so often upside-down and backward to the world's strategic, bottom-line principles. *What if there are body-life plans that God designed that will bring the results and impact hoped for by the best strategist? What if there are tactics in God's arsenal that will bear the fruit of vibrant, sustained, long-term health, extending Kingdom purposes here or anywhere in the world?*

Maybe, according to David Platt, every local church does not need to have all of the contemporary "essentials" for a successful church: a great meeting place, a good performance, great video screens, a good worship leader and band, a charismatic communicator, sophisticated programs for children, and professionals driving the ministry.[15] Maybe mission agencies do not need to stay focused on their primary plans of action in a given country when the Spirit of God begins to work in unplanned ways that were not a part of the original strategy. Maybe God wants to reveal new things to us in this process of considering His mission and His purposes. What strategic actions has He prepared for us to execute *His* target objectives?

It's likely that, from the standpoint of strategy, God's objectives are more about the people and the relationships already in place. In most cases, though, we simply are not watching the "who." Yet God has already strategically prepared and brought the right people into play. We are so consumed with busyness and the "how" that we are usually training the "who" to fit that "how" plan of action rather than discerning the spiritual gifts and passions of the players already involved.

Without question, Kingdom missional objectives include worshipping God our Father in Spirit and in truth, and doing this through an abiding relationship with Jesus (see John 4:23; 15:1-11). We have been called to make disciples of all peoples (see Matthew 28:18-20) and draw worshippers from every nation. We are called to be Spirit-empowered witnesses at home, in the town and region around us, and to the ends of the earth (see Acts

1:8). We are to proclaim repentance and the forgiveness of sins through Jesus to all (see Luke 24:46-48). On these things we agree and are committed. The visionary mission from God has been clarified.

To fulfill these organic imperatives, God has prepared His primary Kingdom vehicle to be His people, those in whom He now lives and among whom He now moves regularly to have His way in the world. He has prepared us together to fulfill His objectives organically — relationally — through body-life ministry. The Church in its manifold, creative forms becomes the powerful We-army He raised up among His Spirit-filled people in Ezekiel 36–37. Jesus Christ is alive today: in the Word of truth, in the supernaturally powerful gifts enfolded in every body-life part, and in the grace-filled relationships among His people. These realities dramatically affect how we prepare our strategies to fulfill His mandated Kingdom goals.

> He has prepared us together to fulfill His objectives
> organically – relationally – through body-life ministry.

What principles must we consider as we plan and execute our strategies?

Before we answer that, we must address a certain, painful reality. The chances are that God is weary of our humanly contrived and executed plans to reach the world. He is probably weary of our scheming to fulfill His purposes through the next and greatest program coming out of superchurch X or evangelistic ministry Y. Perhaps we are looking and acting a bit too much like the world around us — and doing it often by our own designs and our own choices.

I do not offer these things casually. Given the opportunity to constantly observe Christian ministries, I have discovered that we have made a mess of a lot of situations and communities both at home and abroad. Our well-intentioned plans often are manifested in mixed motives or the personal search for significance played out in teams. It has many times created goals and strategies that are human-designed and driven rather than Spirit-led. It appears that we sometimes stand with Jesus in the desert of temptation but lose His perspective because of our own wants or our desires for efficiency and effectiveness.

I think of one organization that determined it would win the world with one distinctive approach to evangelism. They prepared all of their people with one primary skill set, and that became their exclusive strategy for reaching the world. Intriguingly, thousands of people within this ministry whose primary gifts were pastoring or mercy giving struggled because they could not do the strategy in a way that freed them to be themselves in Christ. As a result, many of those gifted people left the organization, only to bless many other missional groups with their hearts for evangelism cloaked in a pastoral or mercy-type caring.

I think of another ministry that became extreme in their approach to developing defined strategies. The "right" kind of person was needed to fulfill those action plans. Unwittingly, they began to devalue most of the people already working in their mission fields worldwide. Their intent to "do it right" ended up with broken relationships and significantly lessened impact in many areas where their group had been ministering powerfully. They determined to do it consistently "right" and with the "right" kind of skill sets and strategies, and it has backfired again and again. Interestingly, a new focus combining the stewardship of spiritual gifts and unique passions as well as a return to intentional shepherding of relationships has begun. Impact is again increasing in a number of places where such stewardship is enacted.

Finally, I'm seeing many groups put all of their spiritually strategic eggs into the basket of finding and developing one kind of person: the church planter, the church-planting movement multiplier, the strategic missional leader, or some variation of one of those three. Every organization taking this tack is, surprisingly, short of finding the right kind of person. God will not honor such approaches in the long run, because by design such models break down the Spirit-led, body-driven style that God has prepared in us for fulfilling His purposes. He calls us to enact His strategies in a more difficult way: through the challenges of relationship, community, and gifts-based body life.

His grace has been sufficient and His power has still worked mightily among His people in many places. But our plans and strategies have, at times, created problems of gargantuan proportions. Sometimes we are simply not as smart or as spiritual as we think we are.

Consider the following prayer, and pray with me if the Lord so moves your heart:

> *Lord, forgive us for when we presumed that our plan was Your plan for every situation and it ended up not working.*
>
> *Forgive us for when we took a biblical principle and proceeded to misappropriate it unwittingly for our own purposes. That did not bring glory to You and did not multiply anything.*
>
> *Father, forgive us for when we thought we understood Your purposes intimately but actually played out our plans in Western cultural ways that were not helpful to nationals in various cultural settings throughout the world.*
>
> *Forgive us for when we placed more emphasis on the task to be completed than on the people whom You prepared to share together in fulfilling that task.*
>
> *Forgive me for when I held back from something You were*

leading our group to do because I did not like the leader or his style.

Forgive me for when I allowed a broken relationship to block communication in our local church or mission and shared my hurt with others rather than the person involved.

Forgive me for playing up the importance of my own role in a project or situation where You were calling a whole group to play many parts to fulfill Your intended purposes.

Forgive me for raising myself up to receive praise and glory, stealing from You the very praise, glory, and honor that is to be Yours alone. Amen.

Two Essential Organic Kingdom Principles

We know that we need to plan and prepare, and to count the cost of being and making disciples. These are nonnegotiable. We also know that God enfolded people with spiritual gifts such as apostle, prophet, leader, and pastor-teacher into the body of Christ to provide supernatural equipping and direction for biblical courses of action. We know that He placed administration, wisdom, and discernment of spirits in the middle of body life to help us to be careful and thoughtful in the building of systems and executing of plans. But how do God's relational, Spirit-led, and empowered body-life processes affect how we design and implement organizational goals, strategies, and schemes?

1. God has designed relationships to be at the center of His plans and activities in the world.

God designed His people, His chosen dwelling place, to be the center of His activity—in the planning as well as the follow-through. Ephesians 2:22—"And in him you too are being built together to become a dwelling in which God lives by his Spirit" (NIV)—illustrates what we discovered in our Ezekiel 34–37 walk-through in part 1. Our goals and plans need to reflect the centrality of the body life, the We-principle. How we live together reveals so much of the strategies God has prepared for extending His Kingdom.

I received an e-mail recently addressing the centrality of relationships in the development of a ministry strategy. It is from the center of the house-church movement in central Asia. Remember the apostolic team that has broken cultural leadership models by sharing ministry using their complementary spiritual gifts to cover each other's weaknesses and needs?

We just had an AWESOME prayer meeting with the house church leaders today. I'm AMAZED at what is going on. They are starting to actually PLAN and STRATEGIZE together. And, on top of that, today, Nazeer said, "We really need to make sure we get together and we try to get everyone from every location around the country that are connected to the network there." This was after last year when I thought he really didn't see the value in our getting together like that! Sometimes I wonder just how much we are supposed to DO and how much we just SPECTATE at God's mighty hand! The more I let go, the more He does. The spiritual wind continues to pick up here. In that meeting I was hearing talk about new believers, new, YOUNG leaders, how to multiply groups, reaching into new areas, and even a prayer for humility from our "machine gun" brother![16]

The role of community in this movement is so simplified that we are amazed at what God is doing among the fellowship as it expands through natural relationships. Even the strongest leaders are sharing and asking God for humility in welcoming others to share in the work. A multiplicity of gifts is the only way to manage what the Spirit desires to accomplish. The model of "letting go" of control in both strategy and type of people to be involved is crucial to what is happening there.

We see this relational, body-life priority manifested in several distinctive ways in the New Testament, referred to earlier and noted here only in brief. Paul and Peter spent much time laying out explicit guidelines for living out healthy Kingdom relationships in Ephesians, Colossians, and 1 Peter. Husbands and wives, parents and children, masters and slaves, and believers and unbelievers—all of these key relationships were given important and specific guidance. Living out godly relationships is imperative. It drives the household movement of the Spirit—the very thing that is in the center of the house-church movement in central Asia. No need to explain to them why relationships are so central.

Why? Because we are His dwelling place, where relationship with Him is reflected in the "one-another" relationships in the body of Christ. It is also the source of powerful gifts that are to be stewarded in the people God brings to each setting. Nothing on earth is more important than reflecting the relationship of the Father and Son in unity, as we noted earlier from John 17:20-26, each fulfilling their role in relationship to one another. This is very serious and underpins any strategic plan to be undertaken. Unfulfilled goals and objectives, frankly, are often the common result of broken or unhealthy relationships in families and among team members. Sadly, I have observed this reality in thousands of relationships in hundreds of settings around the globe.

As our friend Nancy Boecker reminded me recently: They will know Him by the way that we love each other, as John 13:34 states. It is radical because all strategy counts for nothing if we do not have love. Related closely to love, consider that beyond the capacity to teach, Paul's guidelines for spiritual leadership center on relational character—how one carries himself in day-to-day life with others. Titus 1:6-9 describes a man who is "the husband of one wife . . . not . . . arrogant or quick-tempered or a drunkard or violent or greedy for gain, but hospitable, a lover of good, self-controlled, upright." So much of one's capacity to lead and encourage others is derived from living out healthy, truth-telling relationships. Since we together are the place God lives by His Spirit, our lives together must reflect the love, grace, humility, and power that Jesus modeled for us. And the Spirit seeks to empower those very qualities in each of us as we abide in Christ.

The fruit of the Spirit—love, joy, peace, patience, kindness, goodness, faithfulness, gentleness, and self-control (see Galatians 5:22-23)—is the relational foundation of moving from "I to We." Given this, our well-thought-through schemes have to reflect the strategic importance of relationships in winning and discipling others, and in helping them to learn how to live together in Christ. We have no desire for that Russian to confront us again, asking us to go home "until we like each other" in order to share the gospel more authentically.

Given these realities, be aware that any of the solid biblical strategies for evangelism and discipleship of our day, like the church-planting movements strategy, CPMs,[17] or the Mars Hill/Acts 29 reformed missional strategy, can go awry unless it gives priority to the work of the Spirit through spiritual gifts and relationships. God's economy of relationships, by design, is to reflect and reveal His purposes. Body life reveals strategies through relationships for the church-planting and evangelism directives that will rise up among God's people in a given setting.

2. God has prepared all of His people to be exactly who He wants them to be, person to person, in the whole body of Christ.

If 1 Corinthians 12:18 is true, then how the people of God affect the strategies of God is something we must consider more seriously: "But as it is, God arranged the members in the body, each one of them, as he chose." God has already gone before us and prepared His people. All of the members are prepared to become a powerful We-force in any context, anywhere in the world. The Lord of the universe desires to fulfill His purpose among all peoples in the world through His band of believers. He hand-picks the people whom He sends to pastor this church or partici-pate in that fellowship. He equally calls each one in the body to their exact place of need. That could be a local small group or perhaps in tribal Africa or Asia. He has prepared each one with His chosen design specifications—and called each one to be in just the right context. Given this, how often do we design our strategies with those God-prepared people already in mind?

Welcome to a second major problem I have found in every state and country where I have worked. A sober estimation of each member of a team or group is seldom a part of the planning and execution of ministry strategy. The man-made plan usually drives the people and not the other way around. What if God has prepared His purposes to be fulfilled by His We-economy of relationships? One could seldom know this by how we plan and execute our schemes. We are excited by our plans and tend to fit people into those plans with the preplanned and pretrained skills we want them to perform.

Body Life Design teammate John Blake has sharpened his organizational development skills over the past three years with a master's degree in organizational development. He has been an incredible blessing in challenging our systems thinking about the body-life purposes of God. John's simple diagram below depicts a common sequence for how visionary and organizational goals are set into a strategic action plan. The workers are then brought into the process, directed by the schematics of the plan. They are trained according to the skill sets needed to move toward the desired outcomes of the strategic plan.

As we considered how this organizational process works most effectively in a body-life model for Christians, we made an important tactical change. John again provided the insight that clearly reflected our thinking. If God designed the people to be just who and what He desires, don't we want those people to shape the strategy?

In Ephesians 4:11-16, God places His people together to mature and come together in unity of purpose and relationship. How can the people, purposefully designed by the Father, not fit in the very center of our strategies? Bluntly stated, our strategies that do not include His people are not His strategies. His design has a chance to be more strategically based on the people and processes He has already arranged.

I will never forget my first attempt to make disciples in a real-world setting. I was beginning to understand my lead gift of exhortation as a pastoral intern working in rural North Dakota. An opportunity opened for me to coach a softball team in the little town of Milton—a tremendous opportunity for one young man and me to win over many of his peers for Christ. This was a team of fairly talented eighteen- to twenty-five-year-olds who needed someone to pull together what had become a struggling team and a season going south with loss after loss. I sensed this was something God had prepared for me, to support fellow believer Jeff, who was already on the team. The team was made up of prima donnas, slackers, several hacks, and some really good ballplayers.

I thought my gift of exhortation might be just the thing needed to encourage these guys, with the deeper hope of several responding to the gospel. Together we set up some team rules: (1) no negative putdowns, only affirmation; (2) everyone was equal, no one better—so treat each other that way; (3) roles and positions for each on the team would change according to the needs of the team and not the desires of the individual; (4) work hard and listen to each other; (5) did we mention no smart-aleck remarks? This was a real problem for most of the team members. I became the leader among equals, the manager who encouraged and made certain that everyone followed our We-determined rules.

We eked out our first victory with a late-inning rally in my first game with the team. Then we did the same in the next game. We did not, in fact, lose a game until the semifinals of the state tournament. But the winning is not the point of this story. One man did come to Christ, and the unity had become so unbelievably real that it could be seen and felt. Our growing team unity and role sharing affected the strategy, both in skills and in relationship building. It changed everything! I still treasure the softball not ten feet from me as I write this, signed by every teammate, that they gave me after the season. I have seldom seen a more powerful example of how a group of people that discovered team unity and played their respective parts transformed both attitudes and results. I knew the teammates could reach their goal of playing well as a team, and we did. Team members were given an opportunity to affect the strategy, and the results spoke clearly to the wisdom of the strategic process.

Consider the obvious parallel to the very American team example: What if God is the strategist and we are the stewards of His body-life revealed plans?[18] How we seek Him together may create new ways of discovering His purposes that we have missed in this season of well-orchestrated vision, organizational goals, and efficiently defined tactics.

Circling back to our central Asian apostolic team who are planting churches throughout their country, where synergism now happens in abundance: Somehow, they have figured out how to share in organic—that is, relationally focused and driven—ministry. Each one plays to his strengths and allows others to step in to cover his weaknesses.

Their strategy grows from what God is doing among them as they approach each new village in a new *oblast* (region) in their country. Every situation is affected by who had the relationship with local people in the new outreach setting. The gospel literally moves from house to house, from family group to family group, in culturally appropriate ways. They are invited into homes to share meals and relationships, and the gospel is shared openly. The follow-up is designed to bring appropriately gifted believers alongside who can assist in encouraging local growth in the new believers. New house churches are thus started. One or more of the team supports that development, bringing whoever is needed while young believers mature. Also, they are watching from the beginning for God to raise up new players from among all the new, gifted believers. Equipping and releasing is the mindset from day one, with the goal of encouraging gifts to be used by all.

A tremendous and truly unforgettable truth is at play around this apostolic team. Remember this reality about teams and body life happening in central Asia: They are playing out God's economy. In the administration of His purposes (see Ephesians 3:2), God not only designed each of this team of Christians with supernatural strengths in their powerful spiritual gifts but also determined each to have intrinsic weaknesses. Why? It was so that each would need the others, the only way that body-life ministry truly works.

This is one of the undeniable ways God designed organic

growth patterns of the gospel to work. Body life has the opportunity to take root immediately, where powerful strengths begin to rise up in individuals alongside the necessary character growth. Both the gifts of the Spirit and the fruit of the Spirit need to be manifested for healthy, organic body life to take place. So the stewards from the apostolic team and other spiritual encouragers who are brought alongside are watchful for both gifts and fruit.

This becomes quite the developing process of mature veteran believers intermixing with new believers in relationship. As they share in both service and sacrifice for the sake of the gospel and for one another, something much more than ministry happens. Body life, unity in the Spirit, and life-giving processes overflow. You simply cannot measure the abundant quantity of fruit or the breadth of results. Their plans do not get in the way, and they are less worried about doing it right than they are living in right relationship as they go. Less is planned to exactness in advance. More happens because of how they play their parts together as a body-life team.

God's Relational Strategy Made Clear

God has given us a very deliberate strategy for accomplishing His Kingdom mandates: We are called to worship Him through abiding in Christ, to make disciples of all nations, and to being Spirit-empowered witnesses who proclaim Him to all. It is ultimately defined in a strategy of organic relationships. We have this privilege of moving out of the spotlight and into body life. This is where all of us together in community become the dwelling place of God. Hear Scott Rodin: "Here is where we learn that relationships define us. We learn that to be God's people we must focus on who we are as people in relationship. . . . God's intent is for us to do the work of the Kingdom within and through the community of believers."[19]

How is it possible for us to gain deeper insight into the nature of His strategy and tactics prepared for us in community?

We have determined that the Father's objectives are not achieved by simply executing the right programs, led by the right professionals, while meeting in the right place. Without question, there is more to this plan for reaching the world than determining the one right methodology with one certain kind of visionary, missional, or church-planting leader. One size does not fit all. It has more to do with living in the power and presence of the Lord together in authentic body life. Ephesians 4:11-16 is a helpful passage for grasping God's body-life strategy. There may be no better summary to understand how He fulfills His desire for us to live and grow in His presence together, and to impact the world. Consider His tactical wisdom revealed to the apostle Paul:

> He gave the apostles, the prophets, the evangelists, the shepherds and teachers, to equip the saints for the work of ministry, for building up the body of Christ, until we all attain to the unity of the faith and of the knowledge of the Son of God, to mature manhood, to the measure of the stature of the fullness of Christ, so that we may no longer be children, tossed to and fro by the waves and carried about by every wind of doctrine, by human cunning, by craftiness in deceitful schemes. Rather, speaking the truth in love, we are to grow up in every way into him who is the head, into Christ, from whom the whole body, joined and held together by every joint with which it is equipped, when each part is working properly, makes the body grow so that it builds itself up in love.

As Paul began, preparation for the ministry is the first priority. We already have been given gifts by the Holy Spirit, as noted earlier in Ephesians 4:7. Some of those followers with verbally powerful equipping spiritual gifts are immediately put into use in functions to prepare the rest of the Kingdom participants for their respective body-life roles. From the beginning, the dynamic to fulfill God's purposes on earth is to be His power, not ours. As Platt explained, "The question is whether we trust his power. And the problem for us is that in our culture we are tempted at every turn to trust in our own power instead. So the challenge is for us to live in such a way that we are radically dependent and desperate for the power only God can provide."[20] God designed body ministry to be built for power. God's power is released through gifted body members from the very start.

The five formative roles found in verse 11, which some theologies define more as offices than gifted functions, are no more or less important than the others they prepare for ministry. They are functions that are vital to the equipping or preparing of the rest of the body. They simply are gifted stewards who yield themselves as instruments for God's mysterious purposes, modeling for others in the body that same trustworthy availability He requires of every member of the body.[21] As modeled by Paul, Apollos, and others in 1 Corinthians 3:5-9, these equippers and builders are simply "fellow workers" in God's field. That way no one can develop a heightened sense of self-importance because of his or her gifting or role.

Paul continued at the end of verse 12 and into verse 13 to clarify that the work of ministry is not merely about the actual tasks in ministry. His goals go beyond effective or efficient task fulfillment to the "building up the body of Christ, until we all attain to the unity of the faith and of the knowledge of the Son of God, to mature manhood, to the measure of the stature of the fullness of Christ." God first prepares us for body-life commitments that include being a steward of the powerful gifts He has given to each of us. The preparation for ministry has to include the stewardship of relationships so that unity among us is one of the primary outcomes. It is choosing to live in one accord in faith and in conviction of belief that results in a shared maturity in Christ. Put simply, like the cream-filled cookie: we grow up together in Him (a) in the Word, (b) in powerful, shared ministry by gifting, and (c) in relationship to one another. That makes us a people prepared for the full extent of life and ministry in which we share life together, even as we saw revealed in Acts 2.

When you consider the process of God's equipping and building us together—for decades, centuries, now millennia—you know that He is busy connecting relationships. He is constructing part of His holy temple throughout every state in our country and every nation around the world. All lines on this blueprint of relationships, with shared spiritual gifts and collective passions for varied people and places, are under the lordship of Christ. That is why we grow up into Him, who is the head, because we cannot grasp or understand His mysterious ways and means to fulfilling His purposes.[22]

> Maturity is as much a body-life process
> as it is a personal holiness issue.

It is whom our Lord brings and how He moves in amazing ways that show just how organic and unplanned—in human terms—all body life really is. The fact that He grows us together in maturity unto Himself is not only hard to fathom, it is also a priority we now must grab hold of as we move forward. Maturity is as much a body-life process as it is a personal holiness issue. *Lord, bring us to sincere understanding of this essential spiritual reality of unity.*

By our abiding together in Him and growing in the Word, we grow out of childhood and gain spiritual wisdom "so that we may no longer be children, tossed to and fro by the waves and carried about by every wind of doctrine, by human cunning, by craftiness in deceitful schemes" (Ephesians 4:14). Our unity protects us from the blustery winds and waves of deceit all around. This verse dials in on this very issue of human strategies and schemes and why they are so dangerous. We literally can get "blown out of the water" if we buy into plans or tactics that appear visionary or results bearing but are ideas driven by the passion of man. *Oh Lord, may we heed Your word of warning about plans needing to be grounded in Your Word. Make us alive by Your Spirit, and encouraged in Your body.*

The conscience for effective stewardship of relationships comes next in verse 15: "Rather, speaking the truth in love, we are to grow up in every way into him who is the head, into Christ." Truth telling that is face-to-face and done in love, without a mixed or insincere motive, is the heart and soul of healthy, fruitful relationships in the body. Trust is earned in honesty and authenticity, providing a safe place for both the weak and the strong. Gossip and slander have no place, not even as prayer concerns. Such gives the Evil One a foothold that tears at the very fabric of God's dwelling place among us. To create disunity among us is to lessen the accessible power among the gifted players and to break the bonds of love that hold the body together.

That is why damaging relationships and destroying team unity are the Evil One's top priorities. Can you see this now? The energizing power and the grace-filled love of the gospel most vividly reside in the life of the whole body, not in the greatness of one individual. Paul said, "We are to grow up . . . into Christ, from whom the whole body, joined and held together by every joint [ligament] with which it is equipped, when each part is working properly, makes the body grow" (verses 15-16). This is not simply an issue of personal spiritual growth. It is about spiritual formation taking place in community. It is a We-issue of lordship. He desires us to grow up together as this living body.

God's call to make a sober estimate and find my fit in the body is an imperative for following Jesus. It is so that we all —together—can grow up into Him. A mature body, disciplined by the Scriptures, empowered by the gifts of the Spirit, and built up through grace-filled, truth-telling love, creates a formidable action plan for making disciples of all nations.

All of these things, according to verse 16, are inextricably tied together. First, we are joined and held together by every supporting joint, every weight-bearing ligament. The joints and ligaments create the bonds that make a body a body. In our Body Life Design process, we distinguish between verbally powerful equipping spiritual gifts, energized to equip and release other believers, and action-oriented supporting gifts, designed to supernaturally give, serve, and help. Every one of these gifts is essential, no one more important or less strategic in God's design. Without all supporting joints and ligaments, the body would simply break down. You see, we are "joined and held together by every joint [ligament] with which it is equipped, when each part is working properly." It is so mysterious that God designed His strategic course of action to include all of us. Without the framework of each one of us, the body simply breaks down and becomes less effective.

If you want strategy, there's nothing more strategic than "when each part is working properly." We need all of us, the various equipping joints and all the supporting ligaments, because we make up a body rather than a project or a plan. Part of how we grow up together as this unified body is driven by the multiplicity of roles played by every part in the body. We do not need for each of us to be a multiplying church planter nor a strategic visionary leader nor an evangelist so that we all evangelize the same way. We need all of the gifts or we are ill-prepared and ill-suited for the task of reaching the world. God's action plan is that we strategically use the whole body of players and gifts.

God has designed an environment in which the Holy Spirit can dynamically work among and through His people. Everyone is of absolute significance in this organic construction model. God's building is filled with His people and held together by His Spirit.[23] This model will affect the way we live together and the way we work together. It allows for more diverse and dynamic options. It will affect the way we discern vision, as input from the parts will give wider and deeper counsel into what God has purposed among our team or ministry.

God's plan will also affect the way many play their parts, because suddenly they are validated for who they are and not for what new skill they learned. They will engage as owners of their body-life calling, not renters waiting for someone else to do the work. If you want ownership from all the players, this will do it.

The shift in ownership will move from a few really talented leaders to the full multiplicity of body parts just waiting to be themselves. Patrick Deneen summarized this principle very nicely: "To use a metaphor common to both the ancients and in the Biblical tradition, the body as a whole 'precedes' in importance any of its constitutive parts: without the body, neither the hand, nor foot, nor any other part of the body is viable."[24] When all find their fit, the body enacts the purposes for which God prepared it. And the whole body grows and matures.

It appears that God is pretty smart, living among His people and engaging them as His multidynamic army prepared to change the world. This organic strategy has possibilities. Consider the central Asian apostolic team modeling for house-church leaders the joy, power, and fruit of sharing ministry by focusing on individual strengths and releasing weak areas to others. I am seeing more and more of this kind of organic processing, and it is pretty exciting. God has prepared the body of Christ to be a life-giving, powerful force in every setting where the Church lives.

Summary

The organizational and management influences on the Church in the Western world are legion, providing real blessing and also creating new challenges. Strategic planning, goal setting, and management concepts have increased the quality of ministry in many Christian organizations in the past thirty years. The gift of administration is often the least used spiritual gift in the body, and the implementation of healthy systems, procedures, and fiscal accountability has been a blessing to churches and mission agencies. I for one, through my business colleagues as well as ministry partners, have grown tremendously in areas of administration and planning. I have also learned to ask for help from these administratively gifted brothers with whom I share ministry in our Leadership Initiative work alongside ministries.

On the downside, these influences have also created tensions that often go unnoticed. Many ministries are under growing pressure to become more "corporate." Some may lose perspective on how to function as the dynamic life-giving body of Christ and become more goal and strategy-oriented. Increased expectations that come with the high-producing, "leader in the world" mindset of our culture sometimes place unusual pressure on ministries and individuals. At times Christians are asked or directed to learn skills for ministry that take them away from their powerful gifting, and thus hinder Spirit-empowered body life. The drive for "Christian productivity" can also create a mixing of motives and a sense of "moving up" to greater impact and bigger numbers in reaching the lost or in planting churches. How do we match this with God's call and Jesus' model of servanthood and collaboration in body life where neither individuals nor specific organizations are to be raised up in praise and honor?

God never intended that we put our faith in well-developed

systems, strategic plans, or in certain types of visionary leaders or church planters. He desires that we learn to trust Him and Him alone and that we find strategies in part through the people whom God brings to every situation, so that the power and the glory are His when great things happen.

Given this background, we have developed some Body Life Design principles that encourage stewardship of believers' spiritual gifts and ministry passions. We are seeing organizations become more intentional in the stewardship of both those unique qualities and the matching commitment to steward healthy relationships. Brian has enabled us to see real impact in a corporate setting, and we are working with a number of organizations seeing fruit by giving more strategic focus to these stewardship priorities. God's power through gifting is realized through more players, and the synergism from unified, healthy body life allows God's Spirit to live and move in surprising ways. There is wisdom in moving ahead in not our strength and plans, but in the power of the Holy Spirit.

Ephesians 4:11-16 gives us a helpful biblical model for understanding the way God designed the organics of body-life strategy. He uses gifted equippers to prepare all members of the body to serve powerfully through their gifts, and then calls this body to unity and maturity together. Speaking the truth in love becomes an essential body-building lifestyle for all players. Body equippers and body supporters also build up and sustain our ever-expanding life together, as each part does its work.

Application Steps

1. Try a new strategy. Making notes on a whiteboard or flip-chart, ask all team members how they understand the goals of your team. Next, ask where people are most passionate regarding these goals. See where there is potential overlap

and growth opportunities based on the people God has brought to the room.

2. Individually make a list of names. Include people who are closely connected to the day-to-day operations of your team and people who you believe would potentially have a significant positive impact on your team. Share your list with the group and discuss what stewardship of their gifts, strengths, and passions means for your team.

3. Have each person share a work or ministry task that is very draining or fatiguing to them. Break the task into a maximum of three pieces. Example: Collect the trash, take it to the road, bring back the container the next morning. Discuss how you could share at least one piece of the responsibility with others on the team.

4. Make a list of your group's "strategies." Select one, and transform it to a relational focus. This may include eliminating all processes or procedures outside of person-to-person communication or perhaps downgrading or adjusting the metrics of measurement.

Questions for Discussion

1. Reread Proverbs 16:9. According to this verse, how do our planning and God's working relate to each other? Does God help those who help themselves? Why or why not?

2. What are the strengths and drawbacks of bringing corporate approaches into ministry planning?

3. Discuss the ideas of Christian productivity and downward mobility. Can they coexist? If so, how?

4. Look again at the diagrams contrasting "vision-strategy-people" with "vision-people-strategy." What is the central message the illustrations communicate? What would that look like in your work environment?

1. Oswald Chambers, *My Utmost for His Highest* (Grand Rapids, MI: Discovery House, 1992), August 10.
2. Paul G. Hiebert, *Anthropological Reflections on Missiological Issues* (Grand Rapids, MI: Baker, 1994), 120.
3. Max Weber, *The Protestant Ethic and the Spirit of Capitalism* (London: Routledge Classics, 2001), 76.
4. Weber, 26, 31.
5. Dr. J. Robert Clinton, "Leading with a Developmental Bias," November 16, 1996, 3–4, http://www.impactleader.org/articles/?p=8.
6. Peter Block, *Community: The Structure of Belonging* (San Francisco: Berrett-Koehler Publishing, 2008), 44.
7. Block, 73.
8. Paul R. Ford, *Knocking Over the Leadership Ladder* (St. Charles, IL: ChurchSmart Resources, 2006), 17–68.
9. R. Scott Rodin, "From the Field—Becoming a Leader of No Reputation," *Journal of Religious Leadership* 1, no. 2 (Fall 2002): 3.
10. Phill Butler, *Well Connected: Releasing Power, Restoring Hope Through Kingdom Partnerships* (Colorado Springs, CO: Authentic Publishers, 2005), 66.
11. Butler, 26–27.
12. Rodin, 6.
13. Rodin, 6.
14. Rodin, 4.
15. David Platt, *Radical* (Colorado Springs, CO: Multnomah, 2010), 49–50.
16. E-mail to author from an unnamed partner in central Asia, May 14, 2012.
17. David Garrison, *Church Planting Movements* (Monument, CO: WIGTake Resources, 2004).
18. Gary Mayes, undated personal note to author in preparation for writing this book.
19. Rodin, 4.
20. Platt, 45.
21. Richard J. Mouw, *Uncommon Decency* (Downers Grove, IL: InterVarsity, 2010), 174.
22. Starla Shattler, "God's Construction Zone," *HopeSet*, October 6, 2010, http://starlashattler.blogspot.com/2010/10/gods-construction-zone.html.
23. David Long, "The Spirituality of Leadership," 2007, 5.
24. Patrick J. Deneen, "Community AND Liberty OR Individualism AND Statism," *Front Porch Republic*, July 29, 2011, http://www.frontporchrepublic.com/2011/07/community-and-liberty-or-individualism-and-statism.

Part 3

Body-Life Leadership Applied

When we're used to seeing something in a certain way, it is hard to imagine it being another way.

— ORI BRAFMAN AND ROD A. BECKSTROM[1]

We have seen an extraordinary increase in wealth, in food supply, in scientific knowledge, in the availability of consumer goods, in physical security, in life expectation and economic opportunity. What is . . . more perplexing is that those impressive material advances have coincided with a phenomenon: a rise in levels of status anxiety . . . in levels of concern about importance, achievement, and income. And the pace of one's [sense of] deprivation has also increased.

— ALAIN DE BOTTON[2]

If you are who you were meant to be, you will set the whole world on fire.

— CATHERINE OF SIENA[3]

Spirit-energized body life is God's design for the Church. He wants us collectively to be the place where He can live and move and have His way among us, revealing His strategies and providing all the gifts needed to fulfill what He intends for reaching the world. Amazing.

What does this mean for us as we prepare Christians, leaders, pastors, church planters, and missionaries to be witnesses — and equip others to do likewise — in Jerusalem, Judea, Samaria, and beyond? What if there is no right kind of leader, but a range of dynamically gifted players in the body whom God has prepared? God *has* established His plans through His economy of relationships. He has brought the appropriate people to the precise places to fulfill

His purposes. We now have the opportunity to watch and listen for Him in new ways.

This presents us a new, fundamental challenge: understanding who you and I — who each of us — are. We must know where each of us is powerful and how we are weak. The weakness then reveals whom each of us needs in the body around us to expand the Church to God's full purposes. In His economy, He *has* prepared each body part. We do His bidding, watch for His players, and learn His strategies prepared in body life.

Welcome to body-life leadership, an organic approach to ministry. It gives opportunity for sharing ministry together that enables body health and multiplication by its very nature. Our purpose here is not about changing one's leadership style or trying to change someone through specialized skill-set training. Rather, we have the chance to reflect on organic, body-building roles that give an opportunity to more closely align us with God's body-life purposes. We want to free believers to be who God designed them to be in a wide range of ministry roles — not just a few select ones. Then we will watch God multiply the body of Christ into the world and into the next generation through His strategically prepared people.

In this section, I will introduce five organic functions that show how to work in God's economy of relationships in intentional and purposeful ways. Learning to watch for God in the people He has brought together enables us to discover His creative plans already prepared.

One caveat before part 3 begins: God gives us earthly leaders so that we learn how to submit to them. I am not suggesting that we do away with leadership. To do so would be unbiblical. Leaders and leadership are a part of God's design for the Church. We are, though, repositioning the roles of leadership into a stewardship posture that may affect many of our methods.

A body-life leadership approach is what we are about to consider. This approach tactically raises up all believers, not just leaders, to their God-designed roles, with shepherd leaders who steward gifts and relationships. In part 3, we look for impact and implementation in how we:

- Understand the role of leadership as a dynamic movement working with various functions through different people
- Enable shared leadership, releasing God's body-life purposes we may have missed
- Encourage pastors, church planters, missionaries, and other leaders to spend more time watching and listening for God through prayer, the Bible, and His people

Stanley Grenz wrote, "The Father creates the world, through the Son, by his Spirit. The Trinity acted in relationship from the creation of the world, and set our relational model for friendship, marriage, and leadership."[4] What if our strategies actually grew out of our relationships? What if we discovered how to be more effective stewards of those gifted and passionate people God has placed around us? What if the world of body life releases new thinking and acting?

Chapter 7

Accessing God's Creative Input

Every man must find his own race before he begins to run. God has a work for every person that no one else can do quite as well. . . . A race has been set before me; and it is my duty to find out what the race is, and run it, and not waste life in regrets that I cannot run a different one, or life's energies in unsuccessful attempts to do so.

— BIBLICAL ILLUSTRATOR[5]

I led a network with church-planting pastors this week, and we talked about the transition of pastoral leadership. The change is from pastor as CEO to pastor as steward.

— NEIL TIBBOTT[6]

You yourselves like living stones are being built up as a spiritual house, to be a holy priesthood, to offer spiritual sacrifices acceptable to God through Jesus Christ.

— 1 PETER 2:5

God has decided to live among us. We are the dwelling place where He can move by His Spirit and fulfill His strategies through this "being built together" community. As Christ's body, we are alive, powerful, and grace-filled in order to reach a lost world. God's economy is in place. His tactical plans are prepared. The plans are to be fulfilled through His Word and His people.

Given His sovereign role, God is really smart! Let's pay better attention to His organic preparation. As we move into practical application for body life and its effect on leadership by God's relational strategy, be reminded of five foundational body-life principles that will guide us:

1. Who I am affects who we are. So then, let us look at whom God brought to discern more clearly what God intends.
2. From Romans 12:2-3, to discern God's will, it is imperative that I make a sober estimate of who I am regarding the spiritual gifts God has given me, to understand how I fit in the We–body life that God has prepared.
3. I am to steward my spiritual gifts and the gifts of those whom God has placed around me. Doing so will breed powerful ministry far beyond my gifts alone.
4. Three questions that lead from "I to We" in body life: Where am I powerful? How am I weak? Whom do I need? Whom do we need?
5. I am to build unity among those We-relationships God gives around me; this is how He builds my character and the place where He organizes His organic, life-giving strategy.

Who I am affects who we are.

Consider these principles to remind yourself of this enduring unity: God has designed and prepared the individual to fit into the "body-life We." It is the cream-filled cookie: body life is the place where God reveals His Word (1) in the actions of powerful gifts, and (2) in the love of grace-filled relationships.

From chapter 1, remember the starfish, a visual image for organic, life-giving body life that multiplies itself when split apart. This network of life-giving cells gives us an organic image of the way God has designed the body of Christ. He hasn't built this body-life model like a spider with one small control center.

He has prepared His body to replicate itself by putting uniquely gifted parts throughout the whole system of life-giving cells. Jesus, as Lord of His life-giving body on earth, has given the gifts needed in every situation to fulfill His purposes. In this way, multiplying cells don't depend on one earthly control center or leader for direction. Using the shepherd analogy, we expect leaders to gather the lambs, feed the flock, and increase it.[7] Instead, God sees these functions as part of body life. Jesus is alive in the world through His whole body, enabling body-life health and multiplication processes.

He has prepared His body to replicate itself by putting uniquely gifted parts throughout the whole system of life-giving cells.

One other starfish reminder is helpful, letting us grasp God's global economy of relationships. Each starfish arm is organically tied to the others and works in relationship to all the other arms. So it is with how God has designed the body of Christ to work. He has prepared us in a worldwide network of Kingdom cells to function within His economy; that is, His purposes are revealed through this incredible network of relationships. Because He has tied everyone into the body collectively, He is able to cross-fertilize His purposes across a city, a state, a region, or even across countries or continents.

Let's put together all of these principles and images in the form of body-life leadership.

Nehemiah, Steward of the Walls

Nehemiah is our natural starting point for considering body-life leadership because he is often seen as the classic visionary or strategic missional leader, still the most common model in the West. He portrays a number of valuable, godly qualities—traits that are high on the "competency list" for becoming a leader in the spotlight:

1. The priestly way he fasted and prayed for God's people for forgiveness and reunification (see 1:4-11)
2. The bold yet gracious way he approached King Artaxerxes with his desire to rebuild the walls of Jerusalem (see 2:1-8)
3. The intentionality shown as he inspected the walls of Jerusalem (see 2:9-15)
4. The visionary, king-like leadership in his challenge to the people to rebuild the walls: "Let us rise up and build!" (see 2:17-18)

5. The methods for handling conflict, opposition, and conspiracy against the project (see 2:18-20; 4:2-18; 6:1-14)
6. His commitment to end oppression of the poor (see 5:1-12)
7. Though admitting fear of God while doing so, the way he removed unfair taxation on the people because the burden was too heavy (see 5:14-19)

There were other qualities, but you get the idea regarding the capacity of his leadership. God's favor was on Nehemiah, whose humble, repentant heart and subsequent actions led to the rebuilding of the walls of Jerusalem. But the Spirit of God no longer comes to rest only on leaders or judges as depicted in the Old Testament in this amazing, dominant-leader model. No, God prophetically chose to fill every one of His people, as we covered in Ezekiel 36, with His Holy Spirit. He has given a multiplicity of gifts to all in the body, including whatever qualities or actions we include on our list of "essential leadership skills." We are free from having to be Abraham, Moses, Joseph, or Deborah. We do not have to be an Old Testament top ten "Kingdom leader," and we certainly do not have to be Jesus, the only one with all the gifts. You do not have to be all things to all people, you just need to be who you are powerfully in the Holy Spirit. You need to be part of the body of Christ, empowered and privileged to execute such leadership.

The good news is that none of us needs to be all that Nehemiah was. The body of Christ now carries the shared responsibility of fulfilling such a multiplicity of functions that produces communal leadership. Leadership in the body of Christ is a series of functions to be fulfilled by a group of people. By His design, the *functions* of leadership are to be shared.

Picture one big power line (like Nehemiah or Moses), coming

from one location in the city, supplying all the energy necessary for city life. All the energy needs are met through this one centralized location. However, a new method has been implemented. The power now surges through many lines into the city, still coming through the same energy source (the Holy Spirit) but from many decentralized points. The starfish power grid has emerged. No longer is there dependence on a few access points of strength, one or two resource people valued and needed above all the rest. Rather, the dynamic energy to serve the city's needs is shared by many lines situated to meet the various needs.[8] Such is the creativity of God with His people; we are all essential, necessary components in God's power grid, the organic body life of Christ.

I am not suggesting that we remove leaders—only that we discover new ways to share body-life ministry as we lead the people of God into the next generation. Scripture clearly shows us that God calls some people to provide spiritual leadership, as we have referenced earlier. There will always be "leaders among equals" as we learn to follow Jesus as Lord through submission to the earthly leaders He appoints. By design, individuals will be called to be leaders by their respective ministries—not because they are always the best or brightest or strongest, but because God has chosen them to lead.

In regard to such submission, everywhere I go to minister in my work, I practice "followership" with my "ritual of submission." When I arrive in a new ministry setting, I go to the ministry's leader. I immediately let him know that I am fully submitted to him. This simple act and our prayer together acknowledging it symbolizes my submission to the Lord in every setting. This is what sets the context for me to minister powerfully in the Spirit. I submit to the leader and submit to the Lord and His body-life purposes therein.

How we characterize leadership, and how leadership functions in a body-life style, are the issues before us. As we move fully to body-life leadership, post–Ezekiel 34–37, we look at two essential qualities in Nehemiah's leadership that are seldom emphasized.

First, Nehemiah was a true "steward of the walls" of Jerusalem, and of God's people. The segment of Nehemiah most commonly skimmed over is chapter 3. In it we see the names of every family, or a representative of such, who undertook the rebuilding of the walls and gates of the city. The people of God were the ones who rebuilt the walls. This fact was so important that Nehemiah used a full chapter to show this. We actually do not know if Nehemiah ever touched a brick or got his hands dirty in clay. Picture each one of the bricks below as one of the people or families rebuilding the walls.

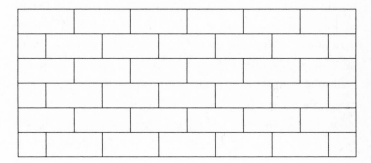

Now you begin to grasp how God was pulling together His people to become His dwelling place. It is a forerunner of the image we see in Ephesians 2:22: "In him you also are being built together into a dwelling place for God by the Spirit."

We see a second shift in leadership focus with Nehemiah's stewardship of the people of God. In Nehemiah 3, beyond leading by vision, he involved all of the people in action. Building the walls of Jerusalem was about much more than brick and mortar or wood and nails — or even strong leadership. It was about bringing a group of people back to a unity of purpose as the chosen people of God. By "stewarding the walls," Nehemiah gave every person a picture of the coming body-life truth: Each one is a player. They all were building blocks on the wall. He engaged the people to once again be the people of God. They were full participants rebuilding His dwelling, an image of the coming body of Christ and the new spiritual temple of God they would become. Nehemiah engaged all the people. This is God's call for this generation of spiritual leaders: to steward the wall of players God has placed around them.

We in leadership are to engage the body of believers to be His body. One brick surrounded by so many more precious stones make up the ever-growing temple of God. Peter said it this way in 1 Peter 2:5: "You yourselves like living stones are being built up as a spiritual house, to be a holy priesthood." Can you see it now? God has brought people all around you to share in the building and multiplying of the body of Jesus in your world. Nehemiah prophetically tended to the interwoven organic, relational fabric of the body, God's dwelling place. Realize now that we are more than bricks set in place. We are living stones sharing together and interwoven together as the full, life-giving body of Jesus.

Let's consider several applications from foundational Scriptures in light of our "steward of the walls" image. First, reflect on Ephesians 2:19-22. We are God's holy temple, being built together as God moves by His Spirit. With Jesus as the cornerstone, built on the foundation of the apostles and prophets, we are all living stones designed to be in relationship with those around us.

Take a quick snapshot of your life "on the wall" that follows—with the changes you would make to allow it to fit more accurately. Putting yourself "on the wall" like this gives you a glimpse of how you fit in the body, and how God has prepared the relationships around you to fulfill His purposes. I encourage you to draw your own wall and begin the stewardship process. Identify who is there around you in life and ministry, both followers of Jesus and seekers already in place organically by God's design. Note that seekers are not yet on the wall, though our hope is that they become followers of Jesus, new and precious stones. See where you fit.

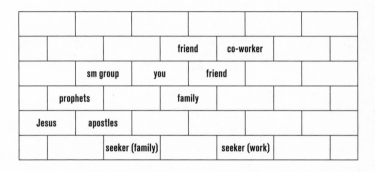

		friend	co-worker			
	sm group	you	friend			
	prophets		family			
Jesus	apostles					
		seeker (family)		seeker (work)		

For a number of reasons, I love doing this exercise with pastors. Almost to a person, their initial response is that there are too many people to care for or encourage. *There is no way I can keep up with all these people in the body, much less love those seekers on my wall.* If we need no other reason to grasp why God has designed the body of Christ to be a whole body and not just the leaders, this is it. God has strategically placed all of us in relationships, for the purpose of relational stewardship—to encourage other Christians and to love seekers of Jesus. The body cares for one another better than one, two, or three pastors or leaders can. As Christians, pastors, teachers, or leaders, we do not need to be everything for seekers. God has placed other people and experiences around them to work in their lives. The body of Christ enables evangelism more completely when all the body parts are playing.

The first fit to find, then, is our relational fit with others around us in the body, "on the wall." We call it being a good steward of your relationships. The second fit is your body-life spiritual-gifts fit, or what I like to call your ministry identity. This is powerful gifts plus your ministry burden or passion for serving in the body. The Romans 12:2-8 passage calls each of us to discern the will of God by soberly estimating who we are, then evaluate our fit in the larger body through our spiritual gifts. Take a look at yourself on the body-building wall.

				teammate		teammate			seeker (friend)
			teammate		teammate		teammate		
		teammate		you		teammate			
	prophets		teammate		teammate			seeker	
Jesus		apostles							
			seeker				seeker (work)		

This time, identify players in a triad, team, house church, or leadership group. Now, what if you were to make a sober estimate of each one of those on your team, to get a better picture of whom God has brought gift-wise? Grasping the power capacity already available among and around you is an intriguing thing to do. It also stimulates thinking in at least two other areas. First, we may catch a glimpse of who might fulfill which ministry functions on the team. It may also reveal partnerships of two or three gifted people who could be much more powerful together than as two or three individuals. This is another great place to ask our body-life questions: Where are you powerful? How are you weak? Whom do you need? I dare say you may learn some unexpected things about who and what God has brought together—and what that means in application—without any hints from me or anyone else.

Grasping the power capacity already available among and
around you is an intriguing thing to do.

I have developed a tool called *Discovering Your Ministry
Identity*, a team-assessment implement that identifies each of the
players' spiritual gifts, team styles, body-building roles, ministry
burdens or passions, and core values. In a team-building setting,
we have everyone write their five sets of results in an organized
fashion on a poster paper and post them on the walls. Then team
members stand back to process the information and observe
whom God has brought to their team. I recently spoke with
Grady King, one of our coaches and a good friend, after he had
gone through this team-building process with a ministry team.
He was overjoyed with how this team building worked. He
watched as the teammates first observed the ministry identities
of each of their partners and then began to share profound
insights about the whole team—and specific aspects of each
person's part. This surprised Grady, especially after he had spent
eight hours looking over each person's results before the team-
building time. The possibilities for effecting plans for team
ministry by identifying the unique qualities of each teammate
are inspired by God Himself. We may have a new tact for discovering God's purposes through the very people He brought
together: watch and listen!

Teams are inclined to go deeper more quickly with such
assessment interactions, especially when there is a high degree of
safety and trust in the relationships present. If there are no relationships of depth, this process gives a huge boost to people
moving to a new level of sharing and trust. Our trusty set of
three questions (Where are you powerful? How are you weak?
Whom do you need?) is a helpful way to do just that. I have

observed this process helping a whole region of struggling, dysfunctional teams in several parts of the world to move to greater trust, healed relationships, and a new opportunity on how to apply strategy together.

I also use another, more sophisticated assessing process called the Grip-Birkman Blueprint[9] in such team-building events. It goes to greater depth on the natural, behavioral side of who people are. It also separates the personality (natural) from supernatural giftings. Through this process, we have actually discovered ways to help individuals distinguish between natural talents and supernatural, dynamic spiritual gifts. This process of moving people from "I to We" in both relational sharing and team strategizing—given such in-depth understanding of the players—has proven invaluable. A number of ministries now use this tool with hundreds of their missionaries, pastors, or church-planting teams to more intentionally steward both spiritual gifts and relationships. Fit is a huge issue when considering *whom* God has brought and *how* He will enact the strategy through those We-players He has brought.

To summarize, let's look at whom God has brought to clearly discern what He intends to do among us. Because of God's wisdom and economy of preparation in each life, we choose to watch the people He brings more intently, to "steward them as a part of our wall." What if we watch and soberly estimate those people whom God has placed around us? Then our plans may actually be carried out by gifted people dynamically prepared by God, each to play his or her varied body-life roles.

As veteran leader-trainer Ken Cochrum put it, "Anyone can be trained to be competent, but only God prepares us to be powerful in specific ways."[10] I contend that body-life power is what we are after, not well-intended skill-set training toward our preferred objectives. This way God's power is dynamically engaged through His multigifted body and He is glorified.

Are you are a leader who loves to offer vision and strategy and then fit people into your plan? You may be surprised when God's design of the people on your wall brings changes to your approach. You may choose to soberly estimate, watch, and steward more intentionally. You may more effectively discern God's purposes prepared through the people He has brought together in a whole new way. He may reveal new roles or even new pieces of strategy because of whom He has brought. God can be so full of surprises when we watch.

Body-Building Roles

Body-life leadership is an organic approach to leadership driven by God's call for us to move from "I to We." There is no one model or style or strategy of leadership that works in all places and at all times to fulfill God's purposes. So we look at options for discovering just how He may lead in varied settings where body life is unfolding and multiplying.

Remember that as we worked through Ezekiel 34–37 and the New Testament verses, God removed the shepherd leaders and then energized the people with His Holy Spirit—person by person and then as a whole army. This set the table for the coming Word, Jesus, and how His presence would continue through the body of Christ by that same Holy Spirit. Leadership now functions from within body life with Jesus as Lord. It is the priesthood of all believers functioning together rather than just a few spiritual powerhouses providing guidance as did Abraham, Joseph, Moses, and the judges and kings of the Old Testament. The Father, in His great wisdom, now offers multiple gifts to execute His purposes through His people. He wants to freely live, move, and have His way in His new dwelling place—His people. He reveals and accomplishes His purposes through the body of Christ, just as He determined it to be (see 1 Corinthians 12:18).

For your consideration, here are five shared stewardship functions for spiritual leadership. These are purposed to build and extend the body of Christ in the world, beginning in each local setting or group. God raises up spiritual leaders in every ministry setting so that we all learn how to submit along the way of ministry together. The functions of ministry, however—how the work gets done and the goals executed—are very much a shared process of the whole. We call them body-building roles. Whenever an individual tries to enact all of these functions by himself, body ministry will be left lacking because Jesus is the only leader who has all the gifts. No more great leaders are to be found, only steward leaders who play their parts while raising up and releasing others to play their body-building and body-extending parts. Since God's purposes are for us to be witnesses, make disciples, and preach the gospel, we bring others along to share the load. Together we steward different functions of ministry to multiply the process and release many to play their respective parts.

We go back to the apostolic team leading the house-church movement in central Asia. Their greatest joy, when realizing their own respective weak areas of service, is allowing others to step into those parts and be powerful. They are released to play their part in shared leadership for the whole body to be built up and multiplied. Their thinking and acting moved from I-ministry to We-ministry, and God is glorified rather than individual apostolic leaders. Their modeling of shared, team ministry shows house-church leaders the very model of shared ministry that will multiply those house churches and grow up new body-building players of all kinds more quickly.

Remember my new training philosophy? I no longer do any training or leading alone. Rather, I always have someone alongside. Not only is the work shared, but new relationships are built and I am always modeling the "pass off" to another partner in ministry. Learners in the room automatically see two powerful styles of trainer, reaffirming that there is not one "right" style.

What are these body-building roles that provide a framework for stewarding God's purposes through the body of Christ? Be reminded that the word "steward" helps us grasp the big picture of these roles. Note that the Greek word is *oikonomia*, which means "stewardship" or "the managing of God's purposes through relationship." It is found in Ephesians 3:2. *Oikonomos* is "steward" or "household manager" in 1 Peter 4:10-11.

Stewards of God's household, tasked with managing His purposes through the relationships He gives, carry out His intentions to make disciples of all nations through these five body-building, body-extending roles. (See appendix A for a short preview of these body-building roles.)

First, access God's creative input revealed through His body, as He has prepared it, by being an

1. Active Listener or Active Watcher
2. Equipping Releaser

Second, shepherd the flock and guide its body-life values for purposes of body-life unity and maturity by being a

3. Team Builder
4. Values Keeper

Finally, realize God's body-life vision revealed through the Word and through members of the body by being a

5. Vision Sharer

Like Nehemiah, now we begin to steward the walls of God's creatively designed, ever-growing Kingdom for purposes of body-building and body-extending. The organic body of Christ is extending its arms, just like our multiplying starfish.

1. Active Listener: Accessing God's Creative Input

Body-Building Role Definition	Role or Function	Motivation for Fulfilling This Role	Indicators of Function Fulfilled
Vigorous Watcher Listens for vision and passion residing in body-life members. Asks before answering. Encourages most powerfully from alongside.	• inquiring • observing • discerning • pursuing	• hearing their heart • valuing their voice • drawing people out • assisting discovery of personal passion	• joy of personal discovery • sense of release and empowerment • new sense of value from being heard • individual passions and visions surface

God designed the body to be His dwelling place, and determined each player to be just who He wants him or her to be. How are you and I actively watching and listening to those whom God has brought onto our team or into our ministry? He has a number of surprises in store.

Regarding the concept of the active listener, we have tended to focus on listening to God through His Word. Amen! But what happens to us regarding body life and the people God brings to us? How do we steward God's creative input in them if not by first being an active watcher and eager listener, one of our core body-building roles? "I'm sorry, could you repeat that? I lost focus for a minute." This world is full of interruptions, from texting to social media to Internet surfing, and on and on. The difficulties of focusing on almost anything amid the busyness of life are real. Maybe it is time to stop, listen, and watch as never before. James 1:19 points the way: "Know this, my beloved brothers: let every person be quick to hear, slow to speak."

As Ronald Heifetz of Harvard University has so aptly said, "Most leaders die with their mouths open." Ever since Samuel found it difficult to discern the voice of God in 1 Samuel 3, it seems that many in spiritual leadership have a difficult time listening. Leaders move to the front and are valued for what they preach or speak or offer in the way of counsel. It often becomes more difficult for them to listen to others whom they perceive may not "hear from the Lord" as much or as clearly as they do.

One of the greatest orators in U.S. history, Abraham Lincoln, had a unique habit I discovered by reading Doris Kearns Goodwin's book *Team of Rivals*. Lincoln spent hours nearly every day accepting visitors in the White House. He loved to listen and interact with common, everyday folk, day in and day out. He acted as a common man who did not take himself too seriously. He portrayed this through his intent to watch and listen to his people. Goodwin wrote, "He sees all who go there, hears all they have to say, talks freely with everybody, reads whatever is written to him."[11] No activity in Lincoln's life more influenced his capacity to see and feel the needs of the people. Lincoln modeled the same behavior during the Civil War by going out regularly among the troops, *watching* and *listening* to the ravaging realities of war in a strikingly personal way.

Thankfully, in the body of Christ some spiritual gifts appear to enable the capacity to powerfully listen to others. That is, to listen in the power of the Holy Spirit to what others are saying. After working with thousands of Christian leaders, and through confirmation of many partners in ministry, I have identified that people with one or more of six particular spiritual gifts commonly demonstrate a dynamic ability to listen. These are people with the gifts of pastoring, wisdom or word of wisdom, helps, mercy, administration, and discernment of spirits.

In our church's gifts-mobilizing ministry, our spiritual-gifts adviser team discovered a very interesting thing. If you ask a person how God works powerfully through him, he commonly can identify two or three ways. It takes maybe two or three questions to bring focus, but amazingly people really understand some of their gifting without knowing the words. If you ask people about who or what or where they are passionate to serve—and they think you really want to know—they will tell you. Why do you think they have never spoken up about their gifts or ministry passions? No one in their church or a volunteer ministry has ever asked them. Active listening is just that: active. It appears that, even with people who are supernatural listeners, we have not validated active watching and listening as an essential spiritual activity. It is time to watch and listen more intently for His purposes in each of our settings.

Stephen Ministries, an "active listening" ministry for laypersons in local churches, has had far-reaching impact for many reasons. I had the privilege to help build the ministry with a team of laypersons at our home church in Albuquerque over a six-year period in the last decade. We stewarded six hundred people into new ministries through their previously untapped spiritual gifts. Through this process, we discovered that every one of the sixty-plus people who became Stephen Ministers had one of the "active listening" gifts, with pastoring or shepherding, wisdom, administration, and discernment of spirits most common. It was also stunning for me to discover that people with the gift of administration ask incredible questions—and most portray an unusual capacity to listen as well. God surprises us with how He wires certain spiritual gifts, or gift combinations, to work.

But one thing is not a surprise. The supernatural capacity to listen to others is a priority in body life. I have not yet mentioned the roles of pastoral care and counseling here. Take note of this enormous segment of body-life ministry. Add to this the growth in the coaching movement over the past ten years that has further validated the role of asking good questions and being an active listener who intently draws out others in conversation.

There's a second imperative for active listeners and eager watchers in body-life ministry: If God has engineered the body to be just as He wants it, gifted person by gifted person, how are we watching the players? How are we seeking to watch and listen for whom God has brought, how they are powerful and where they may fit into body ministry? In our world of job descriptions we often prescribe what we want in a position and then recruit for this position, but afterward do not actually watch how people carry out their roles. Here we have the opportunity to become like Nehemiah, "stewarding the walls"—our walls being the people whom God has given us, and with whom we get to grow and minister together.

I have learned a very simple truth: People act like who they are. British Olympic medalist and missionary to China Eric

Liddell referred to God's gift of his ability to run fast: "When I run I feel His pleasure."[12] God stirs something up in people when they use their gifts—often something perceptible. Watch and you may learn what power God has brought around you. It took several years to learn to position myself in a listening, watching, non-answer-giving style. But once I did, I was amazed at how much people act like who they are. The power of the Spirit rises up, often in ways that are different from a person's natural temperament. I discovered that, after observing a person doing a certain activity for one hour, or over several shorter settings, I could usually identify if a person's gifts were equipping gifts (those powerful in words), supporting gifts (powerful in actions), or a combination of equipping and supporting gifts. Often I could name one or two of their actual gifts. It is amazing how clearly people enact God's powerful design features they have been given, and how obvious it is as they are observed. Yes, active listeners and active watchers often discern how people are powerful through asking questions and through watching them serve.

What if we actively watch people for who they are, observing how they talk and act? We could more readily identify how God has prepared His people to carry out His plans. What if, using a tool like *Discovering Your Ministry Identity* or *Your Leadership Grip*, we help those around us understand more deeply who they are in Christ? Some of God's action strategies often reveal themselves once we understand and pursue how every member of a given team has been dynamically equipped by God.

A Sample Team Action Plan

When I move into a new small group or team setting, I work hard on being a good steward of the relationships in spending time getting to know each person. I watch for powerful, active listeners in the group and very soon ask them to help in this relationship-building process. They always say yes because it is who they are. Along the way, I suggest an assessment-type workbook as a means to understanding each other at a more personal level. And then I become even more intent to actively watch and listen. Several teammates who have one or more of the active listening gifts for coaching are invited to come alongside and help in the process of identifying people's gifts and ministry burdens or passions.

When John Blake came alongside me several years ago, initially I was most excited that he brought a capacity for working with systems that would really help in pioneering the new Body Life Design processes we were building. John has been very helpful there, but it turns out that several of John's spiritual gifts also make him a powerful active listener. I watched in amazement how he came into new situations. He would quietly watch both people's actions and their conversations. Then he would begin to ask focused, thoughtful questions. The power of God was being revealed by John, the active watcher and listener, uncovering new insights, directions, and even giftings in a given situation.

Sometime after the group has done some assessing of gifts, we sit down together and talk about the three questions: Where are you powerful? How are you weak? Whom do you need? We begin to realize different strengths in many of us and look to determine roles accordingly. We are moving away from being strong individuals and becoming a group that shares together in body life. God's purposes, some already on my heart, are confirmed in the hearts of some of those people. But God also provides new wisdom and direction through people's gifts and ministry passions for which I did not plan. We will clarify more about the idea of ministry burden or passion in chapter 9. It plays a crucial role in identifying and executing ministry vision and strategy.

Finally, as we remember that Christ has designed His body to grow, does it surprise you that so many in the body are powerful listeners? Listening is one of our most powerful missional tools in a world that is too busy and too often does not care for people along the way. At work, kids' soccer practice, or anywhere among the maze of overcommitted lives, actively watching for people in need is priority one. Active listening to those hurting or needing a friend is imperative. The love of Christ is revealed in your group or team by inviting seekers into this network of caring, listening relationships. As you listen and watch, ways to express the love of Christ will be revealed. Such accessibility is the key to the lost world around us today. They do not expect Christians to listen because many Christians are too busy focusing on self, the "tasks of ministry," or on internal body-life issues.

2. Equipping Releaser: Enabling God's Creative Input

Body-Building Role Definition	Role or Function	Motivation for Fulfilling This Role	Indicators of Function Fulfilled
Training Coach Prepares and releases others to play their God-designed parts. Enables powerfully from alongside or upfront.	• training • mentoring-coaching • mending • empowering	• freeing people to play their role/part • seeing joy and power manifested in others • enjoying the process of preparing others • desiring "spiritual grandchildren"	• readied and mobilized into ministry • own their personal ministry • move in power • "fit and flourish" in their respective ministries

People with equipping spiritual gifts, *equipping releasers*, are the multipliers of the body of Christ. By God's design, they empower players to extend God's ever-growing building. They invest, train, and multiply themselves into others to prepare the whole body for the work of ministry. As I have observed and worked with spiritual gifts over the past twenty-five years, I have developed a functional approach to identifying several categories of spiritual gifts based on 1 Peter 4:11. The largest grouping is—surprise—equipping gifts, verbally powerful gifts to equip and release the rest of the body to fulfill their dynamic roles.

There is one unmistakable, indisputable reason why the equipping releaser has the largest number of spiritual gifts involved in its body-building, body-extending role. God designed His building, His dwelling place among His people, to grow larger, wider, and deeper with more people. The Great Shepherd's revelation was clear: "And I have other sheep that are not of this fold. I must bring them also, and they will listen to my voice" (John 10:16). Any questions about the meaning of that was settled, among other references, in Acts 1:8. Jesus called His disciples to be His witnesses at home in Jerusalem and Judea, also into Samaria, and to the ends of the earth. When the spiritual gift of tongues poured forth in many languages in Acts 2, the floodgate was opened wide to those peoples beyond Israel. But how would those thousands respond to Peter's message, come into community, and discover their parts in this living body of Jesus? How would the body of Christ be built up and prepared for ministry and multiplication? Equipping releasers would prove to be invaluable players in this process.

The equipping gifts include evangelism, exhortation, knowledge or word of knowledge, leadership, pastoring, prophecy, teaching, and wisdom or word of wisdom. The full range of empowerments provides varying ways for multiplying body life. Let us powerfully build and extend the wall of God's players through these equipping gifts:

- *Evangelize* to enfold or draw people into the Kingdom by accepting Christ
- *Teach* to ground in the Word

- *Exhort* to encourage and train
- *Lead* to orchestrate the many and various parts functioning in the body
- *Pastor* to love, protect, and mend
- Offer *words of wisdom* and *knowledge* to address specific issues
- *Prophesy* to call out decisions of truth

All are unique, all are essential in body-building, and all have a purpose for preparing the body to multiply into the next generation. No one leader, pastor, or church planter could ever fulfill all these body-life functions. Through this process all the gifts of the Spirit are energized for the work of ministry. That includes supporting gifts—helps, service, administration, mercy, and giving. It also includes more of the same equipping gifts and ecstatic gifts growing out of prayer and worship: tongues, interpretation, miracles, healing, and intercession.[13] You must admit that this is quite an impressive setup for the multifaceted ministry Jesus prepared for His body. It is designed to depend on the full range of body-life gifts being played out by the whole body of God's workmanship, created in Christ Jesus for good works (see Ephesians 2:10).

Equipping *and* Releasing

Why call this body-life role the *equipping releaser* instead of just the *equipper*? The answer is both simple and pragmatic. I have observed all too many gifted equipping leaders who forgot to release. For reasons often related to their own search for significance, many want to stay in the center of the spotlight of ministry life. They need to be valued and validated by others. Because of this, they often do not release ministry functions or roles to others. Other equippers love to be needed and so they position themselves as the only one who can counsel, care for, or lead others. Again, they withhold body-life members from their gifted parts. I have had the privilege of leading many team-building events where leaders discover the joy of learning to give away ministry to others at a whole new level. In the process they stop holding onto certain functions for significance reasons; they begin to see body-life multiplication at a whole new level; and they understand more clearly how to multiply themselves into others.

The whole purpose of equipping others is to release them to live out their own powerful body-building roles. In doing so, more new players discover the joy that comes as a by-product of using one's spiritual gifts. Equipping often requires releasing, or nothing happens. I commonly say it this way: I found the enemy of body multiplication—it is often the equipping releaser who blocks the door that opens ministry to others. The equipping releaser can even release ministry roles that relate directly to his or her own gifts, so that God can continue multiplying body life and new players. When I see someone who can powerfully do what I do at a 65 percent to 70 percent level, I prepare to let go part or all of those functions to free that person to use his or her gifts. Whenever I release in this way, God always—I repeat, always—opens up another relationship or context where I can steward anew my gifts. God will keep building His "building" as long as we equip and release, equip and release, equip. . . . He is the ultimate body-builder and body-extender.

This is the way of body-life stewardship for equipping releasers: God gives us people in whom to invest, equip, and release. We are always to be watching for those whom He brings, how they are powerful, and what parts they could play by His design. We do not prepare or train them to be like us, but rather to be powerfully who they are. Such creativity could only belong to God.

It should also be noted that this body-building role is not called "releaser." Many in leadership, driven by the task or action orientation of their gifting or ministry passion, are so committed to multiplying the work that they release to people without training or preparing them. Can you imagine a craftsman in the Middle Ages, say a blacksmith, releasing an apprentice without experience or exposure to the heat and metal shaping necessary to learn his craft? Even though spiritual gifts are energized by the Holy Spirit, learning to use them can take time, preparation, and patience. Learning to use your gifts is like learning to ride a wild horse. The power is all there, but the control and wisdom needed are still to be learned with encouragement and experience. Blind release of younger believers into their gifting, or providing little or no preparation, can lead to failure, burnout, or dramatic gift liabilities coming into play.[14]

Many leaders lead in a way that does not equip and release others in the body to play their individual, specific roles. This helps us understand why God desires no leader to be raised up above others. Many leaders in such a position of authority may choose to retain control of most ministry functions, or greatly limit others being equipped and released. As Sherwood Lingenfelter wrote, "A leader must delegate authority to others with different gifts and then release control, entrusting others to use authority and power appropriately to their roles in the community and body of Christ."[15] You have team members who have proven their will to submit to leadership and portray themselves as one among and not one who lords over others. Give such players opportunity to have authority with responsibility as you call them to step out in stewarding their roles.

An effective steward of the body would never seek to limit powerful body-life ministry from those teammates who are submitted and see themselves as a part of the whole of what God is doing. Such would lessen the power of the Spirit in action, diminish the fruit potential realized in We-body-life action, and steal the joy from many believers ready to play their respective parts. Fact: Equipping and releasing is significantly minimized in many leader-driven body-life models—with a resulting lessening of the power of God revealed. A sad picture of this was recently shared about a fast-growing megachurch. Though their numbers increased, the inward-focused and spider model of leadership was unintentionally devaluing many equipping and supporting gifted players. Many leaders were poorly placed in ministry roles, and often asked to focus on areas outside of their gifting. Powerful body-life members were overly fatigued simply by being misplaced, not heard, not valued, and not embraced for who they were.

Another reason we are not to raise up individual leaders for honor and praise in the body of Christ is found in 1 Peter 4:10-11:

> Each one should use whatever spiritual gift he [or she] has received to serve others, as good stewards of God's varied grace. If anyone speaks, he should do it as one speaking the very words of God. If anyone serves he should do it with the strength God provides, so that in all things God may be praised through Jesus Christ. To him be the glory and the power for ever and ever.[16]

Stated plainly, the reason God's power energizes our gifts, and not our own strength, is so that He gets the glory. Leaders who rise up, or appear to receive more credit or accolade than is appropriate in the body of Jesus, can steal the glory from God. Lord, may it not be so! The spiritual gift of leadership is one of the equipping gifts, not the other way around. It is one part of equipping and releasing. It is one gift among the whole of body life, just as equipping and releasing is one of a number of critical body-building roles. (Here you may want to refer to section 2 of *Knocking Over the Leadership Ladder.*[17])

Finally, equipping releasers function much more effectively when leading or encouraging from alongside rather than upfront. In fact, after working with a plethora of pastors, church planters, apostles, and various kinds of leaders from around the world, I would contend that at least 80 percent of all equipping spiritual gifts operate more powerfully from alongside than upfront. Why? As you are training or encouraging others in preparation for their works of service, when you come alongside you are already halfway out of their way. They are more easily, more naturally, released in this posture. I confess to believing that God designed most equipping and releasing functions to be more powerful alongside because this posture will more quickly multiply others into building and extending the body.

Certain gifts like leadership, teaching, prophecy, and sometimes evangelism are indeed powerfully enacted from the front in a leading and directing sort of way—by God's design. But people with those gifts, I have repeatedly discovered, are also prone to staying too long in the front or in the middle of activity. They tend to lose sight of the releasing parts of their role. Stepping aside or sharing a role to release others after effective upfront teaching, preaching, leading, or training is critical to the multiplication of multigifted body members. Take a moment and look at the list in appendix B of equipping and supporting spiritual gifts. Consider what an amazing thing God has done to expressly energize a body full of people with such powerful gifts just waiting to be used in and beyond the body.

I have had the privilege of freeing thousands of leaders who, mostly for cultural reasons, had lived by the message that they had to be upfront or frontline leaders to be important in the Kingdom. I have actively encouraged them to move to an alongside style of equipping to fit their gifts when such is the case—away from upfront, more visible roles. What is the most common response to this from the 80 percent who are indeed more powerful alongside than upfront? Either a surge of freedom and joy of relief, or a season of weeping because of the years they spent trying to prove their worth and value by moving to the front.

Equipping releasers, let us be about the process of multiplying ourselves through the many gifted people God brings for us to steward by investing, training, and releasing. This can happen through finding opportunities to train young leaders who come alongside you on your part of the wall. It can come in bringing alongside new believers who are trying to find their fit. Take time to call or reach out to people who you feel may be struggling to find their place in the body. The excitement people experience through proper equipping and releasing provides just the catalyst you need. As a partner Tim Roehl says, "We want people to fit and flourish." That is a beautiful description of the equipping releaser in the body of Christ.

Summary

Accessing God's creative input is a truly strategic activity. If He really has prepared the body to be just how He wants it to be, how can we catch and fulfill His purposes? Like Nehemiah, we have an opportunity to become intentional stewards of the walls. We can actively seek to engage the Spirit-empowered players in body life to play their respective parts. In fact, you can build a wall of bricks—precious stones, in Kingdom language—and identify both believers and seekers God has placed around you. You can also build a wall of precious stones for your ministry team or small group, seeking to understand the powerful gifts already accessible in your midst by God's design.

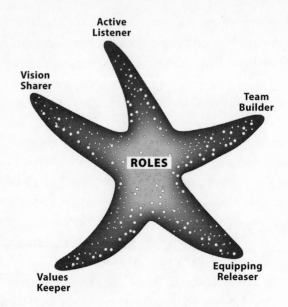

The five body-building roles move us closer to accessing more of God's purposes through the body than current leadership models may allow. Our model reminds one of the organically multiplying starfish, with each arm organically designed to play a distinctive part. When one of the arms breaks off to multiply, it attaches to new body-building roles that God provides to replenish and multiply this new cell.

Some will be active listeners and watchers, powerful observers of "whom God has brought" and "what God is doing." Others will be powerful equipping releasers who, through a range of equipping gifts, are multipliers of the body. Leaders must grasp their essential role of equipping and releasing, or trouble lurks. And many equipping releasers are more powerful as they position themselves alongside others, in preparation for equipping and releasing them. How ingenious of God to prepare many equippers to be powerful in this way, seemingly contrary to many upfront leader–type models.

Application Steps

1. Draw your own wall of Nehemiah as depicted earlier in the chapter. Lay out your wall of relationships that includes believers and seekers in your world. After doing so, consider prayerfully in whom God is calling you to invest more time for building or extending the body of Christ.

2. Draw a second wall of Nehemiah, and again follow the pattern of the second wall depicted earlier in the chapter. This time identify people in a leadership team or small group in which you are an active part. Ask the Lord to show you the priority relationships in whom you are to invest more, and seek what happens as you think and pray about this.

3. Create a mini-courtroom. Create two teams randomly. Take five minutes to prepare and then present the case on one side for "upfront" equipping and on the other for "alongside" equipping. Share with each other the main points.

4. Reflect on these body-building roles: active listeners and equipping releasers. In your current ministry or cell group, what impact do they have? Who directly fulfills those roles? Spend at least fifteen minutes affirming these people and praising the Lord for their part in your team, and identifying how these roles work powerfully in and out of your group or ministry.

Discussion Questions

1. Have you ever worked, played, or served under someone who came alongside you and focused on helping you develop and exercise your unique gifts? How did he or she make you feel? What were the results?

2. Leadership in the body of Christ is a series of functions to be fulfilled by a group of people. How does this definition

compare to others with which you are familiar?

3. Why do you think many people with equipping gifts forget or choose not to release? In what ways does failure to equip and release significantly minimize effectiveness in strong-leader-driven models?

4. We have often heard "Lead or serve like Jesus." How is this statement true? How does the content of this chapter now reshape your thinking about such a phrase, if at all?

1. Ori Brafman and Rod Beckstrom, *The Starfish and the Spider* (New York: Penguin, 2006), 33.
2. Alain de Botton, *Status Anxiety* (New York: Vintage International, 2004), 25.
3. Catherine of Siena, 1347–1380.
4. Stanley J. Grenz, *Theology for the Community of God* (Grand Rapids, MI: Eerdmans, 2004), 102.
5. Commentary on Hebrews 12:1, *Biblical Illustrator*, http://www.preceptaustin.org.hebrews_121.htm.
6. Neil Tibbott, telephone conversation with the author discussing this book, July 2011.
7. Richard Mouw, *Uncommon Decency* (Downers Grove, IL: InterVarsity, 2010), 42.
8. Tibbott.
9. The Grip-Birkman Blueprint assessments are available through ChurchSmart Resources: 1-800-253-4276 or www.churchsmart.com.
10. Ken Cochrum, comment to author during training in Singapore, July 6, 2004.
11. Doris Kearns Goodwin, *Team of Rivals: The Political Genius of Abraham Lincoln* (New York: Simon & Schuster, 2005), 289, 334–335.
12. Eric Liddell, quoted in *Chariots of Fire*, directed by Hugh Hudson (1981; Warner Home Video, 2005), DVD.
13. Spiritual-gift lists are found in Ephesians 4, 1 Corinthians 12–14, and Romans 12. A reference to the concept of equipping (powerful in words) and supporting gifts (powerful in action) is found in 1 Peter 4:11.
14. Spiritual-gift liabilities occur when trying to exercise one's gifts in the flesh, or one's own strength. It is powerless, and can be hurtful or damaging. Liabilities are laid out for each gift in *Your Leadership Grip*, *Discovering Your Ministry Identity*, and the Grip-Birkman Blueprint assessments, available through ChurchSmart Resources.
15. Sherwood G. Lingenfelter, *Leading Cross-Culturally* (Grand Rapids, MI: Baker, 2008), 155.
16. First Peter 4:10-11 in a combination of the English Standard Version and the New International Version.
17. Available through ChurchSmart Resources, www.churchsmart.com, 1-800-253-4276.

Chapter 8

Tending to the Flock

Act as if relationship is primary in every conversation, committee, and circumstance.

— RAY SIMPSON[1]

If I speak in the tongues of men and of angels, but have not love, I am a noisy gong or a clanging cymbal. And if I have prophetic powers, and understand all mysteries and all knowledge, and if I have all faith, so as to remove mountains, but have not love, I am nothing.

— 1 CORINTHIANS 13:1-2

Conversations with these [people] revealed a troubling history of brokenness between Christian workers who had any interest in this country. The brokenness was so great.... "If that individual shows up for any of these discussions, I won't participate." Remember, these were Christians committed to preaching Jesus' power of reconciliation and restoration.

— PHILL BUTLER[2]

I do not ask for these only, but also for those who will believe in me through their word, that they may all be one, just as you, Father, are in me, and I in you, that they also may be in us, so that the world may believe that you have sent me. The glory that you have given me I have given to them, that they may be one even as we are one.

— JOHN 17:20-22

One thing that God will not share with individuals is His glory. Many times in my own life, when seeking the praises of men and women, I have wanted to bring notoriety to myself. But even spiritual gifts, His Spirit-energized power in each of us, are enacted to bring glory to Him, not us (see 1 Peter 4:11). Yet in

John 17, Jesus gives us that very glory, the glory the Father has given to Him. Why did He do this? For our strategies to be world-reaching in their missional impact? For our vision to be crystallized? For us to be raised up as role models for the world as "church-planting movement" creators, facilitators, or whatever language we throw into that newest trend in world missions?

It is clear that Jesus shares the glory God the Father gave to Him so that we would be one, just as He and the Father are one, and thus the world would know that He came from the Father. Human bonds are the essence of how we reflect our fellowship with God. Relationships are the primary means through which He reveals His strategies among His people. One of the ways that abiding in Christ, as Jesus shared in John 15:1-11, is reflected most deliberately is in our relationships—the branches. I understand why Jesus shared these words immediately following in verses 12-13: "This is my commandment, that you love one another as I have loved you. Greater love has no one than this, that someone lay down his life for his friends." Love God, love one another. Wait a minute, those are the two Great Commandments (see Matthew 22:37-39)! Life really is about relationships. It is God's economy, His channel for revealing His grace, power, and love to the world.

The Primacy of Relationships in God's Strategic Plan

In the back of my mind are the words of those Russian believers in the mid-1990s, so thankful that we brought the gospel: "Please send your teams home to America until the team members like each other. *Then* come back and share the gospel." It was—and still is—crushing to grasp the implications of those words. As Christian anthropologist Paul Hiebert wrote,

> Relationships are at the heart of its [Scripture's] message, our relationship to God and our relationships, therefore, to one

another. . . . It is clear that we need to rearrange our priorities. We must make people more important than programs, give relationships priority over order and cleanliness, and spend more time in *corporate* prayer than in planning. We can learn much from the churches in relationally oriented cultures.[3]

Partners John Blake, Steve Hoke, and I, through our Leadership Initiative focus, had the joy of establishing such friendships among the Teso and Bugandan tribes in Uganda. It took me a while to grasp some of the particulars in how they approach relationships in the whole of life and work as compared to our Western patterns. For example, as noted earlier, honoring one's time schedule holds no weight in comparison to honoring relationships within tribal cultures.

Through this I have learned a new sense of natural flow, both relationally and in the Spirit, which takes place in relationally focused cultures. It has helped me to trust God's timing for scheduled meetings. It also helps me to watch even more intently for Him in relational interaction or even strategic planning when things do not happen as I had anticipated.

The most dramatic "relational reality therapy" occurred for me when I was communicating with Simon Peter and Timothy, national leaders of a ministry with whom our Leadership Initiative team partnered. I know that sometimes the question of financial contributions from the West can become an issue when establishing a commitment in such settings. As we spoke about the nature of our commitment to their ministry and our training support to be provided, I mentioned the issue of finances: "I think it important for me to communicate at this point that neither I nor my mission have money to give. The only commitment I can make, for my part, is to commit to share my life with you." Simon Peter looked at Timothy and gave one of those serendipitous glances—implying something to the effect of

"Wow! I think he finally is getting to know our culture. Hallelujah!" It was relationship that they desired, first and foremost, and not material resources or strategies. It is the grid through which they see all of life and its priorities.

In this situation, by complete accident, I had crossed the most important cultural barrier for an American in relating with brothers and sisters from African tribal cultures. In reality, I communicated the primacy of relational investment as the real purpose of our work together. I cannot tell you how God has blessed our team through the relationships we have with Simon Peter, Timothy, Matthew, Franco, Samson, and others in their ministry. Earlier Simon Peter had sent an e-mail to finalize preparation for one of our trips to Uganda. We were in the process of preparing for ten days of ministry together. This trip was designed to expand the work we would do together in the future in other African countries. His closing note in a brief "business" e-mail included my wife, Julie: "God give you safe journey, may your queen smile at you to remind you of those early days of love." Such personal care in a simple, along-the-way communication reflects the ever-central role of organic relationships. These bonds are the life-giving blood of God's purposes among us and to the lost.

Relationships drive everything of substance in the Kingdom of God. His economy for reaching the world is driven by strategies created and prepared through His people, the dwelling place on earth where He works. Relationships provide an amazing perpetual classroom God has set up for His Word to be made flesh and dwell among us.[4]

Relationships provide an amazing perpetual classroom God has set up for His Word to be made flesh and dwell among us.

The greatest impact for me in comprehending God's organic purposes has been capturing this truth: Unity in the body of Christ is both the foundational framework and essential outcome for the Church. Our starting point, Ezekiel 34, has forever changed my understanding of how the body of Christ affects leadership, evangelism, and even strategic planning. Do you remember how angry God was with the shepherd leaders to whom He had entrusted His people?

> Ah, shepherds of Israel who have been feeding yourselves! Should not shepherds feed the sheep? . . . The weak you have not strengthened, the sick you have not healed, the injured you have not bound up, the strayed you have not brought back, the lost you have not sought, and with force and harshness you have ruled them. So they were scattered, because there was no shepherd, and they became food for all the wild beasts. . . . Behold, I am against the shepherds. (verses 2,4-5,10)

Shepherding care was so important for His people that God's discipline for those leaders was to remove them completely. They did not safeguard those in their sheepfold nor pursue those beyond the fold who were lost.[5] It began the sequence of prophetic events in Ezekiel 34–37 that led to every one of God's people being filled with the Spirit, and then corporately filled to become a great army. The promised Good Shepherd, Jesus, gives His life for the sheep to defeat sin and death. At His resurrection, He leaves His Holy Spirit to fill what would become the Savior's presence in the world, the one body of Christ. We have become that army, the priesthood of all believers.

This organic army is now God's dwelling place, an ever-growing holy temple that will grow by the masterful design of its Creator. The shepherding care will be provided, and the body will grow and build itself up in love. Each one is now a grace-filled, power-endowed priest with a role in body-building and body-extending.

God's desire to shepherd His people is a principal reason why a number of the spiritual gifts given by Jesus are focused on the provision of care for His people. Paul challenged not one leader, but the whole group of elders at Ephesus, that they were to be watchful in care: "Pay careful attention to yourselves and to all the flock, in which the Holy Spirit has made you overseers, to care for the church of God, which he obtained with his own blood" (Acts 20:28). Body-building leadership is to realize its crucial role in shepherding the flock. It is not the job of only one person, but of the whole.

In this chapter our body-building roles overview continues with two roles that enable this care giving, mending, and multiplying process: the *team builder* and the *values keeper*. We will see God's priority for building and keeping unity in relationships. It will also provide core biblical values that enable body-building relationships to stay on track.

3. The Team Builder: Building and Strengthening the Team

Body-Building Role Definition	Role or Function	Motivation for Fulfilling This Role	Indicators of Function Fulfilled
Community Connector Gives priority to the people no matter what the process; unity is always a priority. Leads most effectively from alongside.	• unifying • relating • including • bonding	• bringing people together • valuing everyone's contributions • esteeming team members • strengthening cohesion among team members	• unity • camaraderie • shared process • openheartedness/ body-life caring

The team builder works to enable and preserve the grace-driven unity essential to effective, life-giving, shared ministry. Supernaturally enabling the body to function with a priority on growing together as one is the critical function of this vital role. Keeping the unity that Jesus prayed for in John 17 is imperative—for obvious reasons.

As I write this, I am confident that many who read this book, when they focus on the five body-building roles, will highlight the equipping releaser from chapter 7 and then the vision sharer coming in chapter 9. Those two are the two most "exciting" and "strategic" roles in today's church and missional cultures. But as I read Ezekiel 34, I do not understand God to be concerned about whether or not the leaders were calling out the vision. I read nowhere that He was angry that they were not training new undershepherds to multiply the flock. Foundationally, His concern was focused on a deeper issue. He was disturbed about the lack of care and nurture of the people. Vision and strategy are actually outcomes of unified, Spirit-led body life. God was concerned about the need for true kinship and unity among His people. Without this, the people were scattered and received no care or support, with predatory wolves pursuing.

What I have come to realize is that body-life unity is both the foundational framework and an essential outcome of the Church. That is, if body-life unity does not exist or is broken and battered, the vision will likely fall on deaf ears. It will only be a shadow of what it could be as a widely divided and dispersed body of Christ regularly hits or misses with the message. Regarding body multiplication, if the Russians could not see that American Christians loved each other as we shared the gospel with them, the message was lost on the people. That is, independently minded, entitled Christians will struggle greatly to be a team in the way they carry out—or do not carry out—the vision and mission of making disciples.

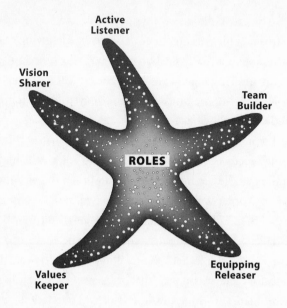

If the We-lifestyle is not dominant among believers, there will be a loss in shared power from the gifts. There will be individual hotspots where gifts are active, but no dynamic, whole-body life as in Acts 2, where gifts rose up together in a most powerful way. Also, the encouragement and building that dominate true community may be seen as secondary and often nonexistent because there is so much focus on the strategic tasks to be completed. In other words, the body will not be acting like the body: growing, building, and extending itself in love. It will be living piecemeal, here and there. The whole body will not have the synergy of working cooperatively like a living organism.

What I have come to realize is that body-life unity is both the foundational framework and an essential outcome of the Church.

It would be like planning to use our starfish system, but with 50 percent of the cells unavailable because they are off doing their own thing, and the other 50 percent not certain that they want to live together with the other cells. It does not work when the cells are not functioning together as a sharing, life-giving group. Team builders are the powerful connectors who encourage unity among those cells. They are the powerful supporting ligaments that hold the body together so that each part can do its work.

The spiritual gifts team builders commonly possess can be one or more of the following:

- *Pastoring*—to shepherd, protect, counsel, and bring unity among members of the body
- *Leading*—to orchestrate people and their gifts together into a common vision, direction, and ministry, releasing many to their God-prepared parts
- *Exhorting*—to encourage, build up, inspire, and challenge to action in body life
- *Mercy*—to love alongside in action, showing kindness, compassion, and sympathy
- *Helps*—to serve and support others in the body so they are free to use their gifts
- *Word of wisdom*—to bring resolution to disputes and sensible counsel to We-issues

It has taken me a long time to understand that the vision for missional lifestyle is to be lived out within a foundational framework of community. That truth is reality because of how God has designed His body to grow: in tandem, with one another, sharing life's work and each other's needs. We are indeed being built together so that God can continue to live among us and fulfill His purposes through us. Multiplication is a by-product of such healthy communal lifestyle.

Team builders see unity and shared ministry as the heart and soul of God's strategy. The various team-building gifts are empowered, different gifts in different ways, to enhance our oneness and enable We-ministry. This will enable His plans to be executed through the body and not simply by a few strong individuals. Encouragement from the team builder breeds encouragement among the rest of us. As the crew of twenty-eight on the *Endurance* survived their days trapped in the snowpack of Antarctica, Captain Shackleton found great encouragement from the optimism his team exhibited. The fascinating part of that story is that Shackleton's very presence and demeanor is what encouraged that optimism in his crew.[6] So it is with unity and team builders. Those who powerfully hearten and build up others literally hold the ship together in ministry teams during crisis or conflict. Some provide a shepherding safety net that allows others to heal amid crises. Team builders gird up the body so that it may be mended, built up, mature, and staying the course together.

As an equipping releaser and vision sharer in my own spiritual gifts, I confess I have fought this body-building role many times over the years. Too often, investing in relationships or working in community seemed to slow down the process of moving biblical strategy into action. But now God's design has become more apparent. God employs relationships as the starting point for revealing His body-life vision and as the power center of the varying body-life gifts available in a team. Stewardship of relationships is not optional—it is the center of the organic starfish activity.

Spiritual Gifts and Love

First Corinthians 12 and 13 provide helpful insight into why team builders are central to God's plan for a healthy, multiplying body. In chapter 12 we find a crystal-clear picture of how the body of Christ works together. Take a few minutes to read the chapter. In summary, the Spirit has given a variety of gifts apportioned to each one as the Father wills. Gifts are given for the common good, not for the individual's benefit but for the good of the whole. These many members with different manifestations of the Spirit are all part of one body and have the joy of functioning that way. That is, we do connected, body-building work together.

Feet, eyes, and noses are all needed and valued. No body part can be set aside or pushed aside. Each is essential to the organic workings of our life together. The unity is such that "if one member suffers, all suffer together; if one member is honored, all rejoice together" (1 Corinthians 12:26). There is great power in the many different gifts, but the true synergy of dynamic ministry is found in community. That is how we who are in Christ are designed. Team builders encourage the process of coming and staying together. They help people understand how they fit together, and they mend broken relationships to restore fullness to the body and its functioning parts.

First Corinthians 13 continues this body-building summary by addressing the heart implications of life together for gifted believers. As in Acts 2 and the parable of the cream-filled cookie, we see the inextricable link between gifts and relationships. In the first few verses, Paul defined that connection. Having angelic words but having no love means that I will come across as a loudly banging gong. If I have prophetic powers but no love, I am nothing. The impact of my gifts is about more than the execution of dynamic spiritual power. The implications are lived out through the filters of friendship, partnership, and team life.

In the middle of 1 Corinthians 13, Paul went on to list the qualities of love. He included patience and kindness, not arrogant or insisting on its own way but bearing and enduring all things. These are all relational, "one-another" qualities. No matter how powerful my gifts, or how impressive my appearance or leadership or strategies, the real litmus test is still love. It is there, in fellowship and partnership, where we grow together and mature in Christ. It is there that we give up our childish ways, the finale in chapter 13. Moving from "I to We" is the heart of gifts-empowered body life. Together is where God dwells and moves to fulfill His outcomes.

> Together is where God dwells and
> moves to fulfill His outcomes.

Team-Builder Responsibilities

In 1 Peter 5:2, Peter was clear: "Shepherd the flock of God that is among you, exercising oversight, not under compulsion, but willingly, as God would have you." No one person is given the responsibility for pastoral care. Rather, it is a shared-oversight issue, body-building and encouraging in nature, that has to be revisited regularly for the sake of unity and health in the body. Peter also makes it clear that this is a willing choice. The elders have been exhorted to make certain this happens.

A recent American TV show, *Friday Night Lights*, had a run of success for a most interesting reason: "Story line after story line on *FNL* is about taking responsibility for someone else."[7] The underlying theme of the show? We need each other. You may remember that this issue became a vital concern for our apostolic church-planting leadership team and how it has multiplied into so many other relationships and new house churches. Such is the core of this body-building role. We were not designed to be independent entities who come and go as we please. We were designed to find our fit and purpose in the context of the whole. Shared responsibility breeds ownership and deliberate care one for another.

Galatians 6:1-2 gives another perspective on the essential need for team builders: "Brothers, if anyone is caught in any transgression, you who are spiritual should restore him in a spirit of gentleness. Keep watch on yourself, lest you too be tempted. Bear one another's burdens, and so fulfill the law of Christ." The call is to support and encourage one another, whether tempted, caught in sin, or coming out of pain. Here is where team builders are most powerful in coming alongside for body-building purposes.

While I can be a great encourager to many, sometimes as an exhorter-prophet, I challenge people in a way that can feel very threatening or intimidating. That is, it may not be done in a particularly gentle way as Paul asked. Here is where I need a gifted pastor or pastor-exhorter to come alongside. Together we can shepherd, encourage, or call out according to the need in the situation. Approaching others in tandem can allow for addressing the various body-building issues as they arise. Sometimes a loving presence without words is most needed in a crisis situation. There I seek out one of our dynamic mercy givers to provide that ministry of presence.

Since body-life parts were built for specific functions, such a range of gifted team builders allows for meeting many different needs in the body. We are set up to serve the common good, as we saw in 1 Corinthians 12:7. As an example, I know a group of house churches who meets regularly to gather material gifts to take to the needy in the larger community. They meet the needs of the hurting, showing a strategic body-extending ministry where a range of team builders and other gifts are used.[8] Such is the way of body life, where we "are standing firm in one spirit, with one mind striving side by side for the faith of the gospel" (Philippians 1:27).

The most common misconception about team builders, with their high value for relational unity and health, is to assume that such a priority will breed an inward focus. Because of the safety and togetherness, if separated from other body-building roles, such unity certainly can turn inward. Also, if a church or ministry is dominated by one or two team builders, it will regularly struggle to look outward. We realize the need for the whole body of Christ and the full range of gifts to be activated and involved. That is exactly why God designed body-life leadership to be covered with a multiplicity of equipping spiritual gifts.

Team building lived out in tandem with other body-building roles provides a safe place for believers to grow together. It is also the base from which evangelists, leaders, teachers, exhorters, and prophets can move out with the gospel. It also provides the most powerful environment—friendships and safety—for welcoming people to experience the love and grace of Jesus. As we will see when we look at the values-keeper role, we are given specific guidance on how to treat unbelievers as a part of Christian lifestyle. Peter Drypolcher, long-time friend and missionary in sub-Saharan Africa for more than fifteen years, talks about how it was the Philippians 2 love modeled by a number of Christians around him that drew him to Jesus Christ. What a window of constant opportunity we have to welcome seekers into our relationships! Consider a most interesting question regarding how we do evangelism: Should we invest most of our energies getting people into churches to hear the Word preached or encouraging them into groups where they can watch the Word acted out in relationships? How about a combination favoring the latter?

4. Values Keeper: Guarding the Body-Building Standards

Body-Building Role Definition	Role or Function	Motivation for Fulfilling This Role	Indicators of Function Fulfilled
Systems Guide Focuses on quality in the process, establishes guidelines, and provides real accountability. Equips most powerfully from alongside.	• organizing • protecting • maintaining • evaluating	• conserving core values • encouraging values-based decisions • bringing quality and depth • providing wise counsel	• Word-based standards • biblical integrity • accountable systems • thorough, wise decisions

Semper Fi.

Latin for "always faithful," *Semper Fidelis* has been the motto for the U.S. Marines for more than a century. It has become far more than a slogan. It represents a set of core values that drive the lifestyle and brotherhood that is the Marines. When you hear *Semper Fi* spoken, you know there is an impassioned commitment behind the words. Note the following words from the Marines website:

> Latin for "always faithful," *Semper Fidelis* became the Marine Corps motto in 1883. It guides Marines to remain faithful to the mission at hand, to each other, to the Corps and to country, no matter what. *Becoming a Marine is a transformation that cannot be undone, and* Semper Fidelis *is a permanent reminder of that. Once made, a Marine will forever live by the ethics and values of the Corps.* (emphasis added)[9]

Behind the actions, attitudes, and motivations of every marine is a set of values. These guiding principles set the standard for life together from the first day of training. Somehow, to this non-marine, there is an aura of invincibility about marines. The commitment of brotherhood for life is very real, and demands a great deal from every marine. But I have never heard a complaint from a marine for the commitment demanded or the promises made. Not one. These standard bearers for authentic commitment and loyalty far beyond words give us the perfect introduction for *values keepers*. These are the standard bearers of the body of Christ.

If team builders represent the heart and passion for body-building unity among Christians, values keepers provide the framework and standards for that body life. You might call them the stewards of biblical Christian culture.[10] Team builders shepherd the process of moving from "I to We," while value keepers provide biblical guidelines and structure that support the organic system God has prepared for His body to function for the common good. They focus on quality of process, established guidelines, and resolute accountability. No body-building role is more important to the long-term spiritual health and multiplication of the organic starfish than the values keeper.

Having grown up in the northern plains of the United States, I have been a lifetime fan of the Minnesota Twins baseball team. I used to listen to their games on my little transistor radio, rooting passionately for my team. I have vivid memories of attending but two games in my youth. Our family drove five hundred miles to see my hero Harmon Killebrew and the team.

In the baseball world, the Twins baseball team is termed a "small-market" club. That is, they have a much smaller fan base and income than, say, a New York, Chicago, or Los Angeles team. No surprise, the smaller-market teams in baseball do not do as well in the win-loss column as the higher-income teams. Surprisingly, over the past ten years, the Minnesota Twins have been among the most successful teams in all of baseball. What has caused this?

I have talked to many Twins fans and baseball aficionados, trying to understand why this has happened. There appear to be some important values-driven reasons for the Twins' success. The management of this baseball club has a long-haul strategy, with a consistent set of core values that drive the organization. They are relentless in remaining true to their values-focused strategy because they have so little margin for error financially.

Here are several important values that drive the club's success: First, the Twins know that they cannot afford to buy high-quality, veteran baseball players, and that they will lose some of their own best players to free agency. So they have an excellent farm system of teams at a number of levels. They groom their own players and eventually give them a chance to excel at the major league level before many teams would allow. Over many years, the Twins have had many highly skilled players who were groomed in their farm system and have made the team successful. The Twins are good baseball equipping releasers because of this.

Second, the Twins highly value longevity. They have had only three managers over the past thirty years. Each manager has coaches who work with the team, and the same guiding principle of longevity holds for them. A number of coaches have been with the Twins for ten or more years, an amazing statistic in baseball. There are more values in play beyond just these two, but suffice it to say that the Minnesota Twins would not be the successful smaller-market franchise they are today if they had not had values keepers communicating and maintaining a core set of principles.

In the spiritual arena, values keepers are essential to God's purposes. He has established a plan of action for reaching the world with the mystery of the gospel of Jesus Christ. As we touched on in previous chapters, we call this "God's economy," in part because of a phrase in Ephesians 3:1-3:

For this reason I, Paul, a prisoner for Christ Jesus on behalf of
you Gentiles — assuming that you have heard of the stewardship of God's grace that was given to me for you, how the
mystery [of the gospel] was made known to me by revelation,
as I have written.

The phrase "the stewardship of God's grace" has also been
translated as "the administration of God's grace." There is a
system God has prepared to fulfill His purposes. Ephesians is
about helping us grasp the essential role of gifting and relationships through that body-life process. I am pleased to remind you
that the stewardship of God's grace is found in His economy of
relationships. Just before this passage in Ephesians 3, in 2:19-22,
we find the framework God is using to fulfill His plans in the
world. It is the household of God that He has prepared, the body
of Christ being built together to become His dwelling place by
His Spirit.

But what principles and values drive this systematic movement of God to reach the world with the gospel through His
people? God has given us His Word, with principles to help us
stay on track and fulfill His purposes. Values keepers are the
guardians of those biblical principles, values, and priorities. They
are the ones in body life whom God has prepared to provide
biblical guidance on core beliefs and accountability checkpoints
to keep us on track. Consider these spiritual gifts God has
designed to fulfill the values-keeping role in body-building:

- *Teacher* — to provide biblical understanding of God's
  principles and wisdom
- *Prophet* — to keep biblical truth on track by calling
  people to action regarding truth
- *Word of wisdom* — to protect the integrity of the Word
  with wise counsel, moving knowledge to action

- *Administration* — to bring quality, order, and organization to body-life processes
- *Discernment of spirits* — to discern values or actions as from God or Satan

These values keepers conserve the core principles from the Word. They encourage values-based decisions, and bring quality, structure, and depth to plans, ministry systems, and critical decisions. I rejoice in these body-life sentinels God has raised up to give guidance from the Word to the body. They offer principled steps we can take to stay on track with His purposes. He provides supernatural power for organizing people and systems to help us remember and enact what He has shown us in His economy of relationships.

As Abraham Lincoln and his talented but cantankerous cabinet led the United States through one of its most traumatic seasons, staying on a principled course was imperative for the president. Kearns Goodwin explained, "Mr. Lincoln's perilous task had been to carry a rather shaky raft through the rapids . . . but cautiously to assure himself with his setting pole where the main current was, and keep steadily to that."[11] In other words, his values-keeping leadership, with a fully functioning team all around him and running on all cylinders, was central to what happened in the country. Peter put a spiritual frame on such conviction lived out in relationships in 1 Peter 1:22: "Having purified your souls by your obedience to the truth for a sincere brotherly love, love one another earnestly from a pure heart." Such are the principles of body-building values keepers as they hold to course direction by the Word of God.

We have no option but to keep visibly in front of us the biblical values that fix our attention on Jesus' purposes for His body. We are to unflinchingly hold to them as God continues to move among us.

Body-Building Core Values

Values keeping for believers is the backbone to our body life together, and our witness to the world. What are some of the core values that drive this Spirit-led movement of God from the Word and through His people?

One fundamental, driving value among us is the call to the lordship of Jesus Christ in all areas of our lives. Scott Rodin eloquently stated the issue: "Before it is about vision casting or risk-taking or motivating others or building teams or communicating or strategic planning or public speaking, it is about Lordship. Where Jesus is singularly and absolutely lord of our life, we will seek to be like him and him only."[12] We are each one a member of His body, with Jesus as the head. No principle is more foundational in our lives as Christians. As Jesus described, "Whoever does not bear his own cross and come after me cannot be my disciple. For which of you, desiring to build a tower, does not first sit down and count the cost?" (Luke 14:27-28). Daily we are to seek Him first and release all life controls to Him.

As we consider our body-building and body-extending lifestyle among those whom God has given each of us, this is the appropriate principle with which to start, praying, *Lord Jesus, have Your way on our wall of relationships. Give wisdom and creativity as we steward those whom You have placed around us, both believers and seekers. Reveal Your purposes and the body-building roles among us as we set out to take the next steps together.*

Another critical body-building set of values that dominates the New Testament Church is the "household code." Though we have referred to these principles earlier, they are among the most strategic passages that reveal how we are to act as the body of Christ toward one another and unbelievers. In Christ, these values show how we are to act in our relationships. Under this code, new relational guidelines dominate the way we treat each other in and beyond our fellowship. Clear guidance is given to husbands and wives in their relationship,[13] as well as principles for parents and children.[14] Slaves and masters are also given specific exhortation on how to act.[15] And, because of our body-extending call to be witnesses, direction is given for seasoned conversation to share your hope in Christ.[16] To be in Christ as a part of His body is to portray a clear-cut set of biblical values to all. Values dominate, and our values keepers provide needed structure and accountability for the body-building Church.

Beyond these behavioral guidelines that affect every part of the believer's daily life, there are many more biblical principles for living healthy, forgiving, honest, and fruit-of-the-Spirit-filled relationships. Since God lives among His people, our relationships manifest His love. While we are to steward our dynamic body-life gifts, the matching call to steward relationships is encouraged in more than a dozen passages in the New Testament. Ministry partner Stacy Rinehart loves to call these the "one another" passages. These are the responsibilities God has given to each of us in the body. God's economy, the administration of His grace, is revealed through these attitudes, actions, and values toward one another. It is the ground floor of Jesus' love for the world.

To illustrate this, here are a few Scripture passages for your reference. After the spiritual-gifts passage in Ephesians 4 and before the household-code guidance in chapter 5, Paul exhorted very specifically on life together in 4:17-32. Peter inserted the same body-life principles between household behavior and using one's gifts in 1 Peter 3:8-17 and 4:1-9. Paul encouraged distinctive body-life care in Philippians 2:1-11 and helpful community-worship guidance in Colossians 3:12-17. On and on it goes.

Body-Building Value Sets

As I have trained the body of Christ in various cross-cultural settings in many countries, certain body-life values have risen up as priorities in almost every setting. During hours spent equipping and releasing believers, ministry teams, organizations, and leaders, these issues came up time and time again. I offer you two companion sets of three foundational principles that I have gleaned through this process. These are imperative for sharing in any ministry setting where body-building becomes a primary process. They are essential for healthy growth.

The first I call the "One Set." If you want to enable Christians to discover and use their spiritual gifts as a means to mobilize your house church, team, group, or overall ministry, these three core values are foundational for every person who wants to discover and steward his place in body life. Without these as foundational values, the organics will undoubtedly break down into disunity. As you seek your fit in body-building and body-extending, realize first that God calls you to be:

1. *One submitted*—the willingness to follow your spiritual leadership is not optional. It is a key part of how we learn obedience to the Father in body life.
2. *One among*—you are one among, designed to fit in and build the body of Christ by playing your unique, essential part. You are not a "superstar" individual, destined for stardom above others, or a "sad sack" lone ranger who claims to have no place to fit.
3. *One who serves*—the call to body life is one of serving others as a part of finding your own place. A servant heart and attitude frees you to be like Jesus and serve rather than waiting to be served. Entitled, self-serving attitudes are not helpful.

Communicating these values regularly and forthrightly on teams and in ministries will provide guidance for every Christian on issues that will *always* arise. When the Spirit begins to move, many will want to live out body life together. These are essential We-principles as a starting point for understanding one's place in the body.

Following the "One Set" values, our second set of foundational principles dial in on our unity in life together. Unity is *the* major target of the Evil One. I hope the reasons will be clear for you after reading this book. Christians are more powerful in body-life ministry because the body of Jesus literally fills out and plays so many dynamic roles in building and extending itself in love. They are encouraged, built up, and matured with others when they move from "I to We." Satan much prefers that we simply attempt to stand alone.

Rather than sharing with you the three main ways the Evil One seeks to break community, let us approach those challenges from three positive angles. I call this the "Body Life Design Team" set. In these four words are three core principles that define what moving from "I to We" means for every believer for whom Jesus died. May these values free you to greater joy, purpose, and stewardship.

First, "Body Life" means that you are absolutely significant in Christ. It is not what you do for God that is important, the works you do or the roles you play. No, "Body Life" means that right now, at this very moment, you are fully and completely significant in Christ because of the cross of Jesus. You are fully accepted, entirely forgiven, and fully released as a child of God. You fit and you are loved.

"Design" means that you also have a unique part to play in body life. Separate from finding your ultimate significance at the cross is the fact that God has wired you to play your unique part in body-building and body-extending. He has built you to be just who He wants you to be.

Do not confuse your significance with your role. Your worth and value at the cross of Jesus is settled. Period. No job, position, popularity, perceived success, or other person can make you any more significant than you already are in Christ. Nothing you can do or say or write or speak will increase your value in the Kingdom. Your role fit, on the other hand, is a part of your God-design and something that you steward as a part of the body. What a privilege to play your special part in one of the body-building roles!

"Team" means that you choose unity. Unity among believers in the body of Christ is not something that happens accidentally.

It is a choice that each of us makes. It is a values decision that allows grace to dominate our relationships. It chooses forgiveness to be an active, ongoing part of daily life. Team means acceptance to include working with people you love but may never like. It is a decision you make again and again in the seasons of life. Jesus died so that we might discover the freedom of choosing to work for—and bear the great blessings of—unity.

Unity can be very difficult when we have to make hard relationship choices for the sake of unity. Captain Shackleton's hardest decision came as his crew found safe haven on the coast and could entertain the hope that they might actually live through their Antarctic ordeal. They threw together a makeshift cover on a small craft that would take four of them to safety across precarious eighty-foot swells in the Southern Ocean to South Georgia Island. Who would Shackleton take? His choices, for the sake of the whole crew, were the bully, the man who most created discontent among the crew, and another who was less than a team player. He put his own favorites aside, taking with him those most likely to thwart unity among the twenty-four who remained. They made the treacherous trip, and returned for their crew.[17] Unity is a choice. Will you choose it?

These three principles start the "I to We" paradigm shift. Often, in discussion, I will come back to these principles. In training, they lay a foundation proving the ground is level at the foot of the cross. As the body of Christ, when we embrace the Body Life Design Team principles at a heart level, the result is dynamic, healthy, and deepening relationships.

Summary

God has placed relationships at the center of His economy. We are beginning to understand that unity in the body of Christ is at the heart of His purposes for reaching the world. Because of this, God has prepared team builders who have particular spiritual gifts that build and strengthen the body of Christ. They see unity and shared ministry as the heart of God's strategy. First Corinthians 12 and 13 give one example of how even powerful spiritual gifts lose their value when exercised without love.

God also raised up values keepers to provide biblical guidelines and structure that support this organic system of believers. They help us stay on track and be accountable to live out healthy, life-giving relationships in God's household. We have so many biblical values that give counsel to living out this life together, as seen through the One Set and Body Life Design Team principles.

Lord, we praise You for making each of us significant in Christ and then for designing us just as You want each of us to be. Help us to willfully choose to build unity of body, even as we grow and mature with other believers as the foundation for Kingdom body-building and body-extending.

Application Steps

1. Team builders and values keepers have huge value for the fit of individuals in the body of Christ and in the expanding of the body of Christ. Spend time creating a chart of what the outward focus (growth aspects) functions and inward focus (unity/fit aspects) functions are for each.
2. Study the characteristics of each team builder and values keeper. Create a small ministry project, and act out how each may approach the situation uniquely. Debrief the experience, understanding participants' unique contributions.
3. Divide into groups of three or four. Take five minutes and create hand motions or actions for the One Set principles. Share with the group, and decide what you feel are the

strongest. If you feel daring, take pictures or record them
and then send them to me at paul.ford@crmleaders.org.
4. Reflect on the Body Life Design Team principles. With
   appropriate transparency, share with the group which of
   these is most significant to you and why. Pray for each
   other.

Discussion Questions

1. "The number one reason people do not want to become
   Christians is Christians." Reflecting on the content of this
   chapter, what does this mean to you?
2. The team builder and values keeper are focused on unity.
   How do these safeguard unity? What role does love play in
   unity?
3. Which part of the One Set (One submitted, One among,
   One who serves) is most natural for you? Which one is
   most challenging?
4. How do you understand the ideas of body life (significance)
   and design (unique role) in the body of Christ? Why are
   they foundational for team unity?

1. Ray Simpson, *Church of the Isles* (Suffolk, UK: Kevin Mayhew, 2003), 77.
2. Phill Butler, *Well Connected: Releasing Power, Restoring Hope Through Kingdom Partnerships* (Colorado Springs, CO: Authentic Books, 2005), 53.
3. Paul G. Hiebert, *Anthropological Reflections on Missiological Issues* (Grand Rapids, MI: Baker, 1994), 137.
4. David Platt, *Radical* (Colorado Springs, CO: Multnomah, 2010), 99.
5. Samuel Adams, "Between Text & Sermon," *Interpretation*, 62, January 2008, 305.
6. Dennis N. T. Perkins, *Leading at the Edge: Leadership Lessons from the Extraordinary Saga of Shackleton's Antarctic Expedition* (New York: American Management Association, 2000), 44.
7. James Poniewozik, "America's Game," *Time*, February 14, 2011, 59.
8. Robert and Julia Banks, *The Church Comes Home* (Peabody, MA: Hendrickson, 1998), 56.
9. "Principles and Values," United States Marine Corps webpage, http://www.marines.com/history-heritage/principles-values.

10. Ken Blanchard, "Your Organization's Culture Is Everyone's Business," *The Leadership Difference*, online communication, January 13, 2011, 1.

11. Doris Kearns Goodwin, *Team of Rivals: The Political Genius of Abraham Lincoln* (New York: Simon & Schuster, 2005), 596.

12. R. Scott Rodin, "From the Field — Becoming a Leader of No Reputation," *Journal of Religious Leadership* 1, no. 2 (Fall 2002): 8.

13. See Ephesians 5:22-32; Colossians 3:18-19; 1 Peter 3:1-7.

14. See Ephesians 6:1-4; Colossians 3:20-21.

15. See Ephesians 6:6-9; Colossians 3:22-4:1; 1 Peter 2:18-20.

16. See Colossians 4:18; 1 Peter 3:15.

17. Perkins, 108.

Chapter 9

Realizing God's Body-Life Vision

Peter, standing with the eleven, lifted up his voice and addressed them: "Men of Judea and all who dwell in Jerusalem, let this be known to you, and give ear to my words."

— ACTS 2:14

With malice toward none; with charity for all; with firmness in the right, as God gives us to see the right, let us strive on to finish the work we are in; to bind up the nation's wounds; to care for him who shall have borne the battle, and for his widow, and his orphan — to do all which may achieve and cherish a just, and a lasting peace, among ourselves, and with the nations.

— ABRAHAM LINCOLN[1]

Preach the word; be ready in season and out of season; reprove, rebuke, and exhort, with complete patience and teaching. For the time is coming when people will not endure sound teaching, but having itching ears they will accumulate for themselves teachers to suit their own passions.

— 2 TIMOTHY 4:2-3

One can argue about President Abraham Lincoln's spiritual pedigree, or the depth of his personal relationship with God. We will leave that for others to judge. There is no question, though, that God used the wisdom, character, and vision of his messages to heal a splintered Union during our nation's Civil War in the early 1860s. John Hay, Lincoln's assistant private secretary who lived in the White House during the president's tenure, offered this perspective: "I am growing more and more convinced that the good of the country absolutely demands that he should be kept where he is till this thing [the Civil War and the abolition of slavery] is over. There is no man in the country, so wise, so gentle and so firm. I believe the hand of God placed him where he is."[2]

President Lincoln's capacity for eloquent proclamation, but with words of the most common of people, has seldom been matched. As one writer summarized, "In a democratic nation, where the rough and ready understanding of the people is sure at last to be the controlling power, a profound common sense is the best genius for statesmanship. Lincoln had demonstrated a perfectly calibrated touch for public sentiment and impeccable timing of new measures."[3] His forthright, uncomplicated words in the Gettysburg Address, the Emancipation Proclamation, and his second inaugural address are examples of such vision communicated to address burdensome issues in a timely fashion. Such periods necessitate the role of vision sharing. It is a crucial part of gathering the people toward a unity of purpose and commitment. So it is in the body of Christ. God conveys vision and intent to the body in many ways, including the written Word and the Spirit-emboldened words of His people.

We move to our fifth and last body-building role, the vision sharer. Commonly this is the role put forth as the most important in the area of leadership in most situations. It is often highlighted first. Frequently, leadership qualities are framed around this skill. I have placed it here, as the last of five strategically important functions, so that we can grasp its importance more appropriately in the full context of body life. The vision sharer cannot stand on his or her own. Other body parts must move around, alongside, or in front, always in shared ministry. Such is true of each body-building role, one of the essential tenets of God's We-economy.

The Kingdom has but one Lord, and all the rest of us have the privilege to steward our God-designed parts that make up body-life activity. Each role is designed by the Kingdom Architect

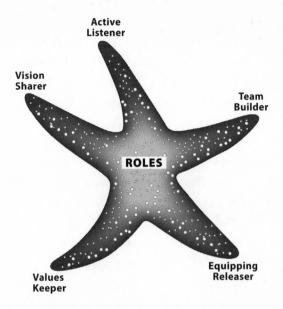

to serve the common good. So it is with the *vision sharer*, one of the essential body-building functions used by God to visibly orchestrate the course for His people. We now seek to understand its unique and essential contribution in building and extending the body of Christ.

5. Vision Sharer: Communicating God's Body-Building Vision

Body-Building Role Definition	Role or Function	Motivation for Fulfilling This Role	Indicators of Function Fulfilled
Picture Painter Powerfully shares vision and values and builds ownership for such. Leads most effectively from upfront or alongside.	• seeing • imagining • inspiring, motivating • pointing	• communicating the "big picture" • capturing the biblical course of direction • pushing new frontiers • enabling others to believe and participate	• clarity of direction • movement toward desired ends • ownership of vision • excitement in connecting others to the vision and involvement

Working in tandem with active listeners, equipping releasers, team builders, and values keepers, the vision sharer is prepared by God to discern and communicate body-life vision. He or she does so both to the body of Christ and those beyond the fold. The Word goes forth to the unbelievers in hopes of enfolding them through confession, repentance, and baptism. The vision of the Scriptures is communicated to both new and veteran believers to understand and act upon its precepts. The vision sharer's role is essential for keeping God's purposes in front of His people, to call out perspective, direction, and orchestrated action steps among the body. Capturing and communicating God's vision and purposes is the heart of vision sharing.

Some of our likely vision-sharer role models have already been part of our discussion along the way of body-building in God's We-economy. We have referred to Nehemiah, our steward of the body-building walls. His sharing of the dream for rebuilding Jerusalem was received in such a way that the people went to Jerusalem *en masse*. His orchestration kept people on task and reminded them of God's purposes even when crisis came in the form of opposition to the building of the walls of the city: "And I looked and arose and said to the nobles and to the officials and to the rest of the people, 'Do not be afraid of them. Remember the Lord, who is great and awesome, and fight for your brothers, your sons, your daughters, your wives, and your homes'" (Nehemiah 4:14). Sometimes a directive word is used by God to calm people, reframe perspective, or provide a ray of hope when hope is hard to find. Such is the dynamic function of the vision sharer.

A pioneer New Testament vision sharer would certainly be Peter on the day of Pentecost. We revisit the scene of Acts 2 to highlight his message about the cream of the cream-filled cookie. Peter was used mightily to provide a vision of what God had promised His people and, now in Christ, was bringing to bear through the power of the Holy Spirit. Step-by-step, he laid out Old Testament prophecy from Joel about the promised Holy Spirit's work among the people. He spoke forcefully about Jesus of Nazareth as the fulfillment of that prophecy and the evident worker of signs and wonders. Though men killed Jesus, God raised Him up and defeated death, Peter explained to the people. He then gave further historical perspective, interspersing references to David. We see modeling of a foundational vision-sharer function through Peter's speaking, particularly his use of biblical texts, both in background and prophecy, to portray truth. He taught the Word as he introduced the Word made flesh, Jesus. Vision sharing has as its imperative the calling out of the Word.

He also revealed the forthright boldness that is a common aspect of the vision sharer's role. Acts 2:36 states: "Let all the house of Israel therefore know for certain that God has made him both Lord and Christ, this Jesus whom you crucified." What was the response to this challenging assertion? They were cut so deeply that they asked Peter and the apostles what they should do. Peter's vision sharing then turned to a specific evangelistic purpose in verse 38: "Repent and be baptized every one of you in the name of Jesus Christ for the forgiveness of your sins, and you will receive the gift of the Holy Spirit." Body expansion happens often as the result of such Kingdom vision sharing, as was the case on Pentecost.

The vision sharer commonly desires a response or action to what is shared. It could be a call to action or commitment by the prophet, evangelist, or exhorter. Or it could be a challenge to the people to follow a course of action by a gifted leader. In Peter's case, it is the call to repent and follow Jesus, as well as the call to body life together. God used this vision sharer powerfully that day as thousands responded, and a new community was formed. It was not the person who was powerful but the

Spirit of God through the gospel—"the power of God for salvation to everyone who believes" (Romans 1:16).

We are reminded by other words of Peter, in 1 Peter 4:10-11, about the dynamic of how the Spirit works in every body-building role—and for what purpose: "As each has received a gift, use it to serve one another, as good stewards of God's varied grace: whoever speaks, as one who speaks oracles of God; whoever serves, as one who serves by the strength that God supplies—in order that in everything God may be glorified through Jesus Christ."

Peter spoke, energized by the Holy Spirit, and the power of God rose up—for the glory of God rather than the praises of men. I love how the people initially responded to Peter's challenge in Acts 2:38 and following. Verse 37 says that they spoke to Peter "and the rest of the apostles." They knew it was God who was speaking and not Peter, so they asked all of the apostles what they should do even though Peter was the speaker. Such is the power of God: He is raised up and speaks powerfully, and each of us gets to play our respective parts in response to His purposes.

The rest of the body-building apostles were very much involved, even as one vision sharer spoke the words. Consider how the vision-casting setting was introduced: "Peter, standing with the eleven" (Acts 2:14). It never was about Peter, but about the power of God. It came through Peter's message with the eleven alongside, and the resulting body ministry. It is all about God's economy of relationship and power revealed through His Spirit-led people.

I remember the first time I was speaking in a ministry setting that I realized it was the power of God working within me by His Spirit. My initial response internally was to release any worries of impressing people. This was God—not me! It was so exhilarating to release that self-seeking, self-serving attitude and simply get out of His way. From that day forward, whenever I know I am vision sharing as a part of body-building, I can make the conscious internal choice to step aside for the Spirit to work. When I remove myself, the Spirit moves people to action in real and powerful ways as I am faithful to steward my gifts as a part of the body.

If I hold on and make myself the center, I quickly become uncomfortable because I realize what I am doing. As I try to exercise the gift in my own strength the results are often unattractive and negative. In our *Discovering Your Ministry Identity* or *Your Leadership Grip* assessing workbooks, we call these "gift liabilities." When we seek to function in our own strength, the power is not there, nor the resulting impact. When we live out our body-building roles in Him, God is glorified and we are powerful—in this case, vision sharing—for the sake of the Kingdom *and* for the common good.

While I have given characteristics of a number of the vision-sharing spiritual gifts, let us stop and acknowledge these specific gifts and their primary functions:

- *Evangelism*—to share Christ one-on-one or in larger groups, in such a way that people respond to the gospel
- *Teaching*—to teach the Scriptures for understanding, interpretation, and purpose
- *Leadership*—to discern and communicate God's vision that enables body-life ministry
- *Prophecy*—to call out biblical truth that demands a response from hearers
- *Exhortation*—to encourage and train people into action through the Scriptures
- *Apostleship*—to share the vision to plant churches and provide direction and spiritual authority for leaders toward this end

An important distinction to be made here is that this body-building role is called vision sharer, not vision originator. All six of these gifts are able to powerfully share vision or direction from the Lord. Usually three are able to consistently originate supernatural vision in the power of the Holy Spirit and guidance of His Word. Gifted apostles, leaders, and prophets do not do this of their own volition, but in the power of the Holy Spirit, for the purposes of building and extending the body of Jesus Christ.

Surprising to some, I found that gifted teachers do not consistently originate vision. Here is what I ascertained: They are able to flesh out directives and guidelines from the Word—see the values-keeper section. Yet teachers often struggle with setting a visionary course of action for a ministry or a church. Once core principles and a direction are identified, they can be powerful in presenting a biblical framework for it, but discerning the overall sense of timely and clear direction can be difficult. I have found those whose primary spiritual gift is teaching greatly value input from others on vision and execution issues, if they are open to such contributions.

> I have found those whose primary spiritual gift is teaching greatly value input from others on vision and execution issues, if they are open to such contributions.

Be aware of a serious concern here. A stunning problem is that we expect ministry leaders, church planters, or senior and/ or solo pastors to discern and originate vision from the Lord by themselves. They are able to do this only if they have an apostolic, leadership, or prophetic gift. It quickly becomes important that we broaden our grasp of the vision-sharing gift.

As noted earlier, I have worked alongside many different types of ministries across the whole body of Christ. I have spent much of that time helping such organizations either build stronger teams or more effectively mobilize their ministry, church, or mission through more intentional stewardship of spiritual gifts. Certain helpful insights about the process of discovering and communicating vision have revealed themselves along the way.

Upfront or Alongside Vision Sharers

The most surprising insight gained is that many vision sharers are more powerful alongside than they are upfront. That is, they prefer an alongside role in sharing vision from the Lord rather than speaking from the front in large group settings, or always from a lead position in an organization. Given our present cultural propensity for the spotlight—see chapter 5—many people assume that communicating vision is something that you should always do from the front. After years of watching and interacting with others on this very issue, it is my observation that more than 70 percent of vision sharers are more powerful sharing vision from alongside—by their own admission. Many leaders whom I have directly encouraged were greatly relieved when they discovered it is okay to share vision and direction from an alongside position. That made sense to them and freed them to steward their spiritual gifts more effectively and appropriately for the common good.

Many have tried for years to be great visionary leaders from the front. Sadly, it has come with minimal fruit and little joy. It turns out that their gift combinations give them comfort, joy, and power when they come alongside and share vision. To be fully validated in one's ministry, they believed they had to assume a position at the front of the room or at or near the top of the organizational chart. This would validate them in leadership, sharing vision, or equipping and releasing others. But this is simply not true—by God's design.

What if God did make many vision sharers—and in this case equipping releasers—to be more powerful in the Spirit from alongside? What if He has a purpose in designing many with these body-building roles to be more powerful as they come alongside others, including a large number of vision sharers? Consider this: The purpose for the household of God is to be the place where we meet with God together. There we are being built together into an ever-growing building of believers. How much easier—and more effective—it would be to raise up new believers if we shared the vision and equipped them from alongside. We would already be halfway out of the way to releasing more players into body-building and body-extending roles. That is why I contend that God has designed many believers to minister dynamically from alongside: the body multiplies faster, more people are touched personally, and many more steward who they are as they fulfill their alongside parts. It is a more relational model as well, designed to organically multiply along the lines of a starfish. This is more than possible if God always brings whom He wants to fulfill what He intends.

> God has designed many believers to minister dynamically from alongside: the body multiplies faster, more people are touched personally, and many more steward who they are as they fulfill their alongside parts.

Back to Abraham Lincoln for a minute. We know him mostly for his eloquent, timely messages—his vision sharing. But there was so much more to Lincoln, as Doris Kearns

Goodwin discovered in *Team of Rivals*. Remember that he also was an active listener of great substance:

> Lincoln thought differently. He trusted the bond he had developed with his soldiers during his many trips to the front. After every defeat, he had joined them, riding slowly along their lines, boosting their spirits. He had wandered companionably through their encampments, fascinated by the smallest details of camp life. Sitting with the wounded in hospital tents, he had taken their hands and wished them well. The humorous stories he had told clusters of soldiers had been retold to hundreds more. The historian William Davis estimates that "a quarter million or more had had some glimpse of him on their own."[4]

Coming alongside in these vivid ways may have been the key to the effectiveness of Lincoln the vision sharer. He also verbally encouraged the troops — literally — from alongside. He enacted his vision-sharer role in a very personal way as an encouraging, body-building storyteller. Such is the substance of his impact, and most of us never knew of this side-by-side role.

I used to think vision sharing worked best in large auditoriums of people who all got to hear the vision together. What I have discovered is that many of those people feel no ownership of the vision because they have no part in it other than hearing. People catch and own the vision when they experience it, or share in its creation, in a smaller setting of believers.

If God has indeed designed many vision sharers to function powerfully alongside, they can share their vision one-to-one or alongside in small groups. People will interact with it, feed back ideas, and own it more quickly and more fully. The same is true for the equipping releaser: one-to-one or small-group training and coaching means more believers personally sharing in the process. They are equipped from alongside and then released to multiply themselves over (and over) again.

This does sound quite organic and starfish-like. So it is with the body of Christ!

Vision Through Body-Life Sharing

We often think of a vision sharer as being the one dynamically gifted spokesperson in a particular setting. There are also situations in which God raises up more than one for various body-life purposes. The first example of such would be Peter with the other apostles in Acts 2 and beyond. No one would doubt that there were others alongside Peter who were also vision sharers with some combination of the gifts just listed. The needs for building and extending the body were so dramatic at this early stage of body life that many vision sharers most certainly ministered powerfully in many different settings.

Acts 15 and the council of Jerusalem give us an example of shared vision sharing. Paul and Barnabas met with the apostles, church members, and elders to address issues related to Gentile conversions. The counsel the Lord gave that day did not come through one brother or sister, but from many believers in the body. Peter, James, and certainly Paul spoke to the issue, and likely others not mentioned in the text. I expected Peter to be the one who would summarize and speak for the group—as he had done in Acts 2. But James spoke decisively and the group came together in unity through his words.

The apostles and elders, led by the Spirit, sent out Paul and Barnabas, again a model of shared visionary leadership moving to action. The good news for those of us who are vision sharers is that God loves to speak through the body to give insight to overall direction or plans for a ministry. Sometimes vision sharers need to listen to other vision sharers, the body of elders, and the fellowship to gain the whole counsel of God. We are reminded that listening to others God has brought gives us the chance to hear the wisdom of God from the people.

Listening for God's vision through the Bible and the body is serious business, even for the strongest vision sharer. The Father desires those of us in positions of leadership to actively listen to others. Even if we are able to discern clear direction from God of our own volition, sometimes He provides other vision sharers or equipping releasers so that we have the opportunity to listen for Him through them. If it were just about communicating the vision in the body of Christ, we would not need active listeners. Sometimes the person needed most by a powerful vision communicator is the active listener. That helps the vision sharer be ready to listen really well to at least one other and not always be the one to give direction in every situation without watching first.

Unity of vision and purpose can also come from a group of people praying and fasting together for the Spirit's guidance. We see several places where vision and direction were discerned through such body life. This is not a surprise given how much we are learning about the organics of God's We-economy. Since it is not about any one individual's greatness, but rather for common good, it behooves us to seek the Lord together in most situations. In Acts 6:1-8, the apostles encouraged a group of godly disciples to select seven from among them, men full of the Holy Spirit and wisdom. The Holy Spirit gave vision and direction to that group of believers from the vision-sharing group of apostles. In Acts 13, the Holy Spirit gave clear direction to a group, including a teacher and a prophet, worshipping together with Saul and Barnabas. It is clear that God can provide vision in such a way that even the vision sharers need to listen, watch, and pray.

Vision Through Ministry Burdens and Passions

What about those vision sharers who are not often able to originate or instigate God's vision simply by seeking the Lord through the Word and Holy Spirit? Without question, as we have already seen from several different angles, God speaks to the body through His Word and through other spiritual leaders. He can speak through vision sharers whom He has brought alongside—and others in the ministry—who are committed to the One Set principles mentioned in the previous chapter. I encourage you to take that one step further and learn to listen to body-life vision from the players in the whole body. What if God has prepared body members with different pieces of vision and direction for a ministry in the form of ministry burdens or passions?

> What if God has prepared body members with different pieces
> of vision and direction for a ministry in the form of
> ministry burdens or passions?

I will briefly mention a related strategy for learning to listen to God more widely through the body, as developed in *Knocking Over the Leadership Ladder*.[5] The introductory statement says it all: "Listen to those whom God brought to discern more clearly what God intends." I call it the "Double Umbrella Principle," and share it here in abbreviated form.

God often gives vision to the leader or leadership team in a given ministry. Also, by His own design and heart for the world, He has prepared a component piece of that vision in every believer in that specific setting. Since He desires to reach the world through the good news of His Son Jesus, He has filled every believer with a burden for a particular group of people, a certain type of ministry, or a specific location. It may be anywhere from the apartment complex next door to a city halfway around the world. As the apostle Paul shared his passion for reaching the Gentiles in Romans 15:15-20, God has prepared every believer with passions of every size and shape all over the world. Take a look at appendix C to see an exercise from the *Discovering Your Ministry Identity* workbook that helps team members discern more clearly what their ministry burden or passion may be.

I have discovered that, if you ask people who or what God has placed on their hearts, they will tell you. Or they will take you seriously enough to say that they need to pray and think about it and then get back to you. The problem? Most ministries, pastors, or leaders do not ask people who or what is on their hearts. We tend to direct people to *our* specific burdens and passions for ministry rather than encouraging them to pursue their hearts' passions. A strong vision sharer usually claims the vision and passion as from the Lord and does not know he would gain wisdom by listening to his leaders or the whole body. That is, unless he watches and listens.

Consider several things from the start as you begin to steward body-life burdens and passions from among the represented people. Not all that people share will be from God or will be able to be fulfilled in that ministry in the short or long term. Such burdens and passions need to be shared with spiritual leadership in part to provide wise discernment as to whether it is from God and if the timing is right for its fulfillment in the body. But learning to listen and watch as discerning leaders and elders will bring us to organic insight from the Lord by the very nature of how He has prepared each one in the household of God. And God will provide new insight on the overall vision, or new specific means for fulfilling the mission, through players in the body. Just remember that the full embrace of the One Set and Body Life Design Team principles is not optional here.

While our overarching vision and mission may not change, God may give clear insight to certain strategic or tactical pieces of fulfilling the mission. After all, we are His dwelling place where He lives, moves, and has His way. His preparation of the body is full and complete. We must watch and listen to the various parts as they interact about heart passions, praying throughout the process, *Lord, teach us to listen and watch for Your Spirit's leading in Your Word, from among the elders or leadership team, and from the body of brothers and sisters whom You have prepared. Bring us together, Father, to talk and pray about how You have burdened and impassioned each of us in our congregation, ministry, or team so that we can capture more of the We-preparation You have already done. Show Your heart and Your passion through Your people, Your dwelling place by the Spirit. Lord, help us to intently steward Your purposes prepared through Your people beginning with spiritual leaders and elders, but also continuing in and through the body.*

Let there be no question: God uses relationships even in vision imparting and in the gathering of His purposes for ministry in Jerusalem, Judea, Samaria, and to the ends of the earth.

The Organic Triangle

If you lead a ministry, group, church, or organization, what if you had a new way to look at whom God brings to you and your ministry? As you consider using the body-building roles as a means to share and multiply both leadership and ministry teams, what big-picture view could help you think through how to work with such a process? The "Organic Triangle" is a way to apply some of this

new learning through several steps in moving from "I to We" in your missional approaches to multiplying the Kingdom. What follows are a set of simple entry points and several starting-point questions for each area about which we shall deliberate. As we go, consider this graphic picture of such a We-strategy that accesses God's creative preparation of His people.

Through the Organic Triangle diagram, you can begin to consider what God has said to you, and may still want to say, as you move toward action in your life or ministry setting. Reflect on the Organic Triangle and its three angles for discerning how God desires to live and move and have His way among your people.

As Langdon Reinke, a pastor and partner in ministry, has suggested, reflect on the three angles of this Organic Triangle as the three critical factors upon which the movement of a ship depends:

1. Discerning navigational direction—We-shared vision
2. Understanding sea currents—"I to We" team building
3. Harnessing the prevailing winds—training body-life leaders and teams

Shared We-Vision

If God's economy is one where shared body life is the heartbeat of His life with us, then the relationships need somehow to be a part of how we seek God for vision and direction. This angle is about setting the navigational direction from the North Star—the Word—and getting our compass bearings as to where we are now. From the Scriptures, God speaks through the leader and leadership team, but also desires to speak through the whole body. We saw this earlier through Acts 6:1-4 and 13:1-3. God reveals His purposes. We need to constantly watch and listen for Him through His Word *and* the players along the way to those desired ends. This gives Him the chance to speak more along the way, especially on the ways and means that we may not have planned.

Lord, teach us to watch for Your new ways, to learn to listen to Your Word and Your body of believers in leadership and even new community members You have brought on board.

Consider one or more of these three sets of ideas and questions as a starting point as you search for organic navigational direction through the Bible, through present compass settings—the people God has brought during this season of your ministry's life.

To your visionary leader or leadership team, after he or they have spoken clear vision:

1. Ask one trusted values keeper, one team builder, one equipping releaser, and one active listener to meet and pray about this question: How do you translate this vision into body life in specific and practical ways? This gives God the chance to speak to the vision through a multiplicity of powerful body functions.

Or ask various ministry or team leaders:

2. What is God saying to the Church about its vision and ministry priorities? Where is He already at work in parts of our body life? Where are people already investing their lives in passionate ministry?

At an annual gathering of the whole church, organization, or group of teams, ask:

3. What is God saying to you personally about our vision and priorities as a body? Who is on your heart to reach in our community, neighborhood, or region? How will

you be a part, each one, in this vision in which God
has called you to share?

*Lord, speak to us about Your vision through our leaders. But
please also give the counsel of Your Holy Spirit through others in the
body. We are listening and watching.*

"I to We" Team Building

Team building is about getting the ship into the right currents
that propel us forward in the Holy Spirit's leading. The seas have
popular currents that many love to follow, but so often God has
prepared a special, deeper current for your ministry. He does this
through the very people He has brought to your part of the wall.
You get to steward those whom God has brought around you to
discern more clearly how the spiritual currents will lead your
ministry or team. The organic current of God leads through
We-sharing and discovering together whom He has brought and
what each one brings to the navigational direction of the Spirit-
empowered current. God is so creative in how He can generate
something new through those whom He brings: newly into leadership, or newly into the broader fellowship or ministry.

> The seas have popular currents that many love to follow, but so
> often God has prepared a special, deeper current for your ministry.

We have this incredible privilege—and responsibility—to
steward the economy of the power of spiritual gifts in and
through those whom God brought. And yet there are challenges
all around, given the varying levels of maturity, commitment,
and involvement of the body parts. Moving from "I to We"

relationally, as we saw modeled in Acts 2:42-47 and 4:31-37, has to be a part of this greater work God is doing. Character and maturity coincide with power and Spirit movement, and so we are called to steward the relationships.

Here are several steps and questions to help you go deeper in developing some organic planning ideas. Your body-builders could frame a process from these that would move you toward deeper relationships and greater stewardship of the dynamic power and grace-filled relationships available.

Ask your whole fellowship or set of teams and their team leaders:

1. Who do you see God raising up in our body who appears to be using their spiritual gifts in a powerful way? Who has a passion to invest in certain people or a place or type of ministry, and how could we confirm their work and equip them more intentionally to play their parts?
2. If we were to attempt to identify powerful values keepers, vision sharers, team builders, active listeners, equipping releasers, or supporting releasers, who would fit in each of those categories?

Address the idea of determining how your whole organization, church, or ministry could gather once, twice, or quarterly just to eat together and to pray. After eating and some time in worship together and prayer, ask people to offer words of encouragement to another person in the room. Words of encouragement are so hard to come by these days, and this could encourage many.

Ask for any in the group who have a real need to request prayer, and have elders and others lead out in gathering others to pray for those specific needs. Four or five different groups could be prepared to listen to needs and to pray so that many in the body are involved with the caring and praying, not just a few leaders.

See what God does through the deepening fellowship that results.

Have each board, team, or set of groups covering your whole fellowship or organization do some type of gifts assessment like *Your Leadership Grip* or *Discovering Your Ministry Identity*, even using an outside coach or trainer, and ask these three questions when you gather:

1. Where are you powerful?
2. How are you weak?
3. Whom do you need?

After groups gather to do this, have all the groups or teams meet together and discover what God did during these times of sharing. Give God a chance to speak among all of you. New believers who were previously less involved will show significant levels of ownership for body life if given the chance to confirm who they are and how they could use their gifts in serving opportunities.

Training Body-Life Leaders and Teams

The navigational course is set by the Word, counsel, and prayer. We are learning to watch and listen more intently than ever for the unique and powerful currents that God brings to each ministry in the growing body of Christ. How do we set the sails properly to harness the prevailing winds? We have our crew well trained to watch for the winds of the Holy Spirit, to know how to prepare others to join in the process of riding in the Spirit. The various crew functions, like our body-building roles, are necessary to keep the ship sailing well and on course. That also means that we must prepare them well for this special work.

So many ships end up at the bottom of the sea because the crew members were simply not prepared to play their specialized roles that keep the ship intact and moving forward. Often they were misplaced in their responsibilities and could not handle what came their way.

How we train our spiritual children and prepare them to equip and release, team build, values keep, actively listen and watch, and vision share determines how many spiritual grandchildren are raised up. This is serious business.

Holy Spirit, propel us forward as we learn to train our shipmates—in this generation but even more so in the next—to fulfill their roles as equipping releasers, supporting releasers, values keepers, active listeners, team builders, and vision sharers.

Consider these ideas and questions:

Watch for two or three people to whom you can devote yourself to encourage and prepare them for the next season of body life. Search out a discipleship resource to share, or do some kind of ministry or service together. This may include praying for someone sick or hospitalized, or friendship evangelism, or doing a short-term missions project together.

If you are already doing this, train others to do the same. As they watch you prepare the next generation, they will learn and follow that model.

Gather a team of trusted equipping releasers, team builders, values keepers, vision sharers, or active listeners. *Make sure* at least four of the body-building roles are present. Talk about the different ways each of you might encourage a group of younger Christians or new families God has brought to your church or ministry.

Decide to do some kind of investing in these people, both one-on-one *and* within groups, to practice "I to We" movement while you are helping others grow spiritually.

Watch for those, older or younger, whom God brings,

and figure out ways for you and others to encourage them to find their fit in the body of Christ. Steward your walls! We are to steward these relationships and play our body-building and body-extending roles to help each precious stone find its indispensable place on the wall of God's rapidly growing building.

Summary

The fifth body-building role that God has prepared to work for the common good is that of the vision sharer. The vision sharer's role is essential for keeping God's purposes in front of His people. It is to call out perspective, direction, and orchestrated action steps in body life. Sometimes we treat this role as more important or special. Rather, its part is as important as our other essential body functions, no more or less. The vision sharer commonly desires response or action to what is shared. It may be the call to repentance and baptism by the evangelist, a call to action by the prophet or exhorter, or challenging people to follow a course of action by a gifted leader, who then helps to orchestrate people and places to serve.

Interestingly, many vision sharers are more powerful sharing from alongside in relationships and groups than from the front of the group or in the lead role in an organization. Not only that, many vision sharers capture more of God's vision by listening to others in the body — other vision sharers, elders, or even members of the fellowship. Uniquely, God has placed ministry burdens and passions in each member of the body. Any vision sharer has the opportunity to help people discover how God has impassioned them — and to listen and watch for what God has placed on their hearts. In this way, God speaks to His whole vision and heart for reaching the world, from Jerusalem to the ends of the earth.

Consider also the possibility of a sixth body-building role, that of the supporting releaser. Their joy is in enabling the process from behind or in support through gifts like helps or giving, and they often end up releasing the gifts of others. It is all about the practical needs—and supporting others in the body in their respective functions—for the supporting releaser.

Let us then begin to reengineer body-life ministry and its body-building roles through God's Organic Triangle. We can take practical steps in how we listen to God's vision not only through the vision sharer, but also through the body. We can fervently practice moving from "I to We" in team building to both deepen our relationships and understand how we fit together, all the pieces working for the common good. As we do this we can merge into an ongoing, enfolding, equipping, mending, coaching, and releasing process with all the roles involved, including the supporting releasers. Learning how to come alongside and regularly prepare to release the next generation of body-builders and body-extenders is our We-centered goal.

Application Steps

1. Give each person a sheet of paper on which to write three words or phrases. Write the first thing that comes to mind when you say "body life," "leadership," and "starfish." Share your answers with one another. How has your understanding shifted through this book?

2. Practice body-life vision. Share one new idea for a ministry project or plan. Have everyone share three things: (1) How they understand it, (2) How they could be a part of it, and (3) Who they think should be a part of it.

3. Draw a picture or use modeling clay to illustrate body-life vision. In groups of three or four, as modeled through the Organic Triangle with the ship's direction, sea currents, and wind power, create an image to explain how you

understand the concept. Share with each other.

4. Review all of the body-building roles. Select which two would best describe God's supernatural power in you. Select also which one you need in the body of Christ. Share the results with each other. Spend time affirming each other for God's unique design and each one's fit in the body.

Discussion Questions

1. Think about a recent successful team or ministry in which you were a part. What made it successful? How was the vision created, communicated, and empowered?

2. How does the source of the vision influence the overall impact? How does shared creation differ from its being developed and shared by one individual?

3. Reread 1 Peter 4:10-11. Why were gifts given? Who gets the glory? What happens when we forget these foundational ideas?

4. What is one core concept that struck you the most from the book? How can you share this concept with at least three people?

---

1. Ronald C. White Jr., *Lincoln's Greatest Speech: The Second Inaugural* (New York: Simon & Schuster, 2006), 18.
2. Doris Kearns Goodwin, *Team of Rivals: The Political Genius of Abraham Lincoln* (New York: Simon & Schuster, 2005), 545.
3. Kearns Goodwin, 596.
4. Kearns Goodwin, 663.
5. Paul R. Ford, *Knocking Over the Leadership Ladder* (St. Charles, IL: ChurchSmart Resources, 2006), 181–189.

Appendix A

Body-Building Roles and Spiritual Gifts

The following chart shows spiritual-gift combinations in body-life language. If you have one or more of the gifts listed as potential for any of the roles below, you likely are powerful in that body-building role.

Gift Combinations for Body-Building Roles		
Body-Building Role	**Potential Spiritual Gifts**	**Potential Liabilities**
Values Keeper — systems guide Focuses on quality in the process, establishes guidelines, and provides real accountability. Equips most powerfully from alongside.	• administration • discernment of spirits • prophet • teacher • wisdom/word of wisdom	• May tend to focus too much on content or process vs. people • May become too concerned with excellence or quality • May overplay the "I'm right" card in some situations • May be overly critical of other people's ideas for change
Team Builder — community connector Gives priority to people no matter what the process; unity is always a priority. Leads most effectively from alongside.	• pastor • exhorter • leader • supporting gifts: mercy, helps	• May get too caught up in internal team dynamics • May be fearful of being too firm or directive • May lose missional focus • May lose balance needed between love and truth

Gift Combinations for Body-Building Roles

Body-Building Role	Potential Spiritual Gifts	Potential Liabilities
Active Listener — vigorous watcher Listens for vision and passion residing in body-life members. Asks before answering. Encourages most powerfully from alongside.	• wisdom/word of wisdom • pastor • exhorter • supporting gifts: helps, mercy • discernment of spirits	• May lose big-picture view • May lose momentum on body-life engagement • May focus too much on the individual vs. the team • May struggle with action focus
Vision Sharer — picture painter Powerfully shares vision and values and builds ownership for such. Leads most effectively from upfront or alongside.	• leadership • evangelist • teacher • prophet • exhorter	• May lose the importance of the vision's details • May try to sell or persuade instead of listening to Spirit • May miss people's needs • May drive the vision and lose touch with team members
Equipping Releaser — training coach Prepares and releases others to play their God-designed parts. Enables powerfully from alongside or upfront.	All equipping gifts: • pastor • exhorter • evangelist • knowledge/word of knowledge • leader • wisdom/word of wisdom • teacher • prophet	• May release, but not equip • May equip, then not release • May push people too fast • May get tunnel vision

Body-Building Roles in Detail

Body-building roles are how you and I steward our God-designed functional part in the body of Christ. They affirm how you fit and play your Kingdom role in missional living and ministry.

Body-Building Role	Body-Life Function	Motivation for Fulfilling This Body-Building Role	Indicators of Role Fulfilled (How Others Respond)
Equipping Releaser — training coach Prepares and releases others to play their God-designed parts. Enables powerfully from alongside or upfront.	• training • mentoring/ coaching • mending • empowering	• freeing people to play their role/ part • seeing joy and power manifested in others • enjoying the process of preparing others • desiring "spiritual grandchildren"	• readied and mobilized into ministry • own their personal ministry • move in power • "fit and flourish" in their respective ministries
Vision Sharer — picture painter Powerfully shares vision and values and builds ownership for such. Leads most effectively from upfront or alongside.	• seeing • imagining • inspiring/ motivating • pointing	• communicating the "big picture" • capturing the biblical course of direction • pushing new frontiers • enabling others to believe and participate	• clarity of direction • movement toward desired ends • ownership of vision • excitement in connecting others to the vision and involvement
Values Keeper — systems guide Focuses on quality in the process, establishes guidelines, and provides real accountability. Equips most powerfully from alongside.	• organizing • protecting • maintaining • evaluating	• conserving core values • encouraging values-based decisions • bringing quality and depth • providing wise counsel	• Word-based standards • biblical integrity • accountable systems • thorough, wise decisions

Body-Building Role	Body-Life Function	Motivation for Fulfilling This Body-Building Role	Indicators of Role Fulfilled (How Others Respond)
Team Builder — community connector Gives priority to the people no matter what the process; unity is always a priority. Leads most effectively from alongside.	• unifying • relating • including • bonding	• bringing people together • valuing everyone's contributions • esteeming team members • strengthening cohesion among team members	• unity • camaraderie • shared process • openhearted-ness, body-life caring
Active Listener — vigorous watcher Listens for vision and passion residing in body-life members. Asks before answering. Encourages most powerfully from alongside.	• inquiring • observing • discerning • pursuing	• hearing their heart • valuing their voice • drawing people out • assisting discovery of personal passion	• joy of personal discovery • sense of release and empower-ment • new sense of value from being heard • individual passions and visions surfaced

Spiritual-Gifts Database

Supporting Spiritual Gifts — power in the actions, designed to serve the body

Gift of Administration

The supernatural ability to provide organization for the goals of the body of Christ by designing and carrying out an efficient plan of action.

Characteristics

1. Like a helmsman on a ship, people with the gift of administration plot the course; or, as in an orchestra, they bring together all the different parts of music for the various musicians to play.
2. Carry vision into reality by putting the details into a plan of action.
3. Tend to be more task- and detail-centered than people-centered, often linear planners.
4. Focus on the details of the vision, part by part, rather than the "big picture."

Liabilities

1. May view people as "task completers" rather than people with needs.
2. May be unresponsive to others' suggestions and changes in plans.

3. May rely on their well-organized plans rather than the Spirit and prayer.
4. May be too careful and block the overall vision with their many specific details.

Gift of Giving

The supernatural ability to give freely, cheerfully, and sacrificially of one's money or possessions for the sake of Christ and His body.

Characteristics

1. Give freely out of whatever resources are available.
2. See money and possessions as tools to serve God, and sets those resources aside for special use.
3. Their giving is often quiet and confidential—no fanfare is desired.
4. Show strong interest and support in the people and causes they support.

Liabilities

1. Giver's own family may suffer because too much has been given away.
2. May be critical of how others spend their money.
3. May expect others to give as they do.
4. May be misled into giving to causes that do not further the cause of Christ.

Gift of Helps

The supernatural ability to unselfishly meet the needs of others, freeing them to exercise their spiritual gift(s). The helps gift focuses on helping to free another person to use his or her gifts.

Characteristics

1. Sees what needs to be done in assisting others in specific ministries and desires to do it.
2. Typically unselfish because of the strong desire to help.
3. Finds great joy in freeing others from responsibilities so that they can share their gifts.
4. Rejoices in the fruitfulness of others.

Liabilities

1. May have difficulty saying no when asked to help, even when they need to.
2. May easily become overextended physically and/or emotionally.
3. May take too much ownership in helping others or in not letting others help.
4. May neglect their own needs and their family's or close friend's needs to help others.

Gift of Mercy

The supernatural ability to show great empathy and compassion for those who suffer physically, emotionally, or spiritually, and to assist them.

Characteristics

1. Show sincere kindness and compassion in their lifestyle.
2. Reveal significant "love in action" to those who are hurting, ill, or downtrodden.
3. Often are drawn to those who may be outcasts or considered outsiders.
4. Attempt to relieve the source of people's suffering.

Liabilities

1. May be too protective of the people for whom they care.
2. May identify too strongly with someone hurting or ill without realizing it.
3. May base decisions on emotion rather than reason.
4. May have great difficulty saying no to need even when they should.

Gift of Service

The supernatural ability to identify unmet needs in the body of Christ and beyond, and to use whatever resources necessary to practically meet those needs. This gift focuses on the acts of service and not the people involved, as with the gift of helps.

Characteristics

1. Resourceful in meeting needs and offering practical solutions.
2. Love to serve, often without receiving any public affirmation. Doing the task is enough.
3. Will often change their schedule to serve others.
4. Able to see needs arising before others see them.

Liabilities

1. May neglect responsibilities at home to serve others.
2. May exclude others from helping by their own drive to serve.
3. May overcommit and wear out physically because of their difficulty with saying no.
4. May find self-esteem needs in "doing" for others rather than accepting themselves for who they are.

Equipping Spiritual Gifts — power in the words, designed to equip and release others

Gift of Exhortation

The supernatural ability to encourage, comfort, challenge, or rebuke others to action in such a way that they respond.

Characteristics

1. Encourages and motivates others to practical application of specific biblical truths.
2. Able to tell others the truth about themselves with great encouragement and understanding.
3. May take the form of rebuke, though people will still feel helped by such an approach.
4. Often more effective in short-term encouragement than long-term counseling or support.

Liabilities

1. May offer "quick fixes" and appear insensitive to long-term needs.
2. May jump to conclusions before listening to the whole story.
3. May offer too direct or harsh counsel at one extreme or be insensitive to the real need at the other.
4. May become more action-centered than person-centered at times because of desire for the person to take practical steps.

Gift of Evangelism

The supernatural ability to share the gospel with unbelievers in such a way that people respond and became followers of Jesus Christ.

Characteristics

1. Share the gospel in such a way that people respond by accepting Christ.
2. Have an ongoing desire to share the good news with many people.
3. Often most effective in one type of evangelistic effort and not necessarily others: i.e., one-to-one, open-air preaching, small-group settings, etc.
4. Want others to share their faith effectively and win the world for Jesus Christ.

Liabilities

1. May motivate by guilt when encouraging others to share their faith.
2. May be very narrow in their evangelistic focus and discount the gifts of others.
3. May see people as "targets" and not as people with needs.
4. Often are seen as overly directive by others, Christian or non-Christian.

Gift of Knowledge/Word of Knowledge

The supernatural ability to receive and share revealed knowledge that was not otherwise known, or the ability to gather and clarify large quantities of biblical knowledge with unusual spiritual insight.

Characteristics

1. Have a clear sense of receiving messages from God regarding things they did not know naturally.
2. May manifest itself by a sense of supernatural insight coming directly out of prayer.

3. Words, phrases, or word pictures may commonly or spontaneously appear in their minds.
4. Some would see this gift as the ability to research and combine large amounts of biblical knowledge in little time, with phenomenal understanding.

Liabilities

1. May respond to false or self-initiated impulses.
2. May inappropriately communicate a personal message for someone in a public setting (i.e., should have been shared personally because of the message's content).
3. Pride may grow because of the "great biblical insights" discerned or messages received.
4. May mistakenly give a personal message to a large group of people, thus creating confusion for many people.

Gift of Leadership

The supernatural ability to provide overall vision for the body of Christ and provide direction for others in such a way that they willingly follow and work together.

Characteristics

1. If an administrator puts the pieces of music together, then the leader is the conductor of the orchestra, involving each person meaningfully in the "music," the process.
2. Provide vision and direction for the overall process, the "big picture."
3. Shares vision effectively with others and is able to involve many people in completing the task; the primary fruit is that people follow.
4. Will appear in charge, even if not identified as the official leader.

Liabilities

1. May forget how much they need others to know and carry out the specifics of the vision.
2. May become insensitive to individuals carrying out details of the vision because of focus on the "big picture."
3. May become overly dominant or demanding if not sensitive to the Spirit.
4. May become prideful of their position or power.

Gift of Pastoring

The supernatural ability to care for, feed, and protect the long-term spiritual needs of individuals or groups in the body of Christ.

Characteristics

1. Able to provide care, spiritual nourishment, and protection for people over an extended period.
2. More person-centered than task-centered.
3. Derive great strength from encouraging and verbally supporting others.
4. Usually counsel and guide many people, whether or not they have had training to do so.

Liabilities

1. May have a difficult time saying no to others, often at the expense of their families and close friends and their own physical, emotional, and spiritual well-being.
2. May be indecisive because of the strong desire to be sensitive to others.
3. May be protective of people and create a situation where people become too dependent on them.
4. May struggle with releasing people to grow beyond their pastoral control—more so than any other equipping gift.

Gift of Prophecy

The supernatural ability to proclaim God's present and future truth in such a way that the hearers are moved to respond.

Characteristics

1. Can be prophetic in either sense: may challenge people by speaking about a future event, or may speak forthrightly about present situations (foretelling and "forthtelling").
2. Proclaim timely and urgent messages from God with authority, calling people to decision.
3. Fruit may include repentance, strengthening, comfort, or encouragement.
4. Role is often to plead the cause of God to His people and/or the world and call out change.

Liabilities

1. May preach gloom, doom, and despair that is not from God.
2. May experience pride and self-centeredness growing out of the authoritative nature of the gift.
3. May communicate inaccurate foretelling when functioning in own strength and not the Spirit's.
4. Can be too blunt.

Gift of Teaching

The supernatural ability to clearly and accurately communicate the truths of the Bible in such a way that people learn.

Characteristics

1. Have a deep conviction to communicate biblical truth.
2. Able to powerfully instruct, reprove, correct, and train using the Bible.

3. Able to pull scriptural insights together in a clear and insightful way.
4. Communicate truth in such a way that people understand what was conveyed from God's Word.

Liabilities

1. May appear to have all the answers, leaving little room for discussion.
2. May communicate too much information too quickly for the average learner.
3. May become prideful of their own learning.
4. May be too content-focused with little or no people-focus.

Gift of Wisdom/Word of Wisdom

The supernatural ability to offer pertinent spiritual counsel immediately in situations where such guidance is needed.

Characteristics

1. Able to apply spiritual knowledge in practical ways.
2. Have a supernatural understanding of situations in which they have no previous knowledge.
3. Offer practical, helpful solutions to problems, i.e., wise counsel.
4. When such gifted people speak, people learn to listen because of the consistently accurate and wise spiritual counsel offered.

Liabilities

1. May offer only human wisdom when functioning in their own strength, causing their counsel to be ineffective in the situation.

2. Forcing a personal view on others is a clear violation of this gift.
3. May become prideful when they realize people really listen when they speak.
4. May begin to believe that they are wise in their own eyes.

Other Spiritual Gifts — gifts that do not fit in the categories

Gift of Discernment of Spirits

The supernatural ability to determine whether a certain action has its source in God, man, or Satan.

Characteristics
1. Able to discern the source of a message or special word as being from God or Satan.
2. Able to discern a person's spiritual motivation to be from God or Satan.
3. Have a profound sense of the spiritual realm, often sensing things in the spiritual realm that others simply do not experience.
4. Often able to help others discover the spiritual source of their problems.

Liabilities
1. May unnecessarily become overzealous in hunting satanic heresy.
2. May be overly judgmental of others and their motives.
3. May be insensitive to the process needed for real change in a person's life when offering spiritual input on source of problems or spiritual warfare.

4. May expect everyone else to be as spiritually discerning as they are, and thus frustrated when others are not.

Gift of Faith

The supernatural ability to trust God with extraordinary confidence, knowing that He will work out His purposes in every situation.

Characteristics

1. Able to trust God to work in supernatural ways, even when the situation seems impossible.
2. Willing to pursue God's will in the midst of enormous difficulties or barriers.
3. Willing to yield to God's will rather than question or waver because of circumstances.
4. Often move out in faith when others are unwilling.

Liabilities

1. May exercise faith without love.
2. May be impatient when others are more timid or careful.
3. May be stubborn and unyielding instead of being willing to listen to counsel.
4. May see concern about their vision as criticism and hindrance to God's work rather than helpful questioning.

What Is Your Ministry Burden or Passion?

In Romans 15:15-20, the apostle Paul portrayed his deep desire for Gentiles to come to Christ. It was not that he disliked the Jews; rather, he was passionate about giving his life for the Gentiles even if it meant going to Spain, as he mentions later in chapter 15. Given this reality in Paul's life, think about your own. What is your ministry burden or passion, the vision or heart concern that captivates your whole life and motivates you to extraordinary levels of sacrifice?

Many ask where such a desire comes from. For some people, ministry burden or passion comes out of the core of heart emotion. It's hard to explain exactly why it is there. For others, it is woven through years of experience, sometimes tied to pain or joy in their history. For yet others, it is tied directly to spiritual gifting such as teaching, encouraging, or helping. As you think and pray about this, consider the following possibilities of what ministry burden or passion God has placed in your life:

- Describes what you really care about in serving
- May reflect a specific activity or be tied to a specific location or type of people
- Willing to sacrifice a great deal to do this in time, money, or creativity
- May realize you are willing to give your life for this activity or people
- May create a new ministry or program if it is needed to

fulfill this heart burden

- For those with supporting gifts, may be serving the vision or passion of another
- Not often that a married couple share the same passion, though it's possible
- May take weeks or months to fully consider what this may be for you; that's okay

Some Examples of Ministry Burdens or Passions

- My passion is to support young mothers who need help with the practical tools of motherhood.
- My burden is to bring conversations around to Jesus into every chat room I frequent.
- I live to equip church planters to start churches in the mountains of northern India.
- My ministry passion is to tutor a small group of Hispanic middle schoolers in our fledgling charter school, helping them to take one academic step at a time to achieve their dreams.
- My wife and I both share a burden to love and serve the many elderly people in our neighborhood, responding to their isolation.
- I love to see the New Testament come alive as I mentor one individual or teach a group of people through a particular book.

About the Author

Dr. Paul R. Ford is a leadership and team-building specialist committed to helping Christian leaders and teams discover and fulfill who they are in Christ. His ministry focuses on training leaders, teams, and ministries, and he has worked in eight cultures and with more than fifty denominational and mission groups, eight hundred individual churches, and ten thousand Christian leaders.

Paul has a BA in journalism from Tarkio College, Missouri, and MDiv and DMin degrees from Fuller Theological Seminary. He is also an ordained pastor with more than ten years of experience in local church ministry.

Paul is deeply committed to his wife, Julie, and together they are an active part of Church Resource Ministries (www.crmleaders.org). They live in Albuquerque, New Mexico, and have one twentysomething son, Stephen, who lives in Washington, DC. To learn more about Paul's life and ministry, visit www.drpaulford.com.

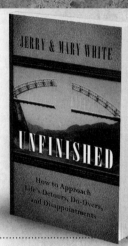
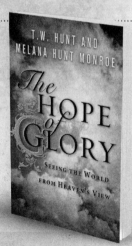